IMAGES
of America

COLLIERVILLE

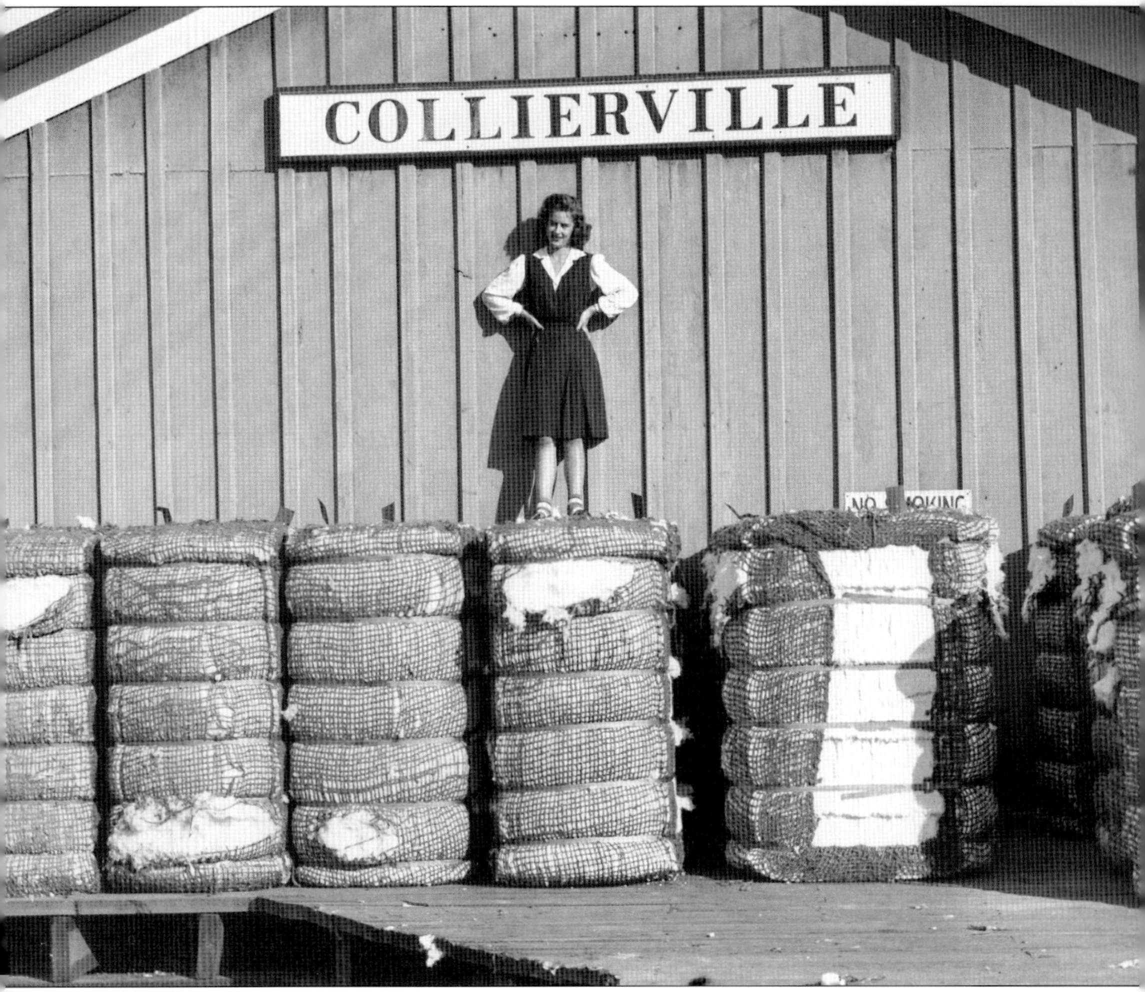

Fifteen-year-old Dorothy Boyd had little idea that this photograph would be remembered years later when she posed on top of cotton bales stacked by the depot for shipment. Her boyfriend, Paul Madison Wilson, took the photograph in 1942. Wilson continued to photograph the town he loved and collect images that would preserve the history of a growing community. Paul and Dorothy were happily married for 54 years.

ON THE COVER: The Cheese Carnival was established by the Rotary Club to promote the dairy industry. Dairy farmers brought their milk to Swift and Company's cheese plant, located on Main and Neely Streets, where it was made into hoop cheese. This gala event would last for several days. There was a queen with her court, band concerts, dances, and parades, and a carnival atmosphere was seen throughout the town. The Cheese Carnival was discontinued after 1940 because of World War II. Swift and Company was purchased by B. B. Annis and moved to Olive Branch, Mississippi, where it continued in operation until 1952. The cover photograph shows the 1939 royal court atop a float at Main and Poplar Streets. The queen is Elizabeth Carrington (Kelsey) from Collierville. Dorothy McGee from Germantown on the far left, and Courtney Gaither from Moscow is standing on the right.

IMAGES
of America

COLLIERVILLE

Main Street Collierville

ARCADIA
PUBLISHING

ISBN 0-7385-4289-X

Published by Arcadia Publishing
Charleston SC, Chicago IL, Portsmouth NH, San Francisco CA

Printed in the United States of America

Library of Congress Catalog Card Number: 2006923858

For all general information contact Arcadia Publishing at:
Telephone 843-853-2070
Fax 843-853-0044
E-mail sales@arcadiapublishing.com
For customer service and orders:
Toll-Free 1-888-313-2665

Visit us on the Internet at www.arcadiapublishing.com

*To the memory of former mayor Herman Wright Cox,
who had the vision to preserve the small town ambience of his beloved
Collierville while leading its progressive development.*

*To the memory of Paul Madison Wilson,
who preserved and captured the history and spirit of Collierville
on film and freely shared his work with others.*

*To Clarene Pinkston Russell,
who has preserved the history of Collierville in writing while donating
the proceeds from her historical work to Main Street Collierville.*

Contents

ACKNOWLEDGMENTS

Organized in 1991 as a part of the National Trust for Historic Preservation, Main Street Collierville has served as a vital organization dedicated to preserving the historic district, the heart of downtown Collierville. Main Street continues to forge the link between past and present small-town charm and the sophistication of urban growth. In preparing this book, we have looked to our membership, volunteers, and community leaders. In 2003, a call went out to the community for historic photographs that could be preserved for future use. Judi Birkitt, town planner, scanned over 100 photographs and prepared a presentation for the annual Preservation Award Evening. In preparing those images for publication with Arcadia, we have formed a committee to gather and identify additional photographs that would be of interest. We are indebted to Dorothy Boyd Wilson, who generously loaned us Paul Madison Wilson's collection, and Clarene Pinkston Russell, whose book and photographs contributed much of the collection and history. Also on our committee were Betty Mann Edmunds and Bill Kelsey, both lifelong residents of Collierville, who were able to find the answers to many of our questions. Joan Crowe, editor of the *Independent Newspaper*, helped with the initial text along with her staff, who scanned several of the images. Leadership Collierville members provided early research and information, and Main Street's administrative assistant, Linda Stamps, did initial "prep work" for the book. Robert Dye, who has published three Arcadia books, including *Shelby County*, truly stepped in and helped us make the book happen! He and his wife, Lisa, have become friends to Collierville. We have begged and borrowed from everyone we could talk with and are pleased that many in the community will see photographs that have not been publicized in the past. Hopefully more photographs will come out of the attic and future books will be published. We want to thank all who have helped Main Street with this project—those who appreciate the landmarks of the past, which give us a sense of stability and belonging.

Laura T. Todd
Executive Director
Main Street Collierville

Nancy W. Bassett
Chairman
Arcadia Book Project

INTRODUCTION

With its downtown a jewel of Victorian-era homes and old churches surrounding a historical town square, Collierville, Tennessee, retains a small-town charm that keeps longtime residents rooted and draws increasing numbers of new citizens yearly. Mild soil and its location between the Wolf River to the north and Nonconnah Creek to the south helped establish the town as an agricultural trade center for cotton and, later, the dairy industry. Once a stagecoach rest stop and later a railroad stop on the Memphis and Charleston line, the town anchors the southeast corner of Shelby County, lying about 30 miles east of Memphis and the Mississippi River. The Union army recognized the importance of the town's location during the Civil War. Battles to take the town were waged on both sides, and in one battle, Maj. Gen. William Tecumseh Sherman escaped capture at Collierville Depot.

The name and even Collierville's home state were in question at various times throughout the 19th century. Jesse R. Collier, a local real estate entrepreneur, advertised lots for sale in the *Memphis Enquirer* as "The Town of Collier" in 1836. Even after its first formal incorporation in 1850, the town also was known as Oak Grove and mistakenly referred to as "Colliersville." Lands that lay south of the Stateline Road (Poplar Avenue) remained in Mississippi until 1838. In 1858, the population was recorded at around 250. There were common schools, funded by local property taxes, and two private high schools, one for boys and one for girls. A coeducational school was available for younger children, and settlers had the choice of four churches to attend: Methodist, Baptist, Presbyterian, and "Campsettlers" (Christian). By 1860, the population had doubled. There were three general stores, three grocery stores, one flouring mill, one hotel, and other professions.

Much of the town was destroyed during the Civil War, but the town sprang back in 1866 around a park that was designated as a "public square." For a time, the park served as an erstwhile zoo with a deer and peacocks contained within a white picket fence. In 1876, a two-story bandstand brought music fans to the town's heart, just as a bandstand does today for spring and summer concerts and several annual festivals and celebrations. More than 42,000 people now call Collierville home. The town covers 18,500 acres, with another 13,700 acres in reserve for future use. A thriving business community includes antique and specialty shops and unique restaurants in addition to larger retail venues and nationally known restaurants. As urban expansion approaches from metropolitan Memphis, the community leaders and citizens strive to maintain and protect the town's unique history, its values, and personality.

"If a community preserves the integrity of its heritage,
that heritage will in turn preserve the integrity of the community."

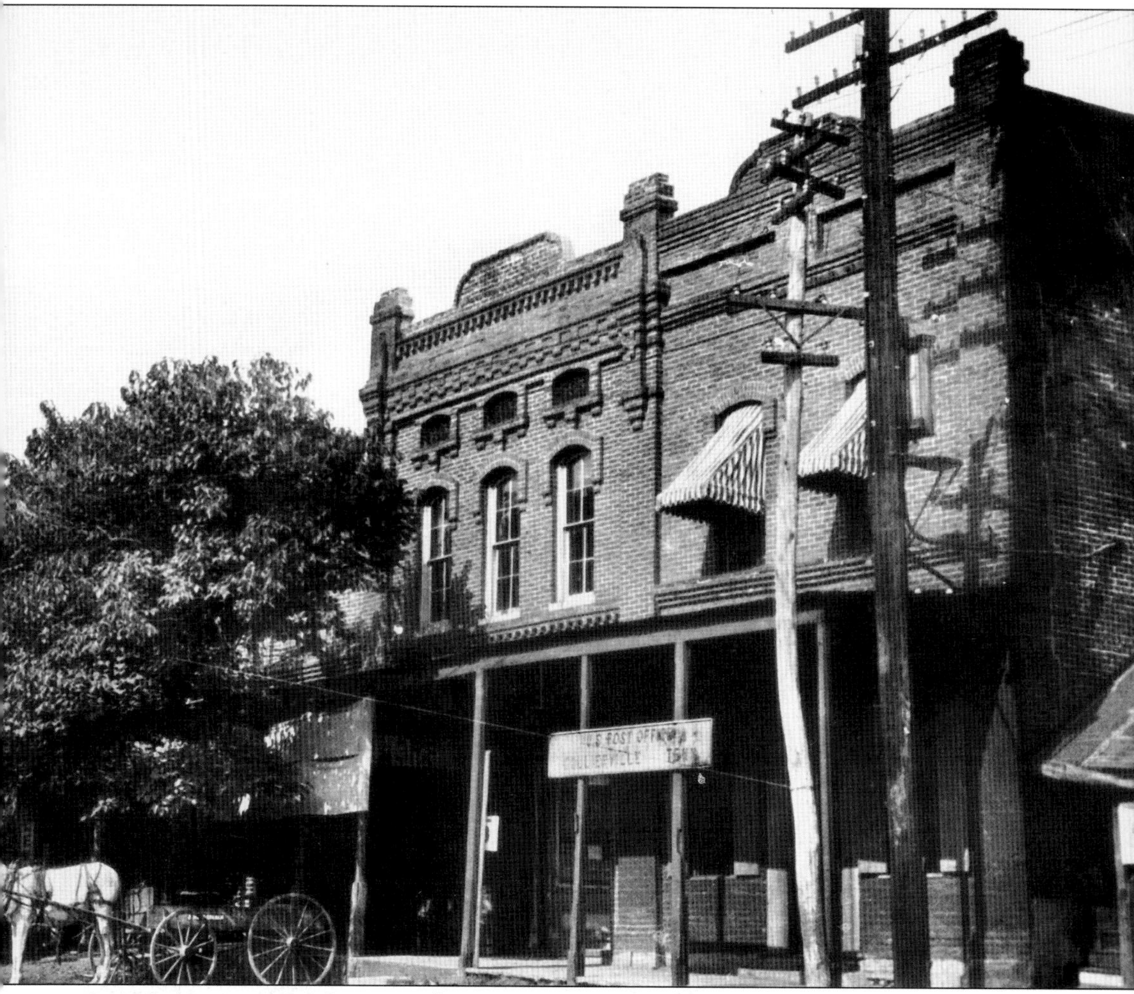

An old photograph of the square boasts a sign for the post office. The earliest post office was located in the middle part of the west side of the square. In this 1907 photograph, it was located at the northwest corner of Washington and Main Streets where the Masonic Lodge is today. It was moved several more times before locating on Center Street in a new facility in 1988.

One

Town Square

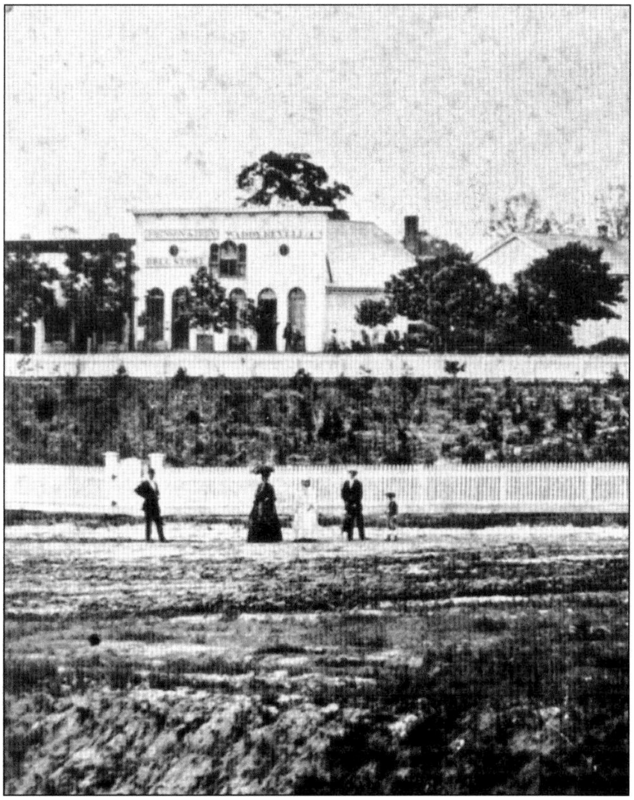

One of the earliest photographs of the Town Square is dated 1880. The photographer is facing north. Note the railroad telegraph pole in the foreground. The acreage was divided and sold into lots. Land purchased by Harrison Irby and Virginus Leake in 1866 comprised the older section of the town's location. In 1870, Collierville was incorporated again as it recovered from the Civil War. The historic square of Collierville was born during this era. According to an 1871 Memphis publication, Collierville was described as "a flourishing little town, pleasantly situated on the Memphis and Charleston Railroad in the eastern part of Shelby County."

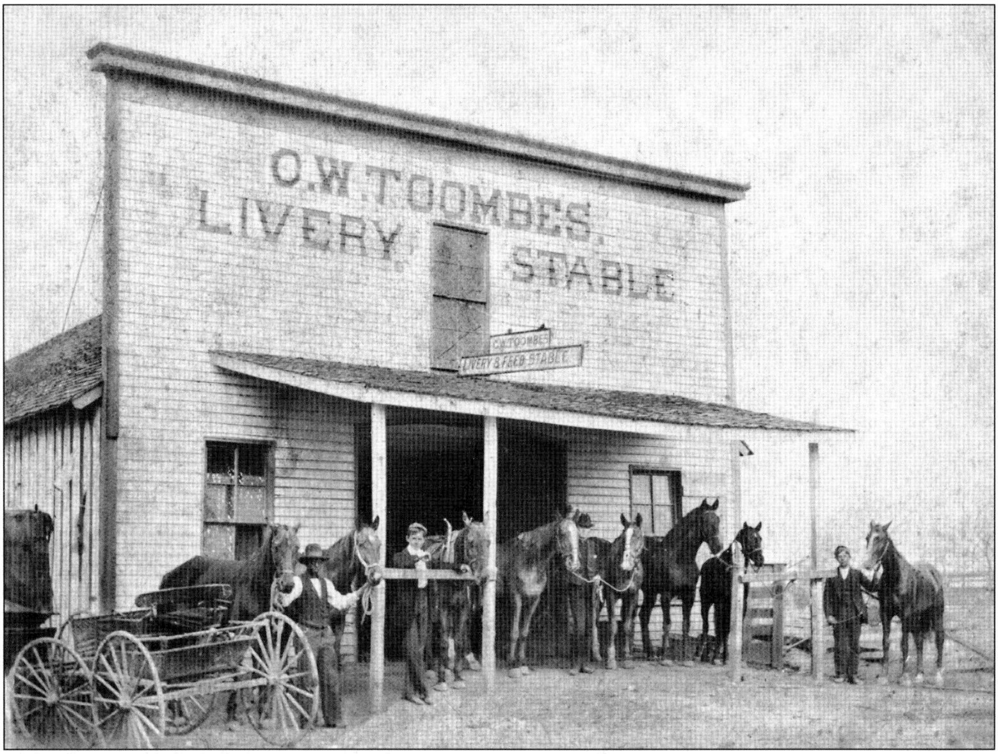

The Toombes Livery Stable was located north of the railroad on Main Street in the late 1800s. Horses and a buggy have been lined up for this photograph.

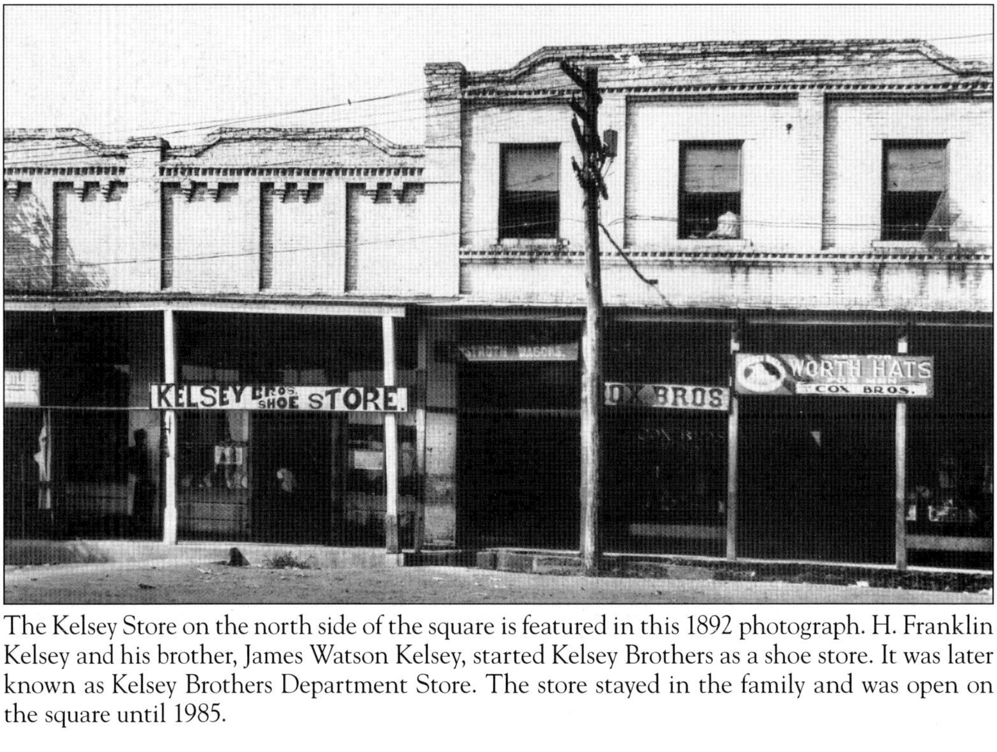

The Kelsey Store on the north side of the square is featured in this 1892 photograph. H. Franklin Kelsey and his brother, James Watson Kelsey, started Kelsey Brothers as a shoe store. It was later known as Kelsey Brothers Department Store. The store stayed in the family and was open on the square until 1985.

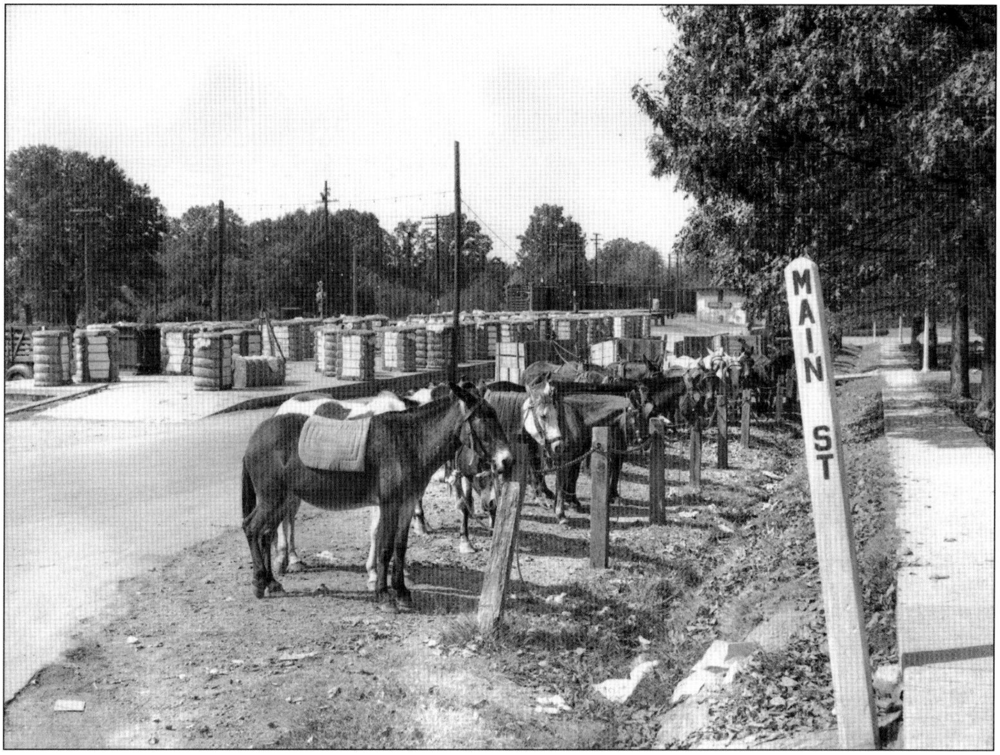

Mules and horses are tied to hitching rails on the corner of Main Street and South Rowlett Street as late as 1948. Railroad tracks with cotton bales on the train platform are in the background.

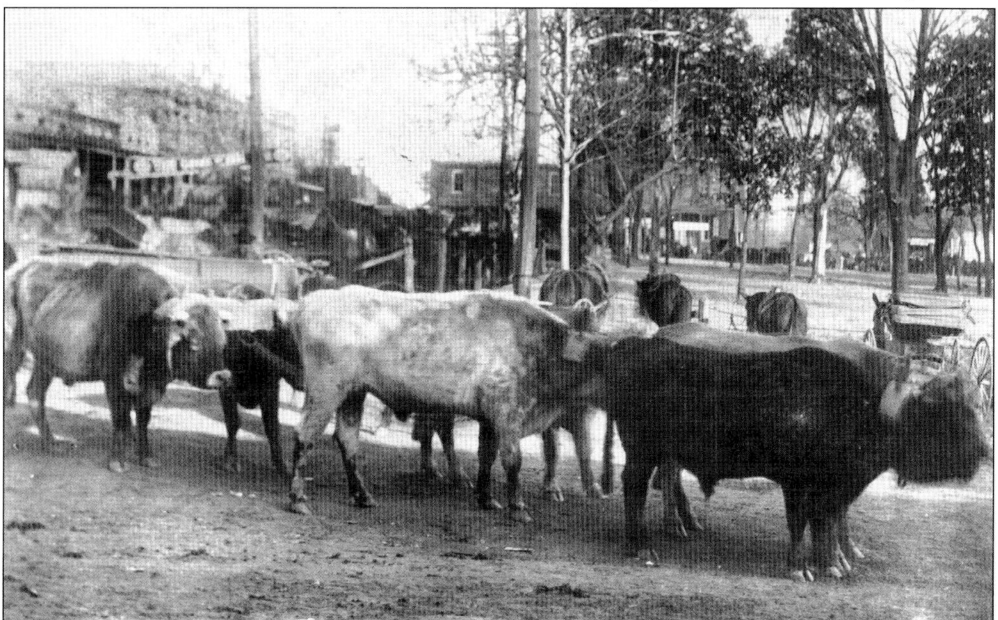

This early image shows cattle being driven through the Town Square on the dirt road. The photograph was taken facing east on the corner of Center Street and Mulberry Street. Note the wagons and horses tied across the street.

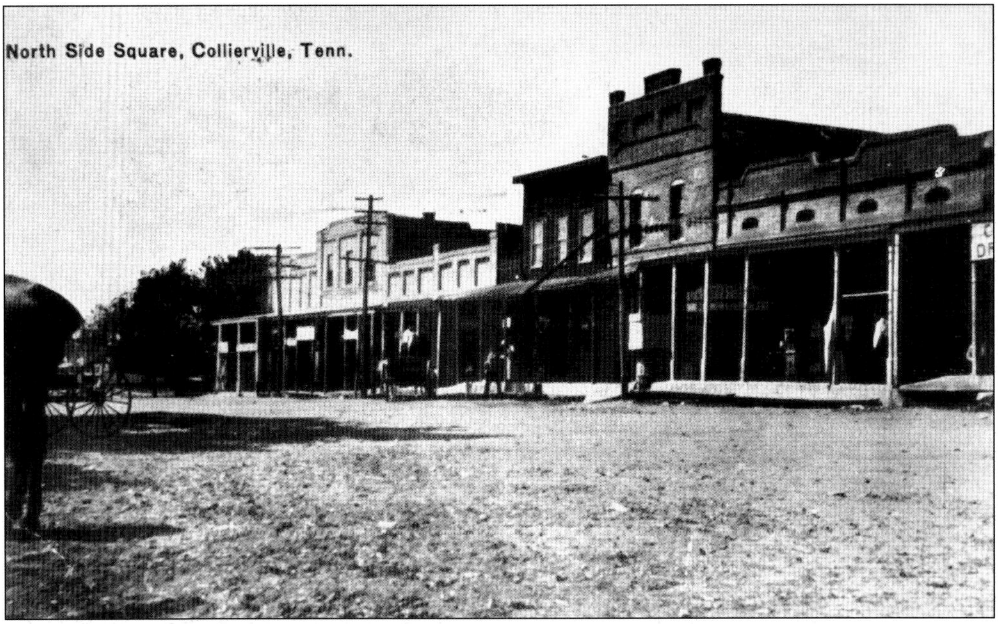

The northeast corner of the Town Square still has dirt streets at the turn of the century. Buggies and horses are tied to the hitching rails. The sign to the far right boasts "cold drinks." The town did not replace the plank sidewalks until 1913.

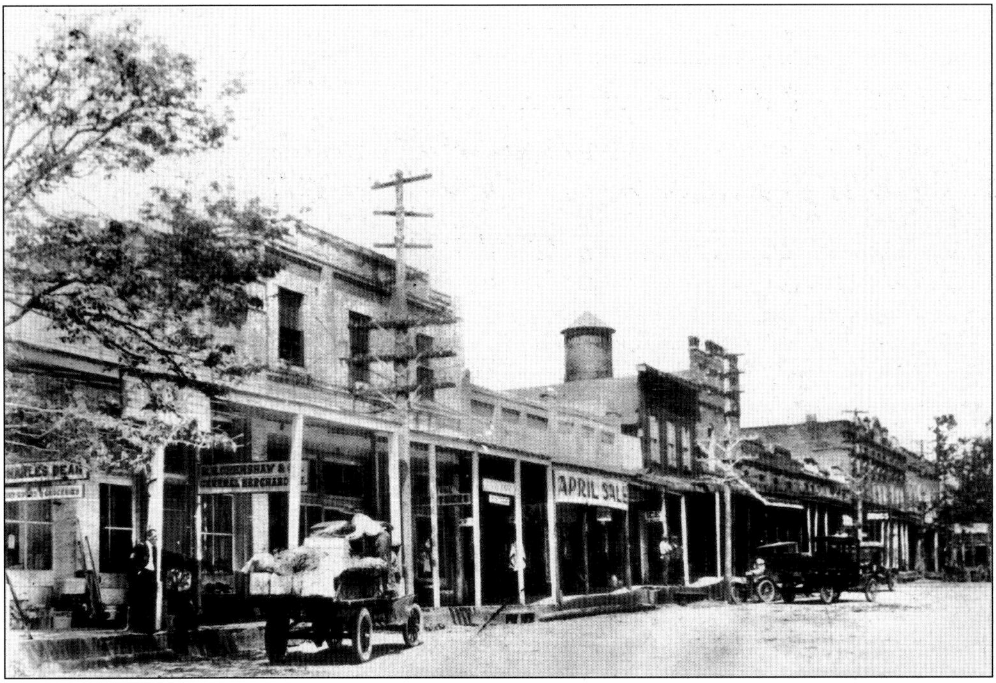

The north side of Town Square, with early vehicles, is featured in this 1900s photograph. A sign in front of Kelsey Brothers promotes an "April Sale." Charles Dean Groceries is at the far left, and H. H. Crenshaw General Merchandise is to its right. The city water tower can be seen in the distance.

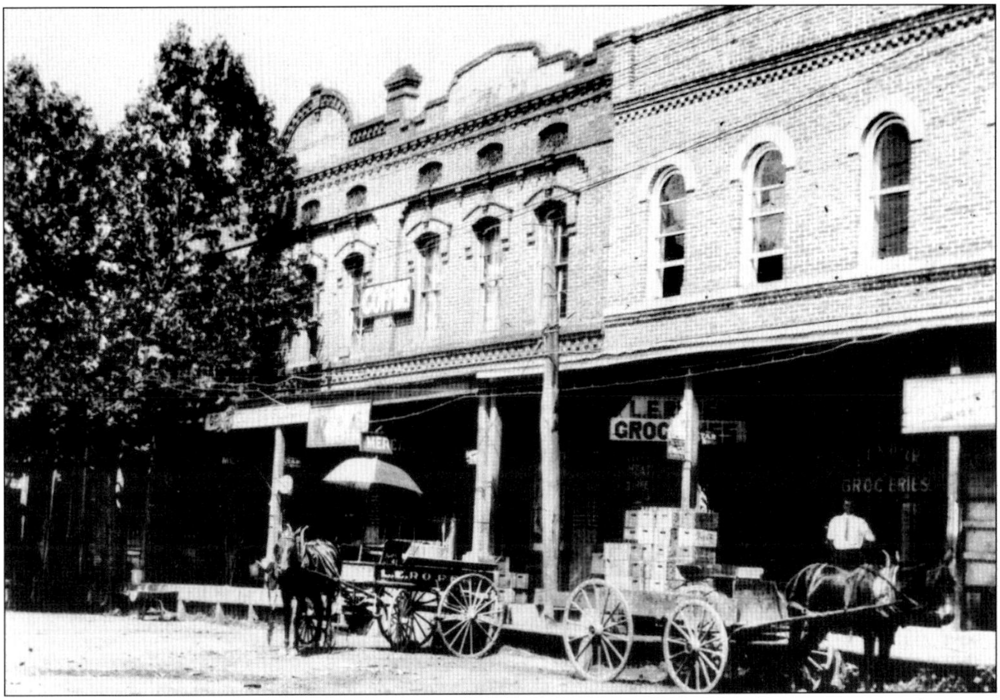

This photograph shows the north side of the Town Square *c.* 1892. L. E. Roper Groceries has two dray wagons in front of the store for deliveries. The wagon with the umbrella overhead for the driver is identified as belonging to "L. E. Roper" on the sides. Groceries were delivered to private homes for the local homeowners until the 1970s, when larger supermarkets opened off the square. Note the sign "Coffins" upstairs on the building to the left of the grocery.

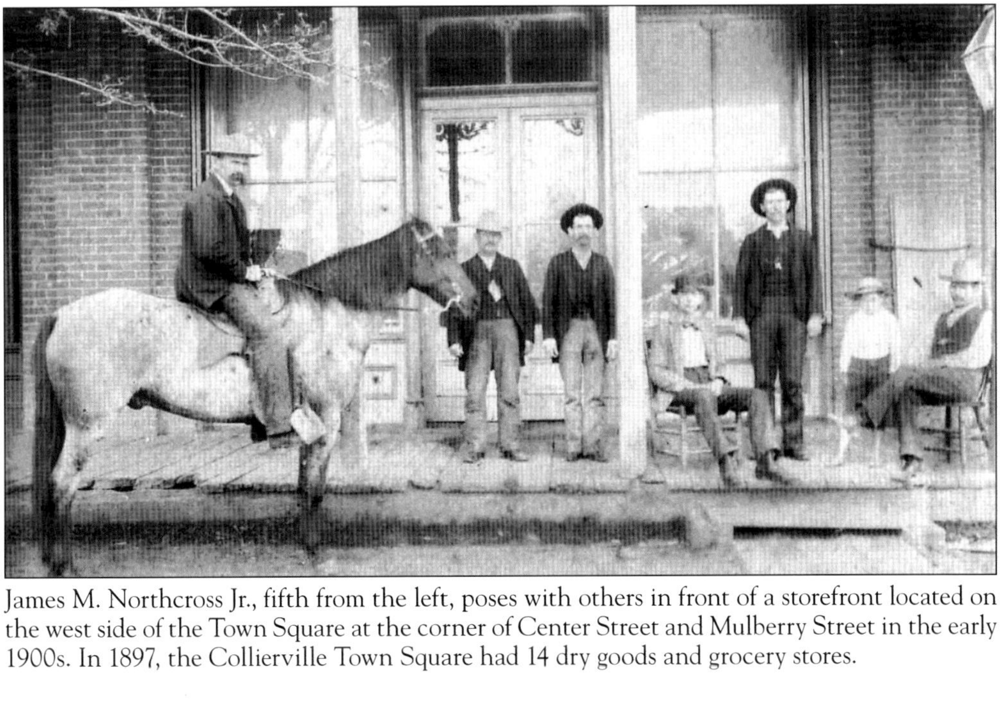

James M. Northcross Jr., fifth from the left, poses with others in front of a storefront located on the west side of the Town Square at the corner of Center Street and Mulberry Street in the early 1900s. In 1897, the Collierville Town Square had 14 dry goods and grocery stores.

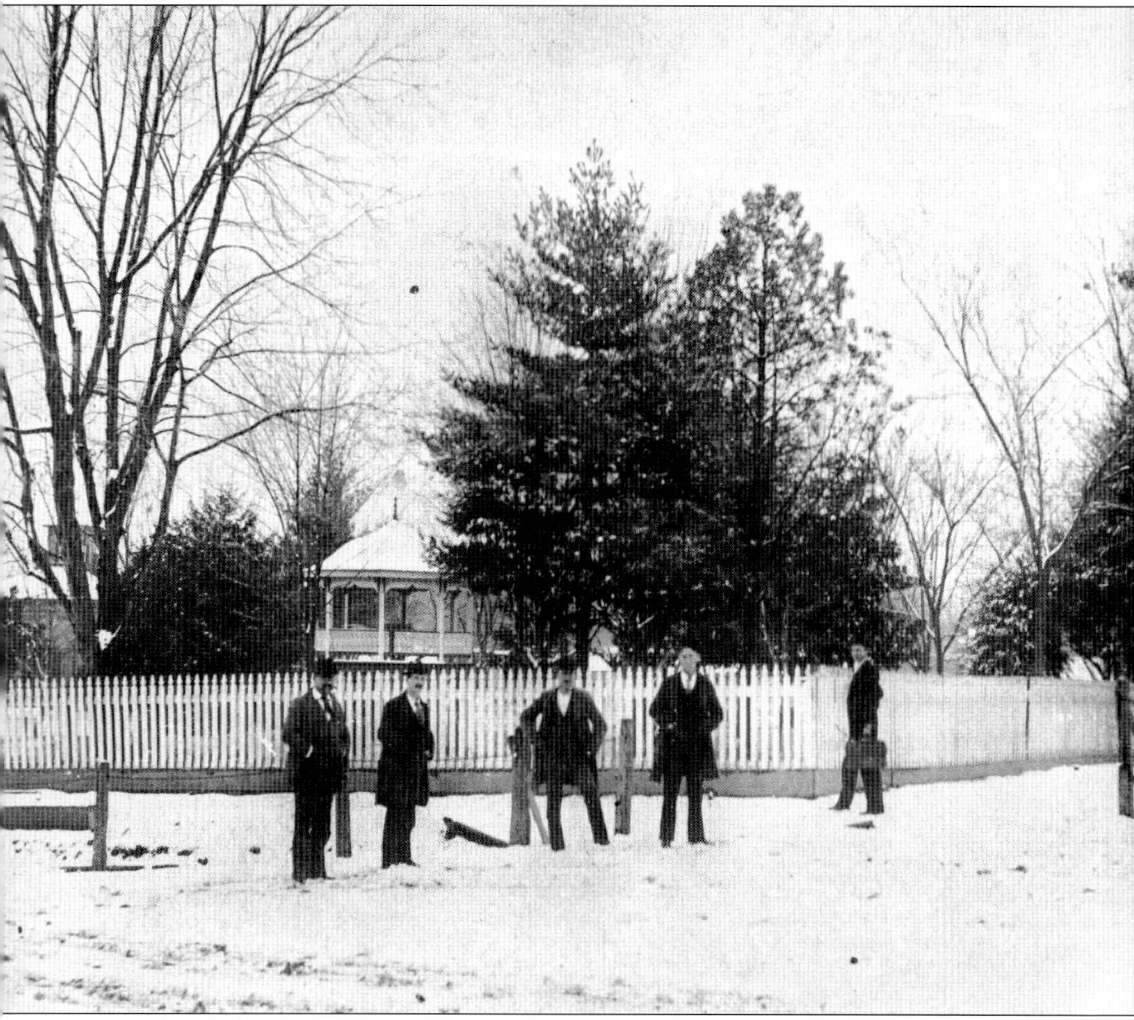

Confederate Park, built in 1872 and also known today as the Town Square, is shown in the snow with the original bandstand in the background. This photograph, taken in 1900, shows, from left to right, Dudley Jones, unidentified, James Powell, W. H. Brown, and unidentified. Unlike most Southern towns, Collierville is unique to have a park in the center of its business district even though it is not a county seat. The "Public Park," as it was known in early deeds, later was named Confederate Park. In 1872, a white picket fence enclosed the park, where peafowl (peacocks) and deer were kept. Wiley Washington McGinnis and his employees hauled dirt and trees to the park from the Wolf River bottom. By 1890, many businesses were around the square, including banks, dry goods stores, groceries, liveries, hotels, saloons, druggists, physicians, blacksmiths, and others. Today it is a place to meet friends and family and enjoy a relaxed pace of life.

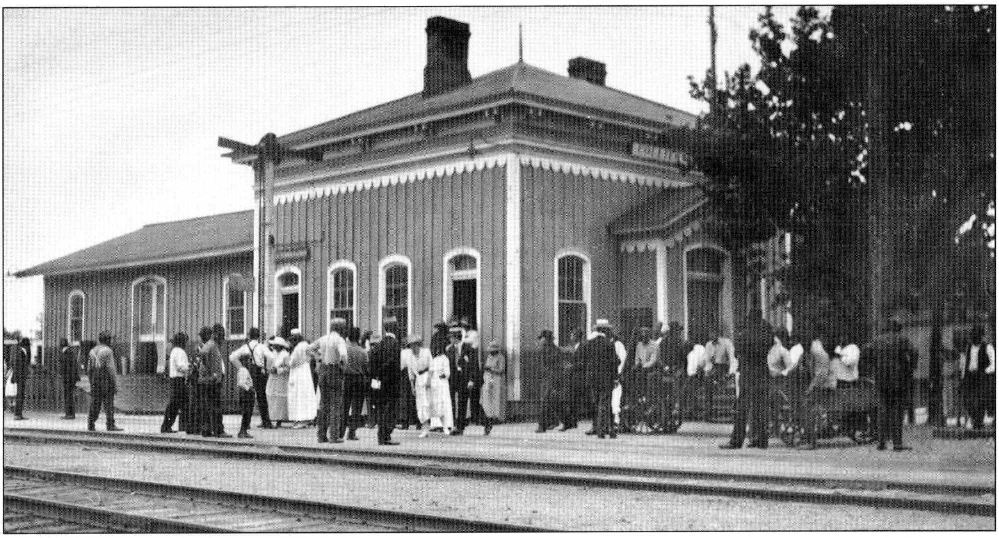

The Collierville Depot was constructed in 1885 and was located west of the present-day structure. A large cotton platform adjoined the depot on the east side, with an icehouse on the west side. For many years, a commuter train called the *Sommerville Accommodation* transported passengers to and from Memphis. The train ran from 1856 until 1930. The train, operated for many years by engineer Mike Brady, arrived each morning at 7:00 a.m. Brady retired in 1930 after 50 years of service. A round-trip ticket to Memphis cost around 20¢ in the 1920s.

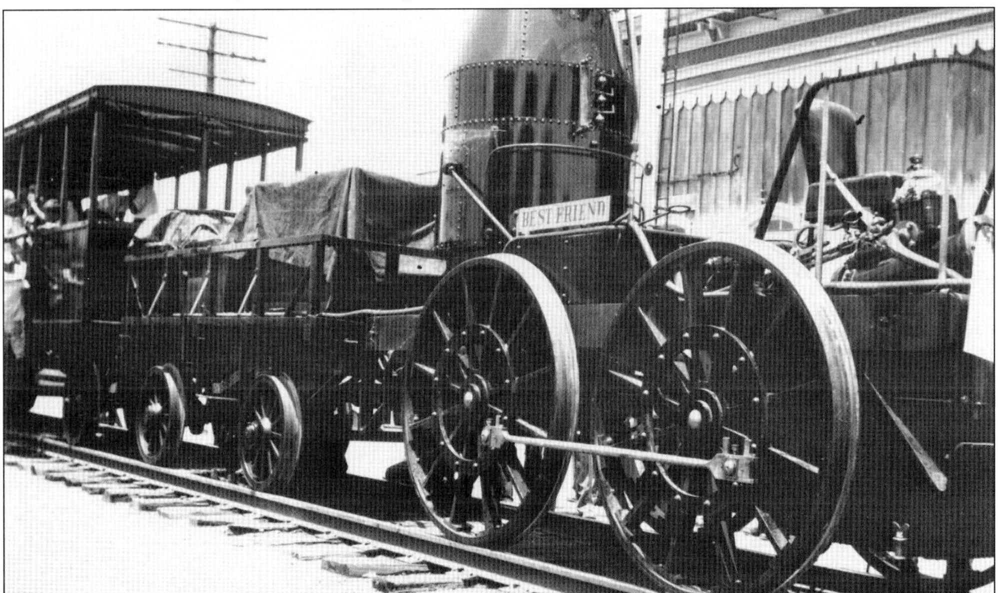

This 1929 photograph shows the *Best Friend of Charleston* replica, built from the original plans in 1928 to commemorate the 100th anniversary of the South Carolina Canal and Rail Road Company. The original steam engine was built in 1830, was used in regular passenger service along a six-mile route off of Charleston, South Carolina, and could transport its passengers at an amazing speed of 25 miles per hour. In 1831, the engine's boiler exploded, injuring the crew and destroying the *Best Friend.* Southern Railway operated this replica on excursions across the United States. The photograph is taken of the replica adjacent to the depot pictured earlier.

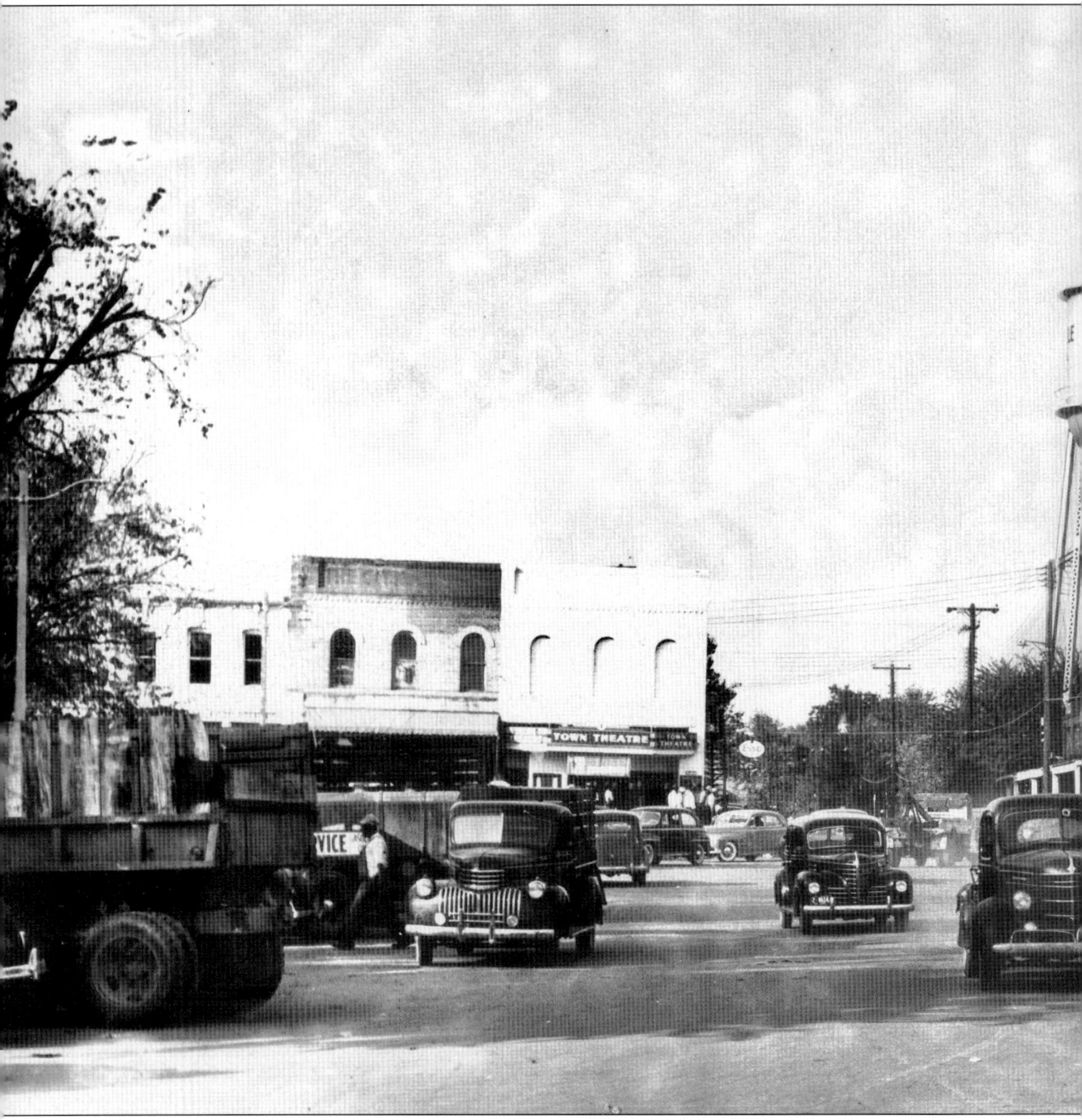

By 1940, the town of Collierville had become a bustling community. With a growing population, the businesses around the Town Square and depot were thriving. Shown facing south was a movie theater, and facing west was Treadwell and Sammons Groceries and Meats, McGinnis Service Station, city hall, a café, and the Collierville Cash Grocery. The town's water tower is shown in the distance. Shopping centers, apart from the downtown, were not built in Collierville until

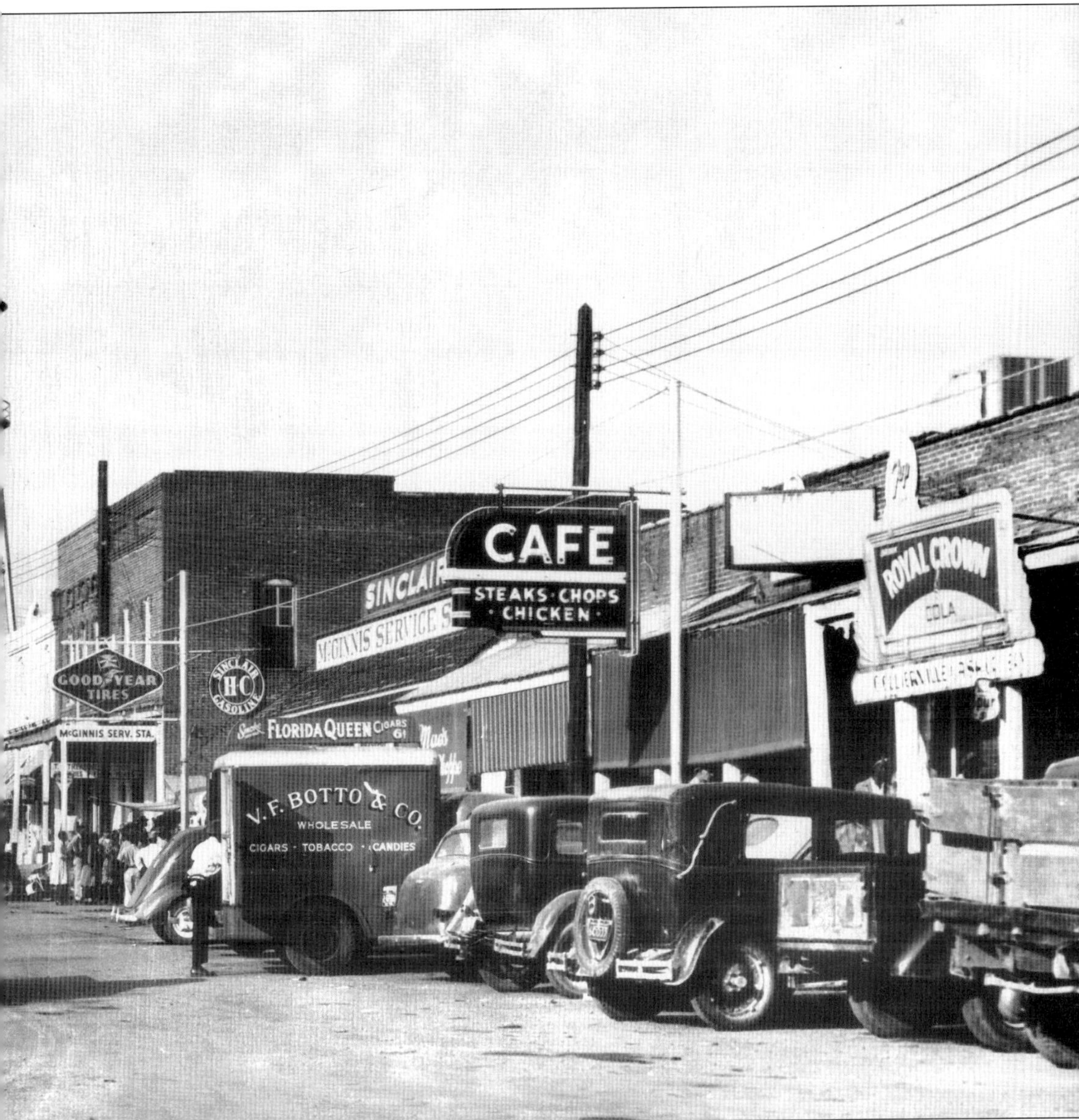

1960, which allowed the community to retain its rural and small-town atmosphere. Industry in the 1950s also contributed to the development of the area outside downtown. In 1990, the town of Collierville participated in a streetscape program under the National Trust for Historic Preservation. The restoration of the historic buildings to the original or appropriate design has helped preserve the business and historic district. Today it remains a vital part of the town's activity.

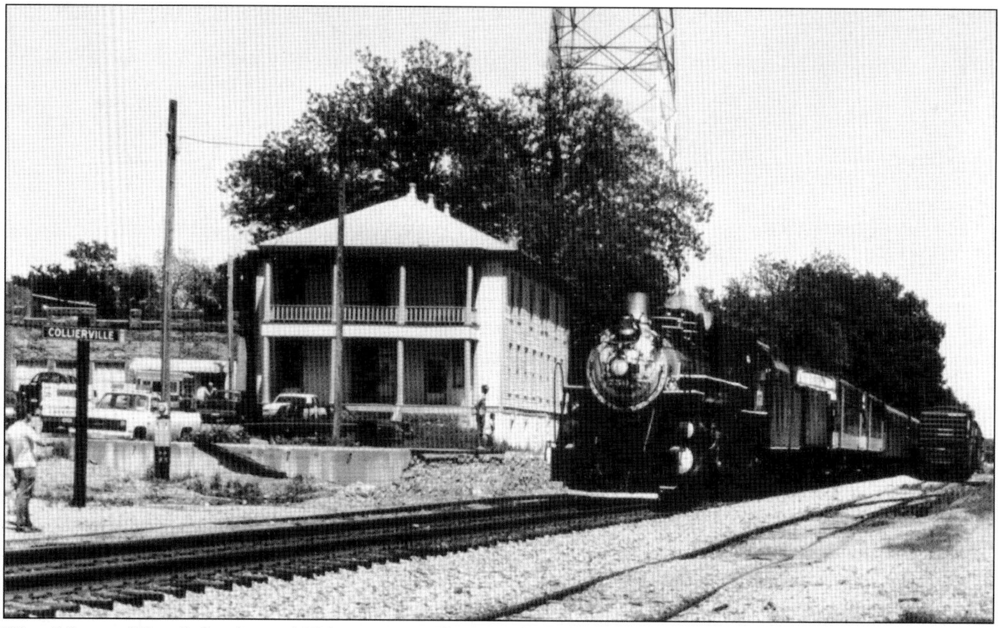

The Hester Hotel, built in 1892, was on the north side of the railroad tracks on Main Street. This hotel as one of the earliest buildings on the square for train passengers. The train stop later served as a boarding house for many years but was destroyed by fire in 1986. Many of the stores on the east side of the Town Square, south of Washington Street, at various times were destroyed by fire but rebuilt.

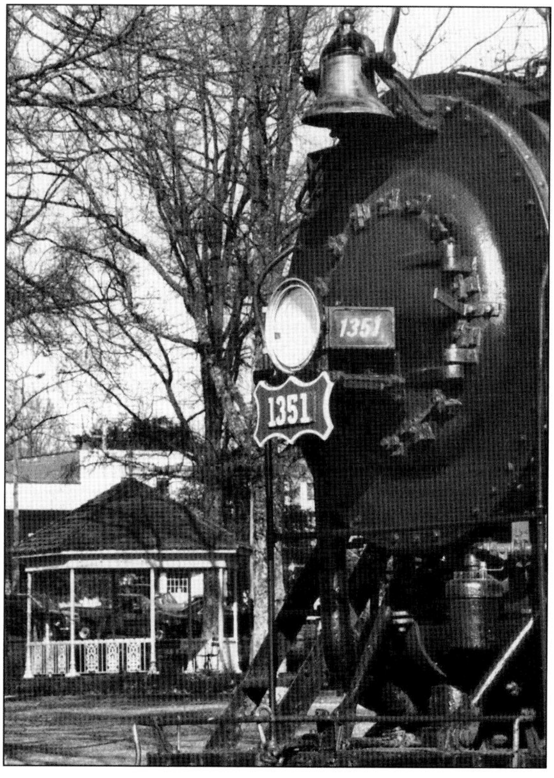

Engine 1351 weighs approximately 230 tons. Among many other duties, it pulled troop trains during World War II. No. 1351 was retired in 1952 and spent many years at the Memphis Fairgrounds and the Defense Depot.

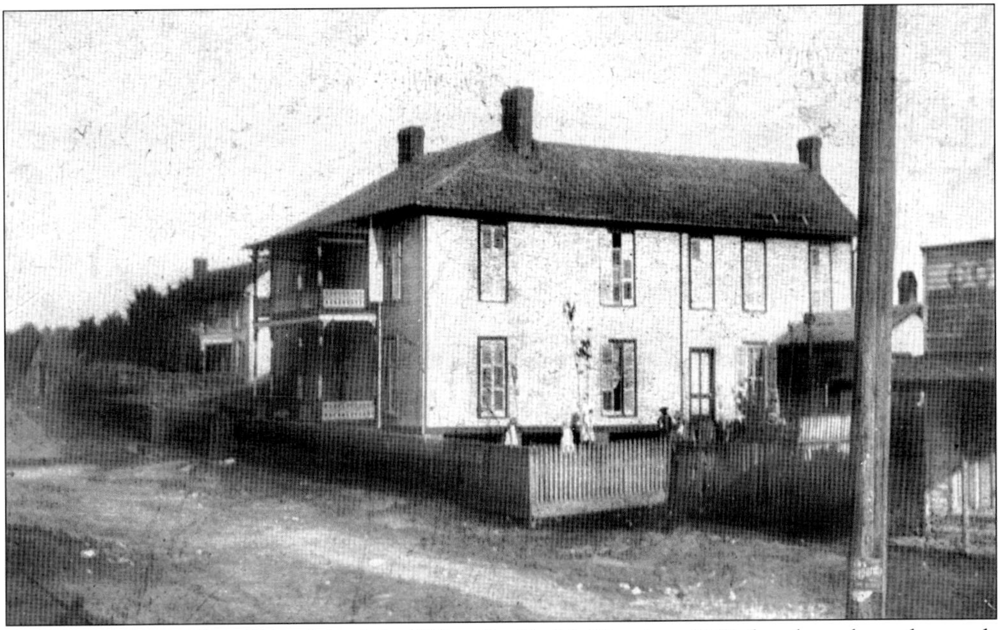

The McGinnis Railroad Hotel, built by Wiley Hinkle McGinnis *c.* 1889, faced north on the south side of the railroad tracks on South Rowlett Street. The hotel housed many of the railroad workers and local boarders. The original Majestic Cooking Stove from the hotel's kitchen is on display in the window of the McGinnis Hardware store today. Many of the original interior features were removed before the building was demolished in 2002.

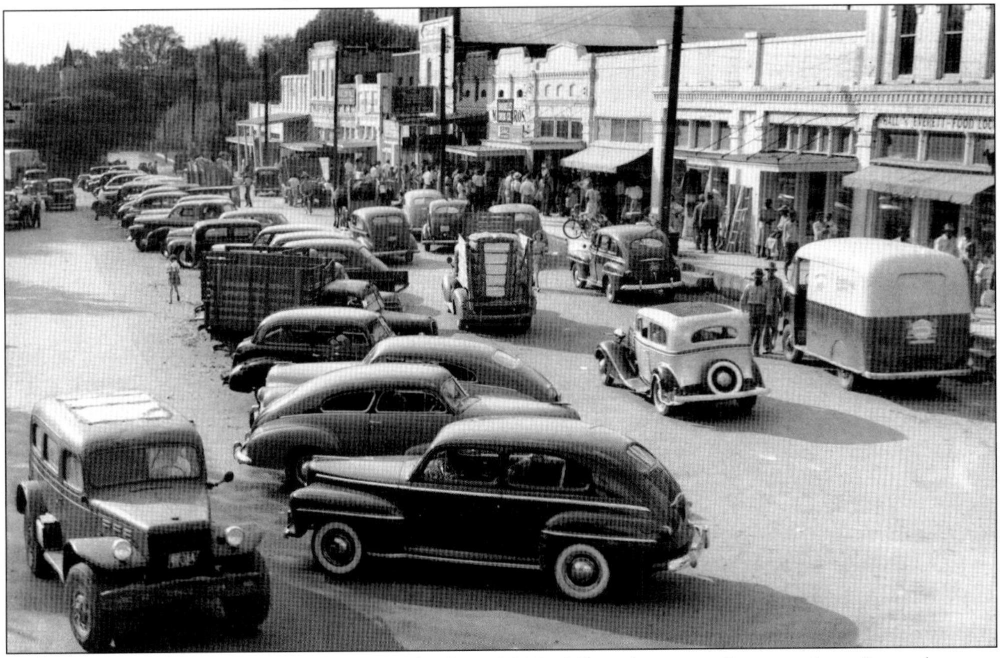

This was a busy day on the square in the late 1940s. The photograph was taken from the east side of the square. Saturday provided an opportunity for farmers to come into town and purchase goods. Stores were closed Thursday afternoons and Sundays. In this photograph, the milk truck can be seen parked on the north side of the square.

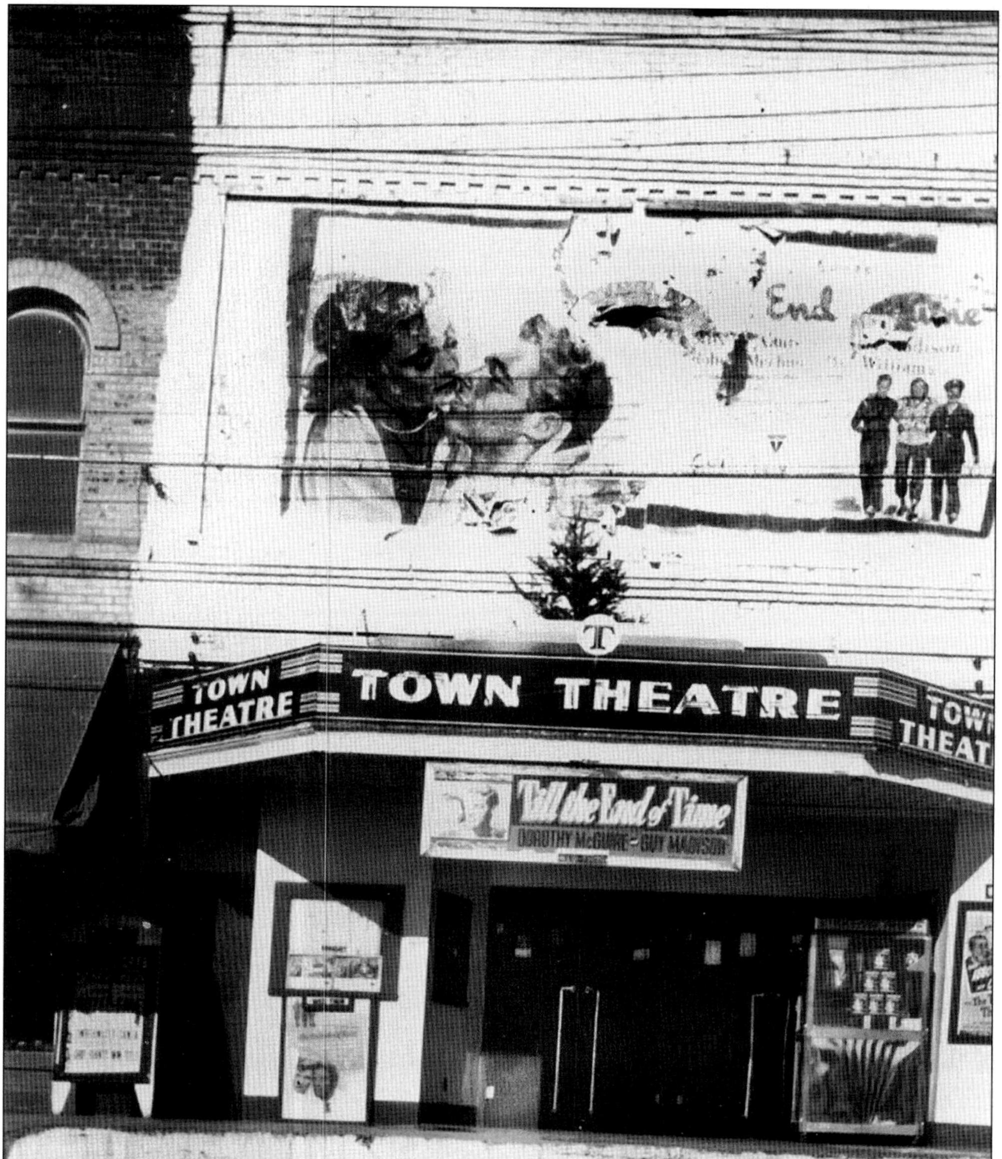

The Town Theatre, owned and operated by the James Haynes family, was located at Mulberry and Main Streets and provided many pleasant memories for Collierville residents. Sam Barrett popped popcorn, and Carl Rutledge ran the projector. Beulah Haynes and her daughters, Sallie, Pat, and Joy, collected tickets and ran the theater. Black residents sat in the upstairs balcony. The theater was destroyed in October 1955 by a tornado. The building was repaired and used as a grocery store, a fireplace shop, and, after a recent renovation, is now used as a Bible museum.

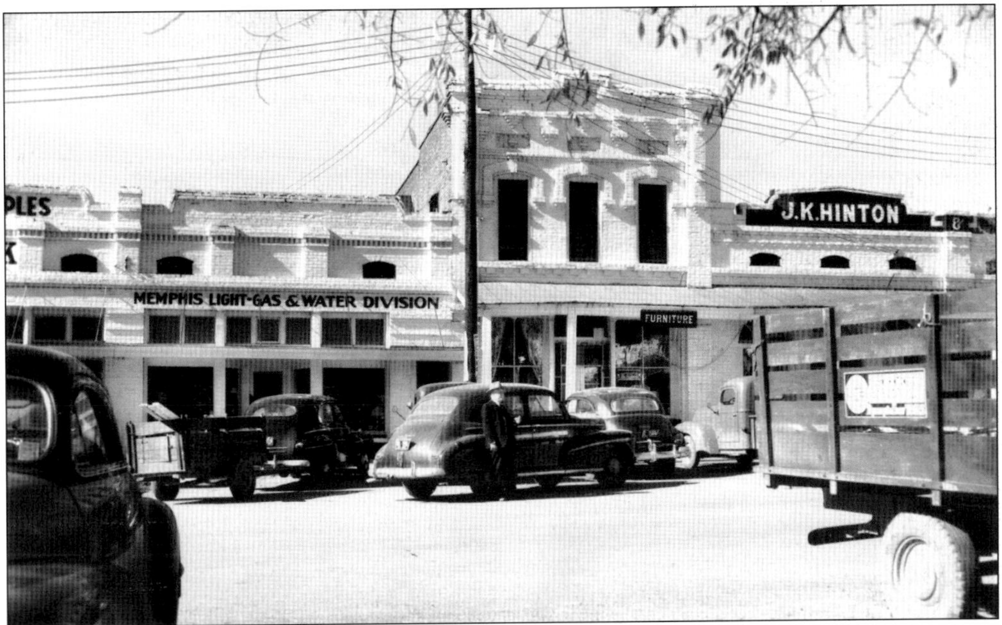

McGinnis Hardware on the corner of the west side of the square is located in a building built in 1879 by T. J. Morris. It was originally built as a lumber and hardware store and is still used and operated as such today. Though heavily damaged by fire in 1996, the historic building has been totally restored. The two adjacent buildings have been used as a saloon, bank, barbershop, insurance agency, and Memphis Light, Gas and Water office.

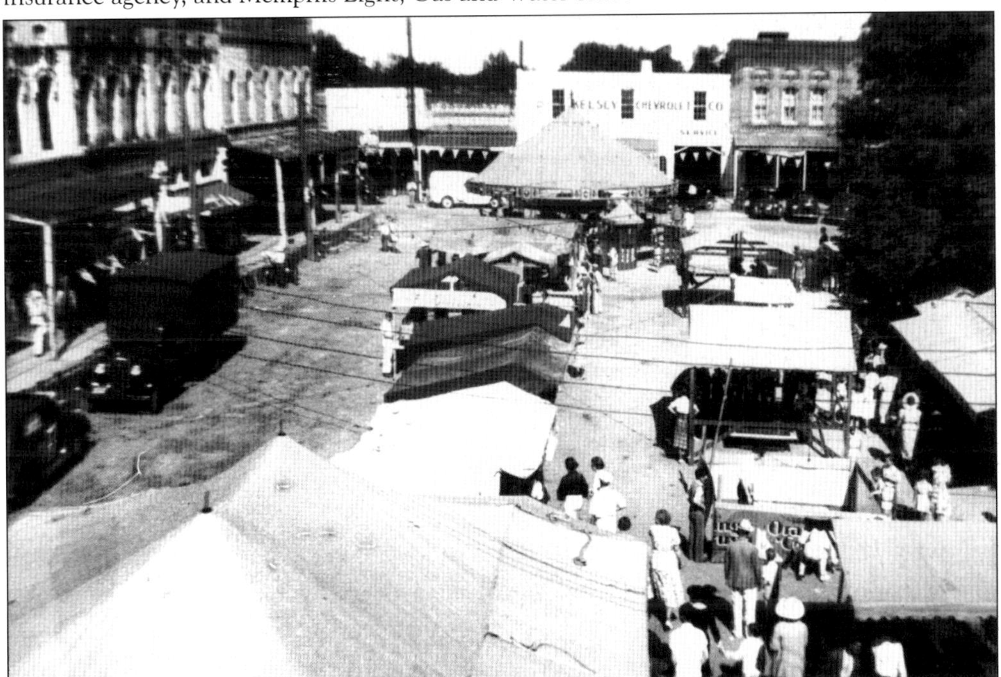

A 1937 photograph taken atop the Ferris wheel at the Cheese Carnival looks east on Mulberry Street. The Cheese Carnival's rides were set up in the main part of downtown for several days to be enjoyed by young and old alike. Kelsey Chevrolet can be seen in the distance.

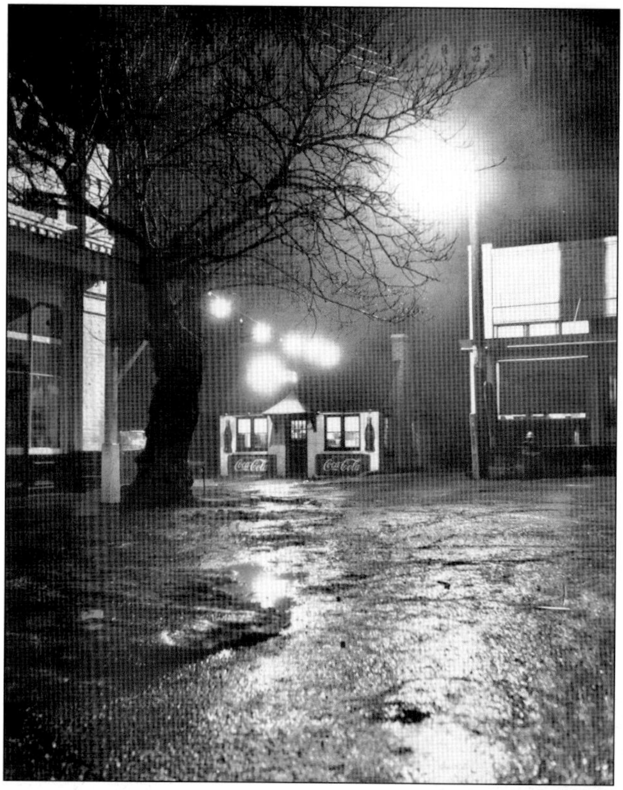

Teenagers frequented the Toddle House Grill on Mulberry Street at the northwest corner of the Town Square in 1948. The last mulberry tree on the Town Square is outlined in the shadows. Behind the tree was a tall water spigot for public use. Two carved gourds were used for drinking. Today a Bank Tennessee branch is located at the site and is the only bank to remain on the Town Square.

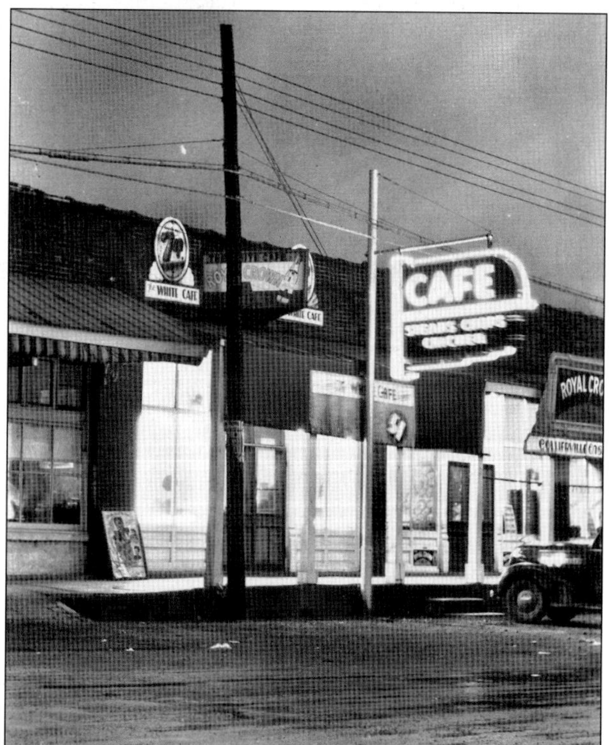

The White Café on Main Street was known for its curb service. Customers could pull up in front of the café and blow their horn. The building to the left of the café was the town's first movie house in 1928. That building was later divided into a beauty shop and general merchandise store. In the 1940s, the *Collierville Herald* was located here.

Two

TOWNSPEOPLE

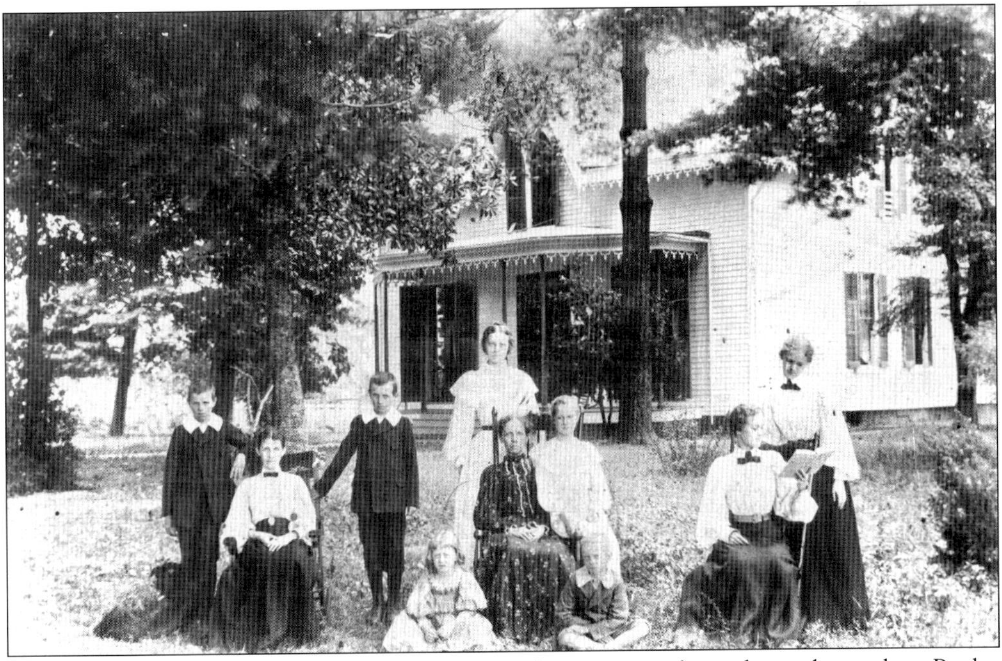

The Deloach/Cartwright family poses in front of a two-story frame home located on Poplar Avenue, west of Collierville. Thomas Hill Peters built the house in 1840. This photograph gives us a glimpse of the antebellum elegance that existed at that time. The Josiah Deloach family lived in the house during the Civil War. Deloach, who was a Union sympathizer, entertained Gen. Ulysses S. Grant at the home in 1862. Two of his sons served in the Confederate army, one in the Collierville Wigfall Grays. Even though Josiah was considered a Northern sympathizer, he owned slaves but opposed secession. When Grant was elected president after the war, he appointed Deloach postmaster in Memphis. Josiah Deloach was spoken of as a man of remarkable influence and great wealth, but after the war, like most Southerners, his lifestyle changed.

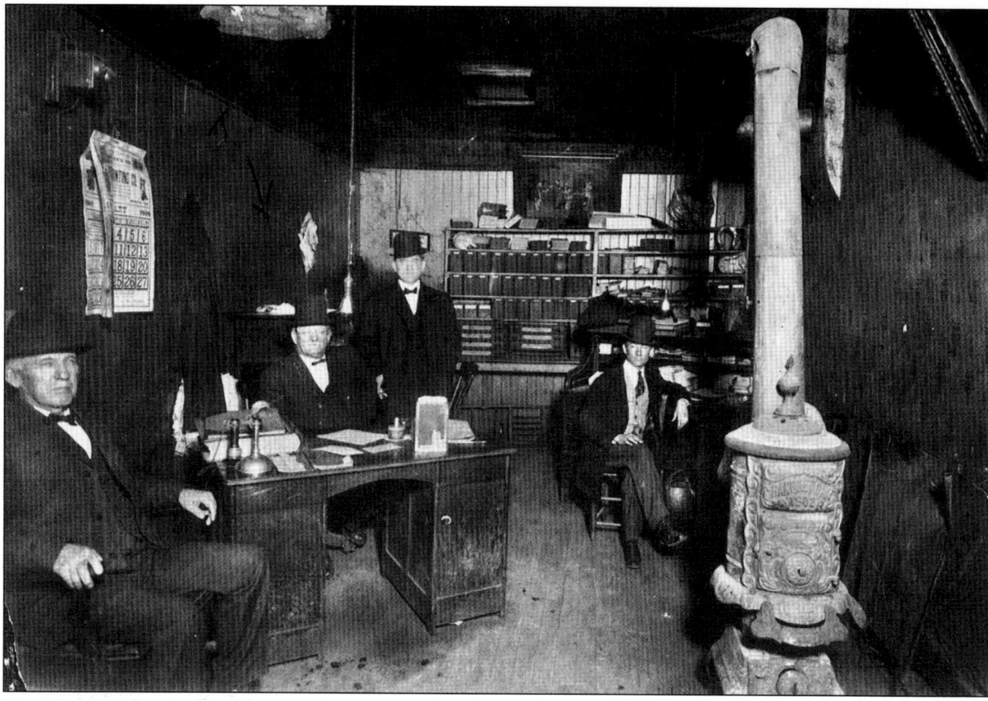

The man at the desk is Thomas Theodore McDonald, who was a three-time mayor of Collierville. He is surrounded by town officials in 1904. John Pittman Humphrey, also a past mayor of Collierville is the first on the left. The other men in the store are not identified.

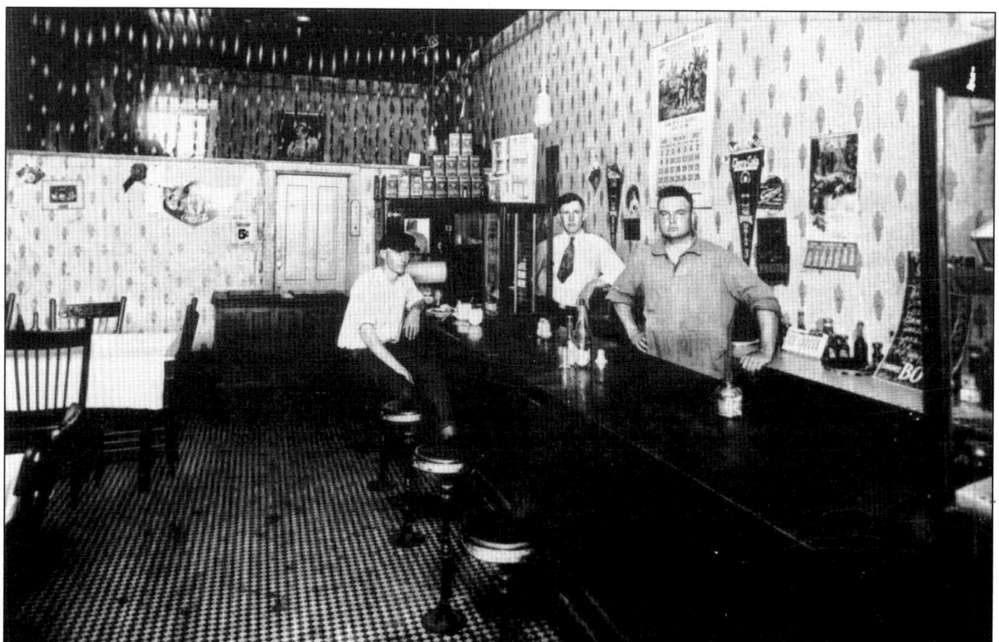

The White Café, shown here in 1922, was located on Main Street, south of Washington Street. Henry Schrader, the owner, is in the photograph. The restaurant featured steaks, chops, and chicken. The building became a heating and air-conditioning business in the 1930s.

Dr. David Thompson Waddy (1828–1892) practiced medicine for a short time in Collierville. After the yellow fever epidemic, he opened a pharmacy and mercantile business. Dr. Waddy was a devout member of Collierville United Methodist Church. He died only a short distance from his home in an effort to obtain medicine for Mattie, his ailing wife. Mattie died less than a year later, and they are both buried in Magnolia Cemetery.

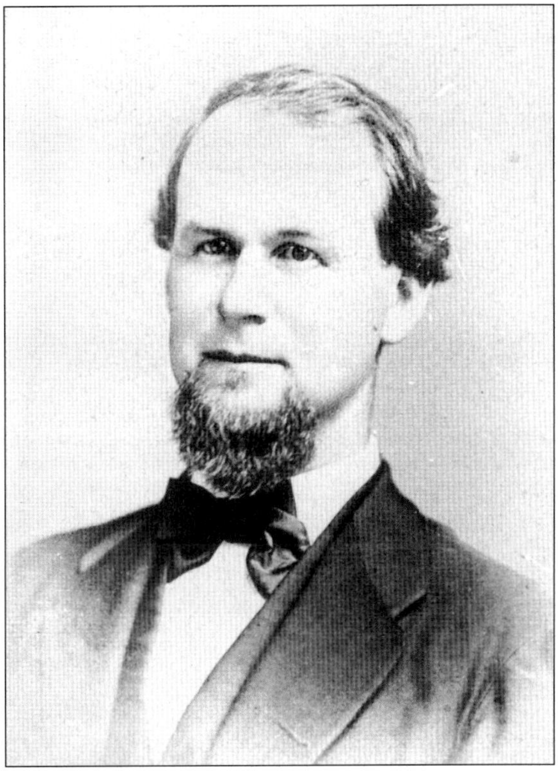

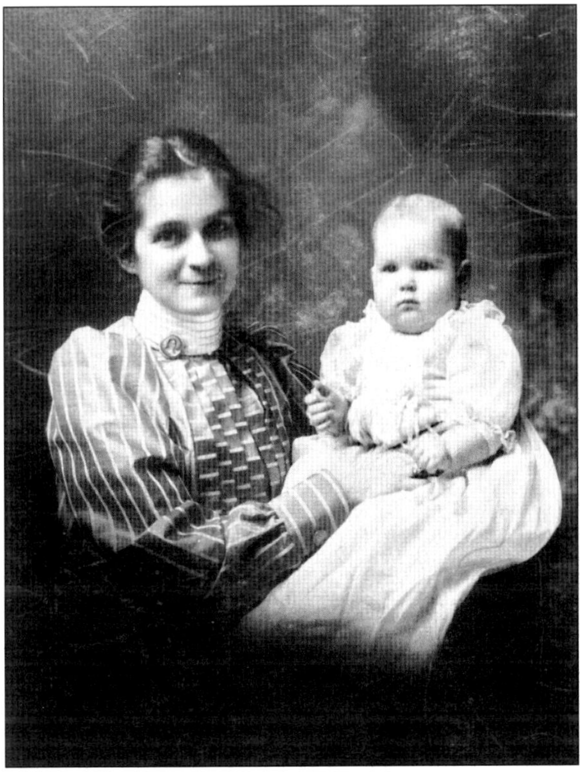

Martha Rebecca Waddy Childress (1869–1948) was the daughter of Dr. David Waddy and his wife, Mattie. She is pictured with her daughter, Martha Childress, who was born in 1898. Martha Rebecca was a well-known pianist. She was married to John Jones Childress, who was related to the Jones family that established the nearby Ames Plantation.

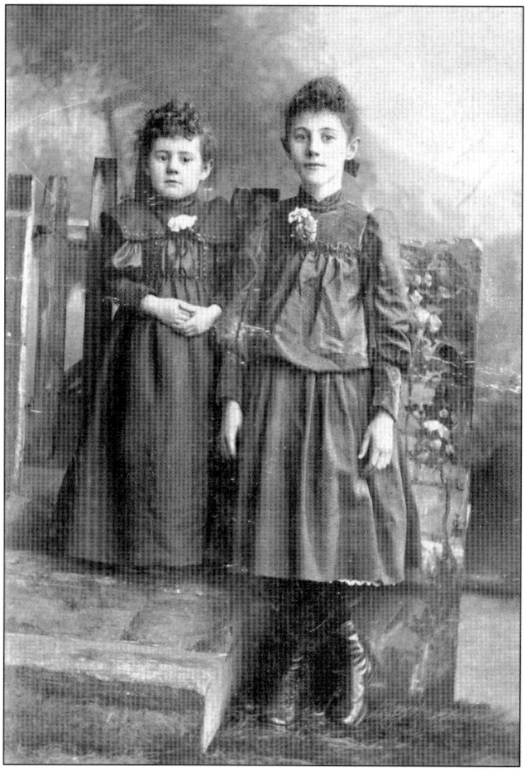

Tinnie Mae Cox (left), born in 1902, and Birdie Cox, born in 1889, were just children when this photograph was made. Tinnie died at age 27. Birdie Cox married Maynard Livingston Wingo but also died at an early age. She was 21.

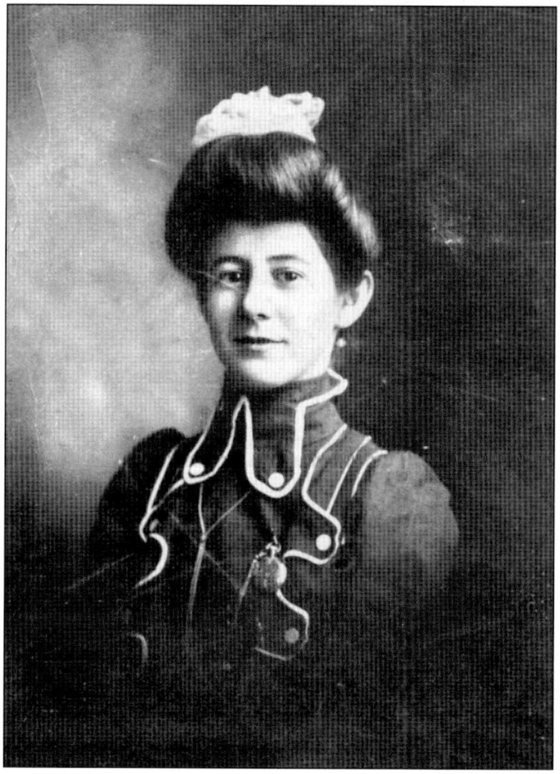

One of the Cox daughters, thought to be Tinnie Mae, was photographed in the 1920s. The Cox family was well known in the community, and portraits of ladies at a young age were desirable as family keepsakes. The ornate design of her dress was common for a formal photograph. Young ladies were encouraged to show a happy expression in their photographs but not to show their teeth.

Fred Eugene Hart Sr. was a dapper young man when this photograph was taken. Born in 1885, Hart married Mary Alice Petrowski in 1912 and was the father of three children. He passed away in 1927. He was very active in his Sunday school at the Collierville United Methodist Church, and his descendants still live in Collierville.

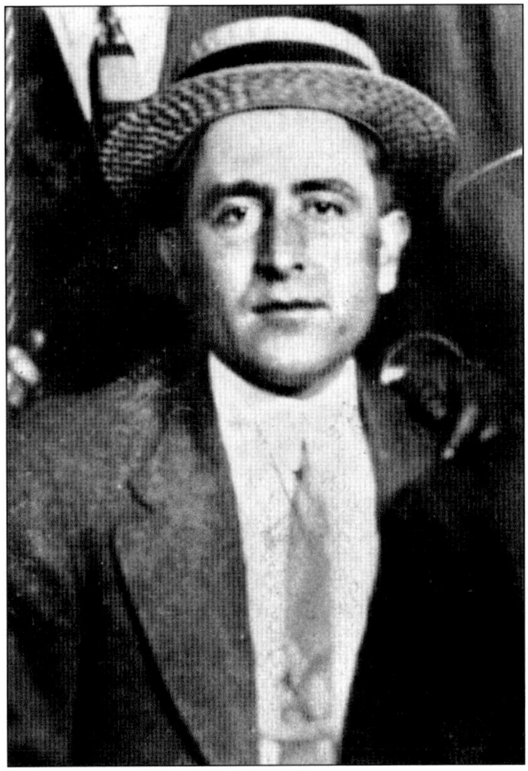

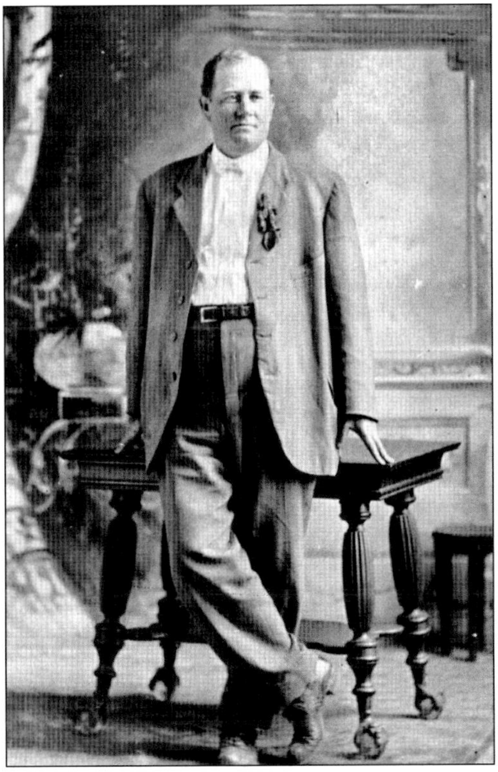

John Wright Cox Jr. was the father of Herman Wright Cox and grandfather of Mayor Herman Wright Cox Jr. At one time, he lived in Cayce, Mississippi, and rode his horse into Collierville. People used to say, "Here comes old man Johnny Cox." He ran a saloon on the square in Collierville, which is where this photograph was taken. He later moved into a house on Mill Street.

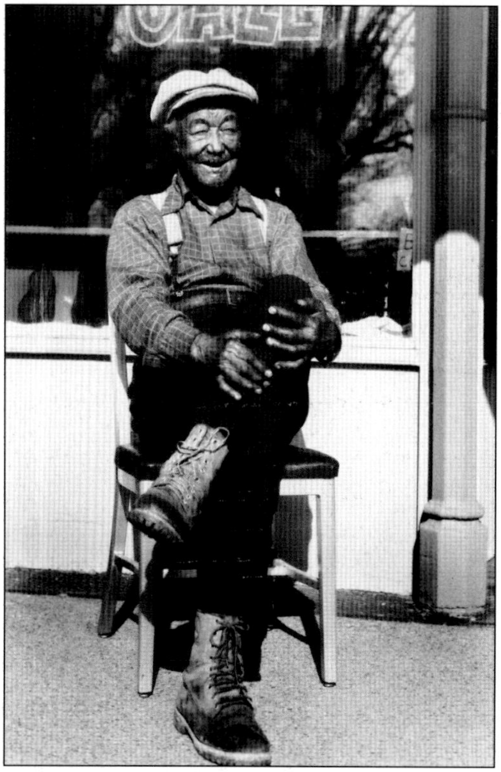

Tom Stewart was well known and loved in the Collierville community. He carried the mail in a large wooden cart to and from the train to the post office. Tom was born on a farm near LaGrange in 1885 and worked as a crewman for the Southern Railroad lines between Grand Junction and Ridgeway stations. He moved to Collierville in 1925 and worked as a drayman for many of the firms around the square before taking a job with the post office.

A familiar scene in 1947 for Collierville residents was a truck unloading cotton bales that would be stacked along the railroad tracks close to the depot. Saturday was a big cotton day for the community. When Center Street was opened to the square, it afforded residents a better access to the businesses on the Town Square.

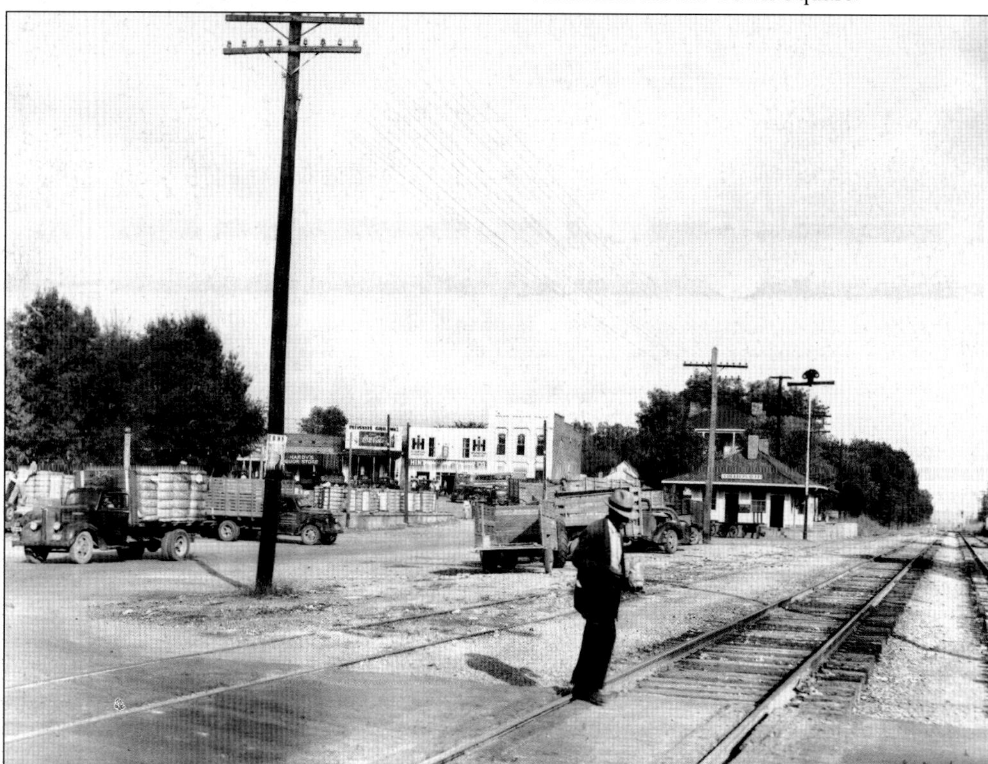

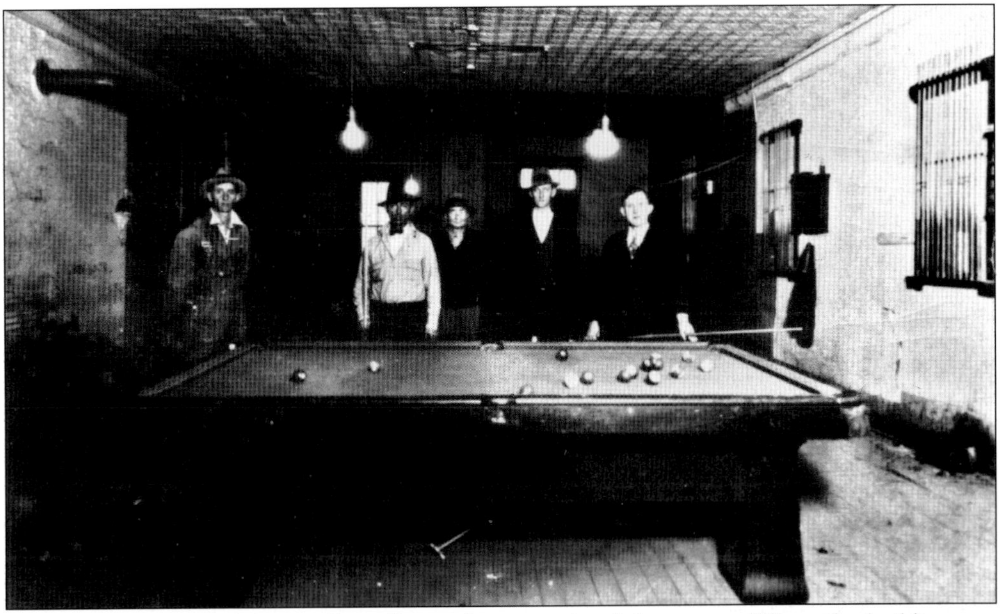

A pool hall was located in Collierville on the east side of the square. When the building was purchased by B. Paul Wilson at a later date, he ran the pool hall for several years. This property remains in the family.

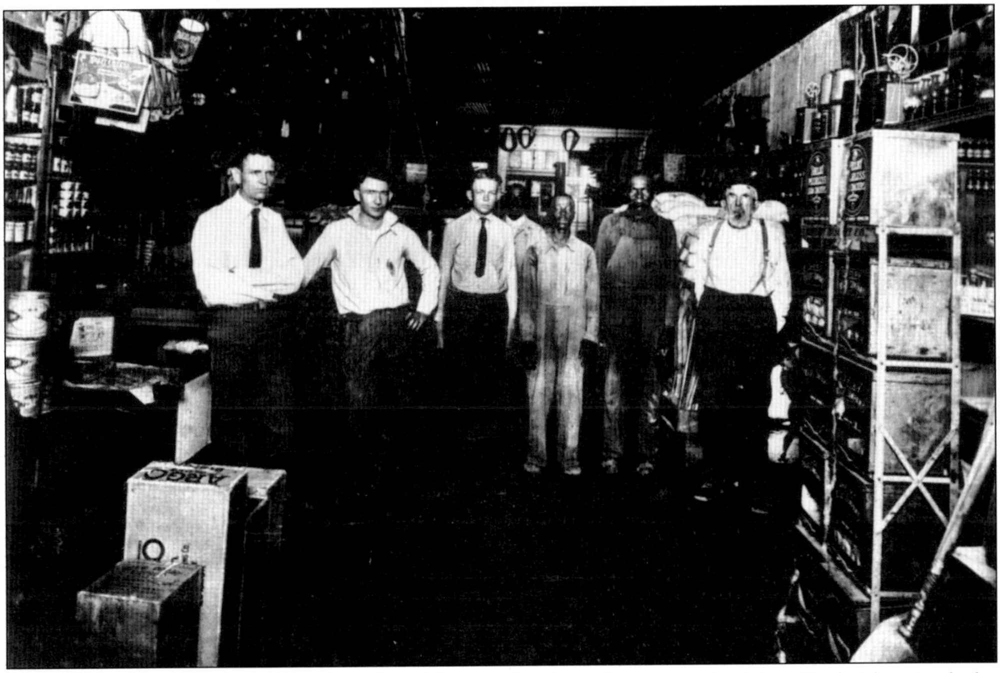

Three men in this 1930s photograph at Hinton Brothers Store can be identified. They include, from left to right, James Karr Hinton, Britt Baldwin, and Herbert Hinton. The general mercantile business was located on the west side of the town square at Center and Mulberry Streets, where the Hewlett and Dunn store is now. James Karr Hinton was also the leading buyer for Collierville and the surrounding cotton-growing community. He was known for dealing fairly and represented Collierville in the Tennessee legislature.

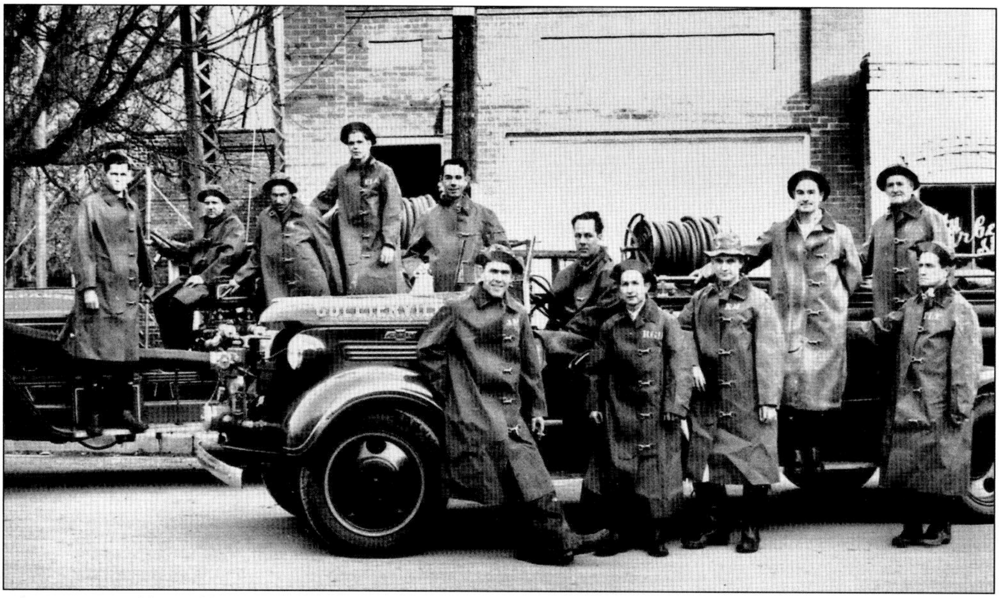

The 1946 Collierville Volunteer Fire Department consisted of, from left to right, Willard Ewing, Lin Kelsey, Joe Ridgeway, Tommy Shepherd, Fire Chief Edgar "Sorghum" Morton, Curtis Cox, Fred Hart, Garner Rutledge, Howard Jamison, Earl Parker, H. L. Sigrest, and O. C. Dean. Volunteer firemen received $1 per fire and were required to meet once a month for training. A $5 bonus was given at the end of the year if they didn't miss a meeting.

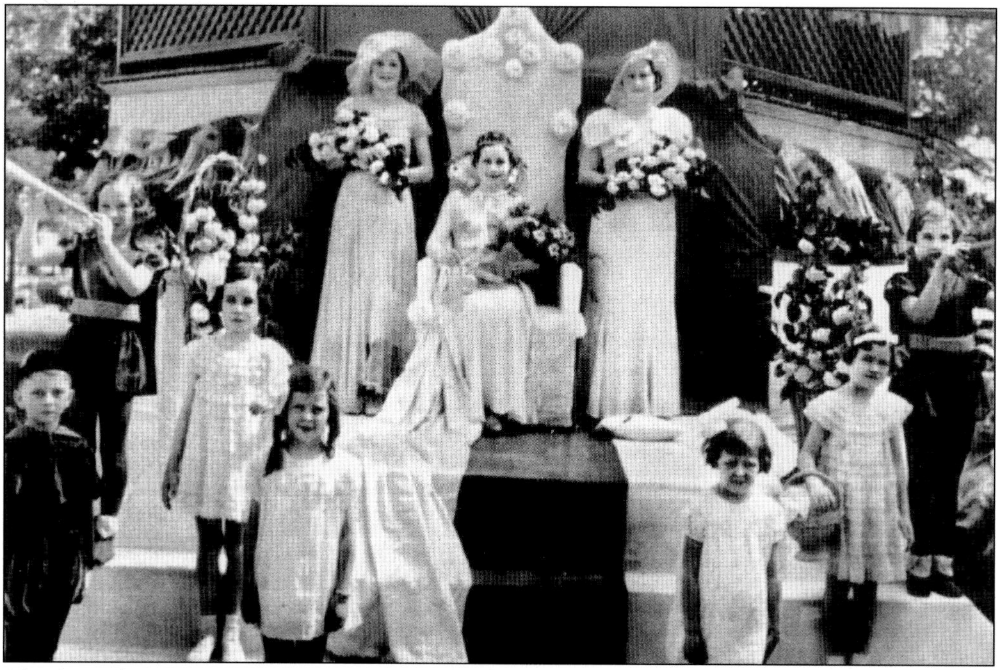

The first Cheese Carnival, in 1935, included Frances Piper as queen. Her maids were Lerdeanya McCandless (left) and Martha Hughes (right). The court included from left to right, Billy Hutton, Joanne Harrell, Kathryn Lynch, Mary Frances Lynch, Kelsey Ann Jones, Florence Kirk, and Virginia Kirk.

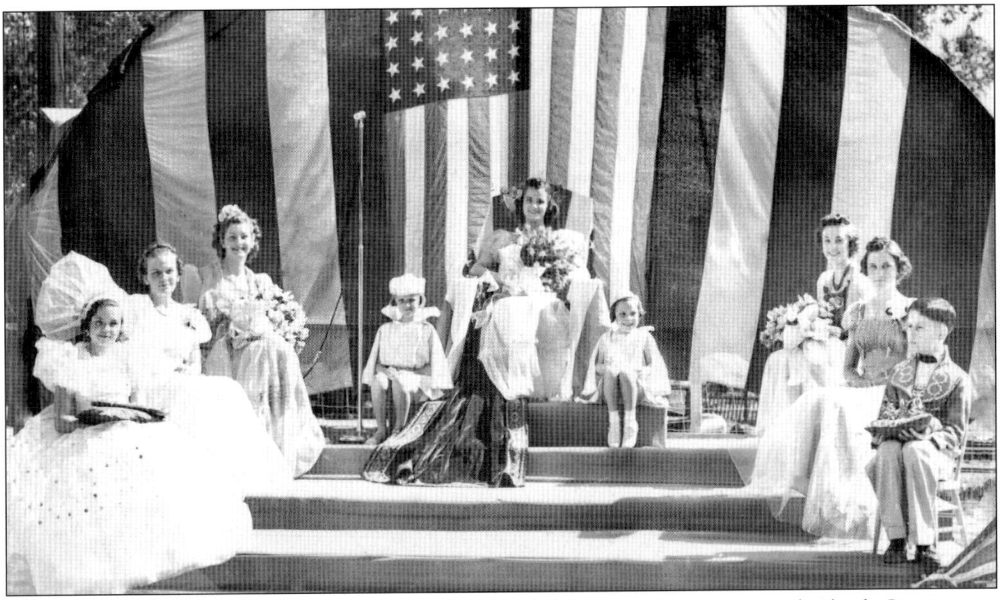

The Cheese Carnival ceremony was the highlight of the community events. Elizabeth Carrington is the queen in the 1939 celebration and is featured on the cover. This picture depicts the royal court during the formal ceremony. Those in the court are, from left to right, Virginia Cartwright, unidentified, Courtney Gaither, unidentified child, Queen Elizabeth Carrington, unidentified child, Dorothy McGee, unidentified, and Stuart Bohan.

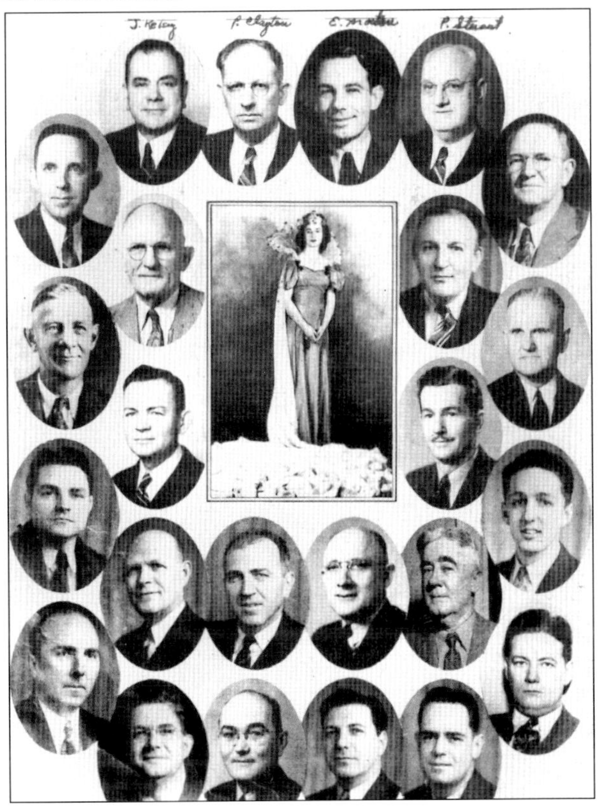

The Cheese Carnival of 1940 featured Sue Ann Jones. This is a photograph with the Rotary Club members, who were a sponsor of the Cheese Carnival.

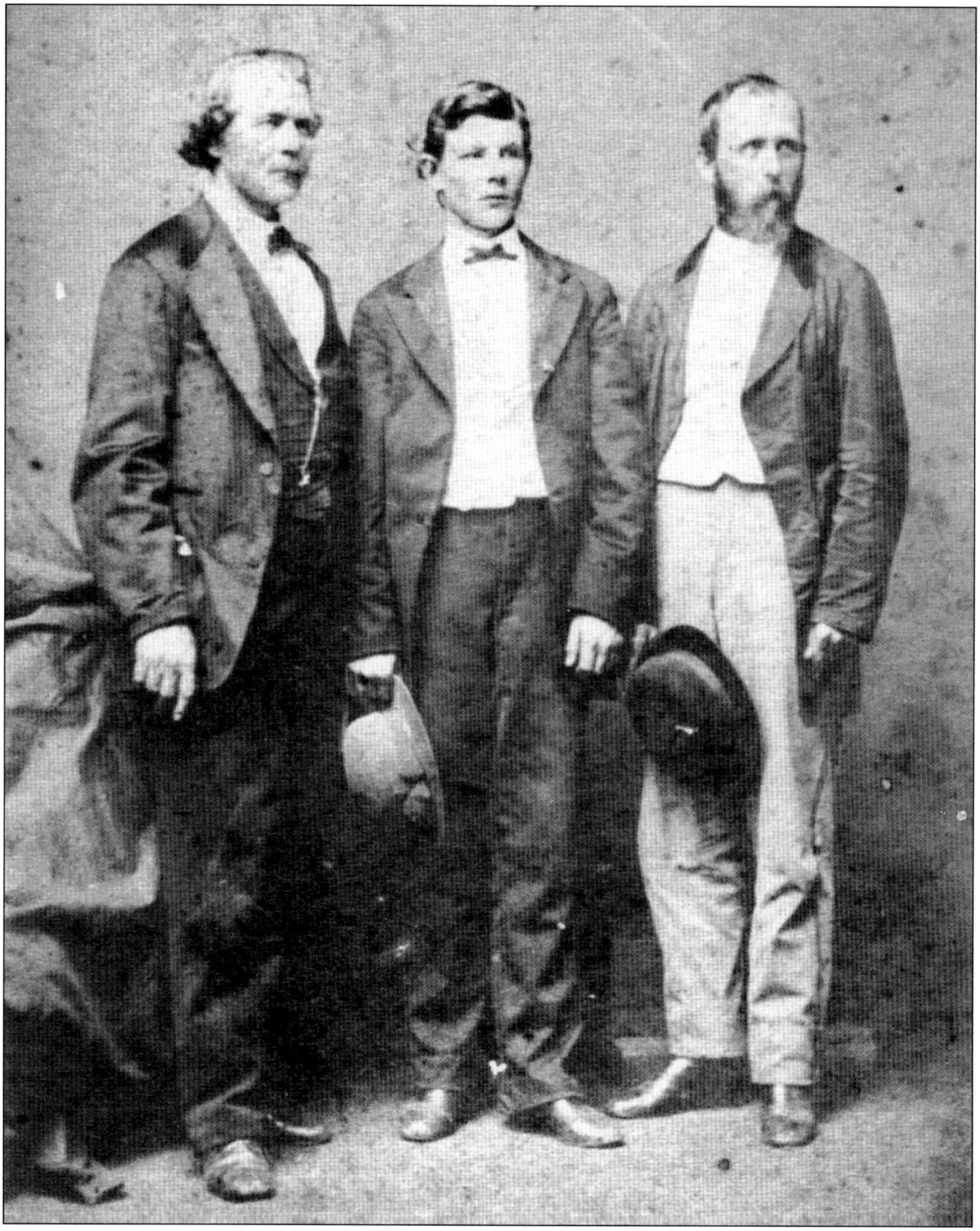

The three men standing are early settlers of Collierville and are, from left to right, Dr. Virginius Leake, Tingnal Jones Leake, and Dr. John Wesley Koen Sr. Dr. Virginius Leake was born in Virginia in 1822. He and his wife, Martha Anderson Field, came to Collierville and built the impressive home, Greenlevel. He was a state senator at the time of his death in 1873. Tingnal Jones Leake was born in 1854 and was the third child of Virginius Leake. He married Emma Keane in 1878 and died at Greenlevel in 1916. Dr. Koen and wife Elizabeth moved to Collierville prior to 1847 from Montgomery County, Tennessee. Dr. Koen was very active in the formation of the early village, as his name appeared on many early deeds and wills as a witness. He also owned large acreage in the area. The family tells of how he often made calls into the rural areas and would fall asleep on his return trip, but his faithful horse would bring him and his buggy safely home.

Tingnal Jones Leake was born in 1854. He attended Virginia Military Institute and married Emma Laura Keane. They had nine children. As Tingnal began to study law, he wrote home after the first year of law school, said he was too honest to be a lawyer, and transferred to Illinois University to become an engineer. The photograph at right shows Tingnal as a young cadet. Family member John Leake visited the school and was able to identify the uniform from the 1874 class. When Tingnal returned to Collierville, he became a cotton gin contractor. The photograph below shows Tingnal as a young businessman. Tingnal died at Greenlevel on February 5, 1916.

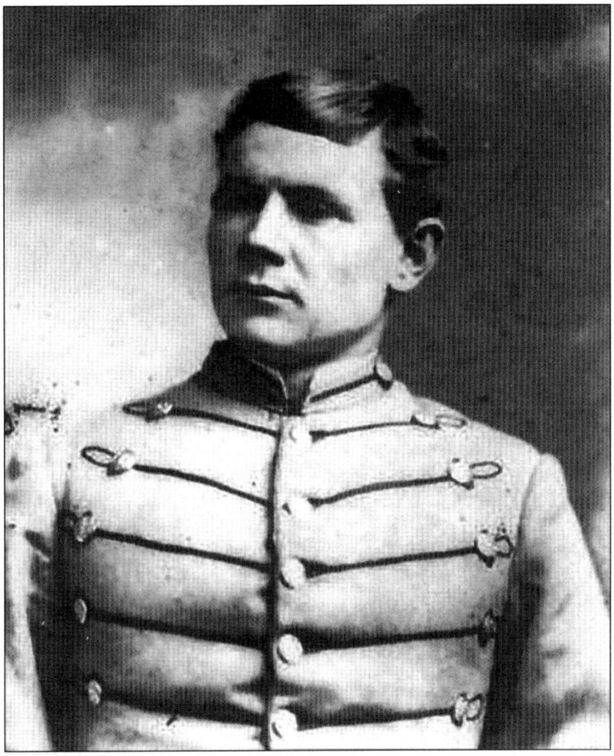

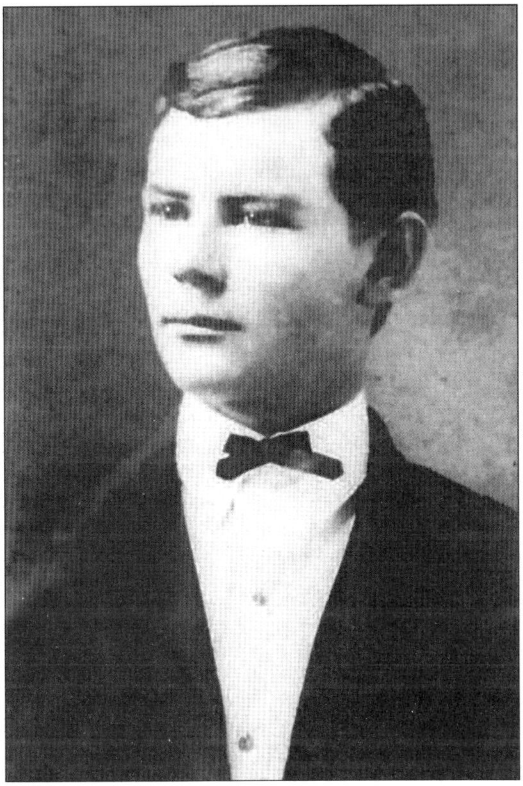

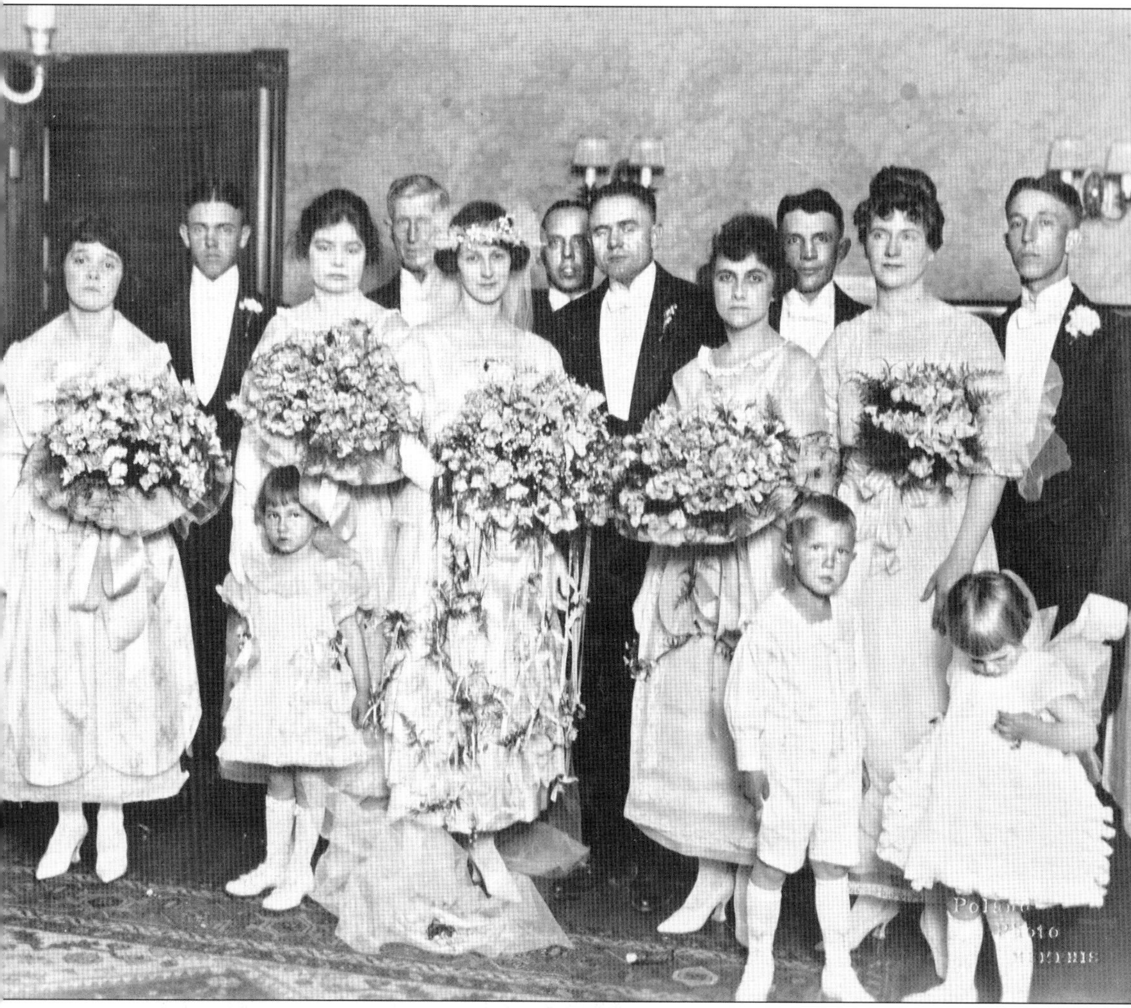

The wedding party of Milton and Alice Mann poses for their photograph on April 14, 1920. From left to right are (first row) Lillian Humphreys, Carrie Mae Mann, Alice, Milton, Virginia Kirk, and Helen Cartwright; (second row) Baxter Crawford, James B. Cartwright (father of the bride), Rev. L. H. Estin, Frank Alley, and David Cartwright; (children) Martha, Jimmy, and Helen Cartwright. The wedding was held at the bride's home. The Cartwright family's nursery and gardens provided the beautiful flowers.

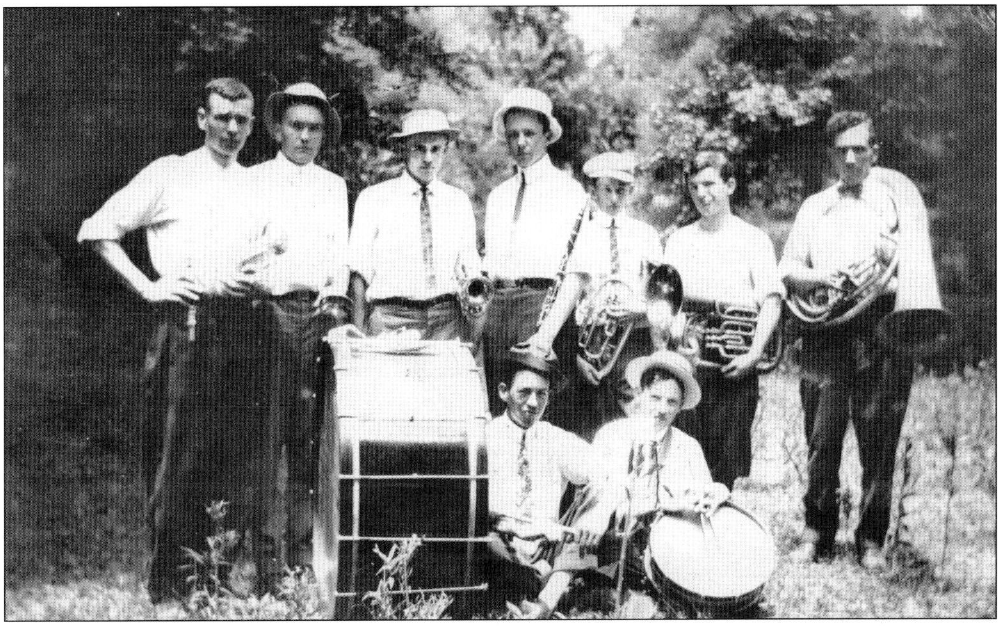

The local Collierville band in 1912 was popular at many social gatherings. The band members are, from left to right, (seated) Taylor Jones and Granville Biggs; (standing) Warren Clay, Franklin Harrell, Milton Mann, Emmet Cox, Cecil Cox, John Algood Humphreys, and unidentified.

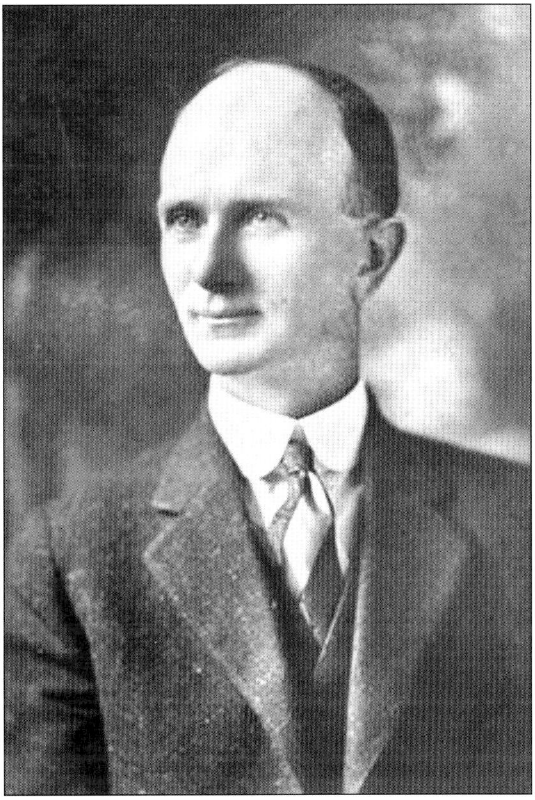

William Newton Craig and his wife, Beulah Hinton, moved to Collierville from Mount Pleasant, Mississippi, around 1902. Craig operated a "furnishings" or general merchandise store called Hinton and Craig with his father-in-law, Sam Hinton, on the north side of the square. He also traded in cotton and served at one time as president of the People's Bank of Collierville. He was an elder and Sunday school superintendent of the Collierville Presbyterian Church.

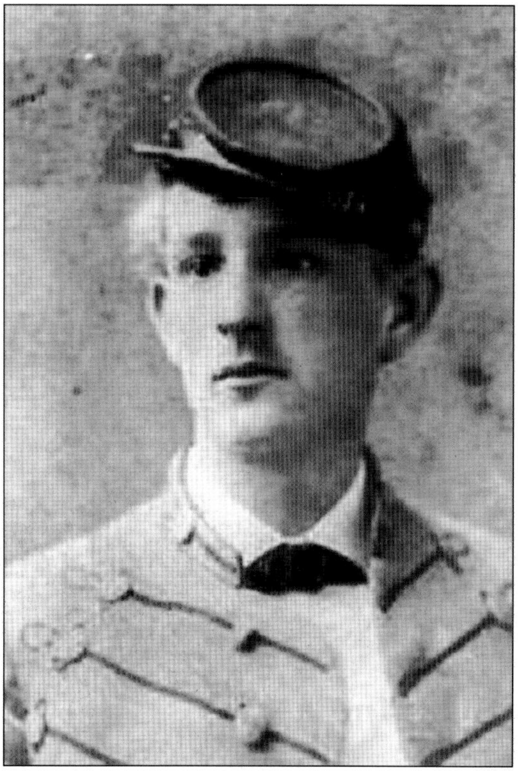

Millard Feild Leake was the second child of Dr. Virginius Leake and his wife, Martha. He was born in 1853. Millard is pictured in his Virginia Military Institute uniform with kepi. He married Alabama Irby and had five children. Even though his family was devout members of the Disciples of Christ Christian Church, Millard became a Methodist preacher. He preached in Collierville and West Tennessee. He is buried in Forest Hill Cemetery in Memphis.

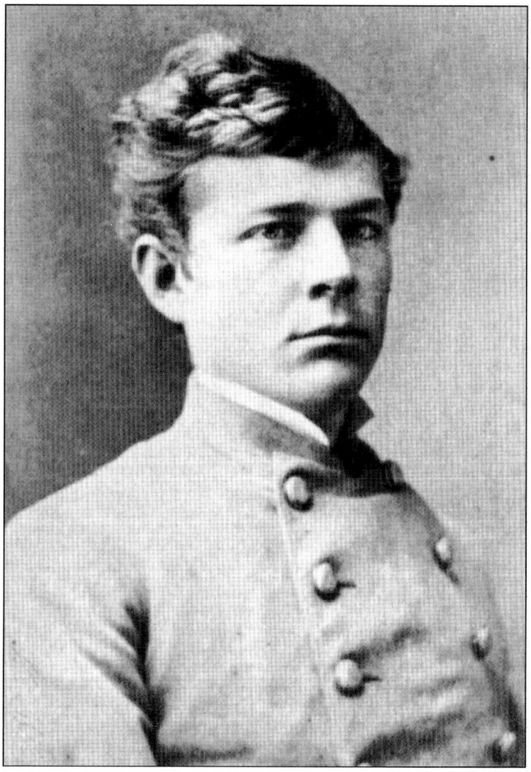

Elgin Kossuth Leake was born in 1852. He attended Virginia Military Institute and practiced medicine in Collierville. He was mayor of Collierville for 23 years. He married Martha Biggs and had seven children. His family had the first automobile and the first telephone in Collierville, and they started the Collierville Water System, which was purchased by the Town of Collierville. Elgin was a charter member of the Collierville Disciples of Christ (Christian Church).

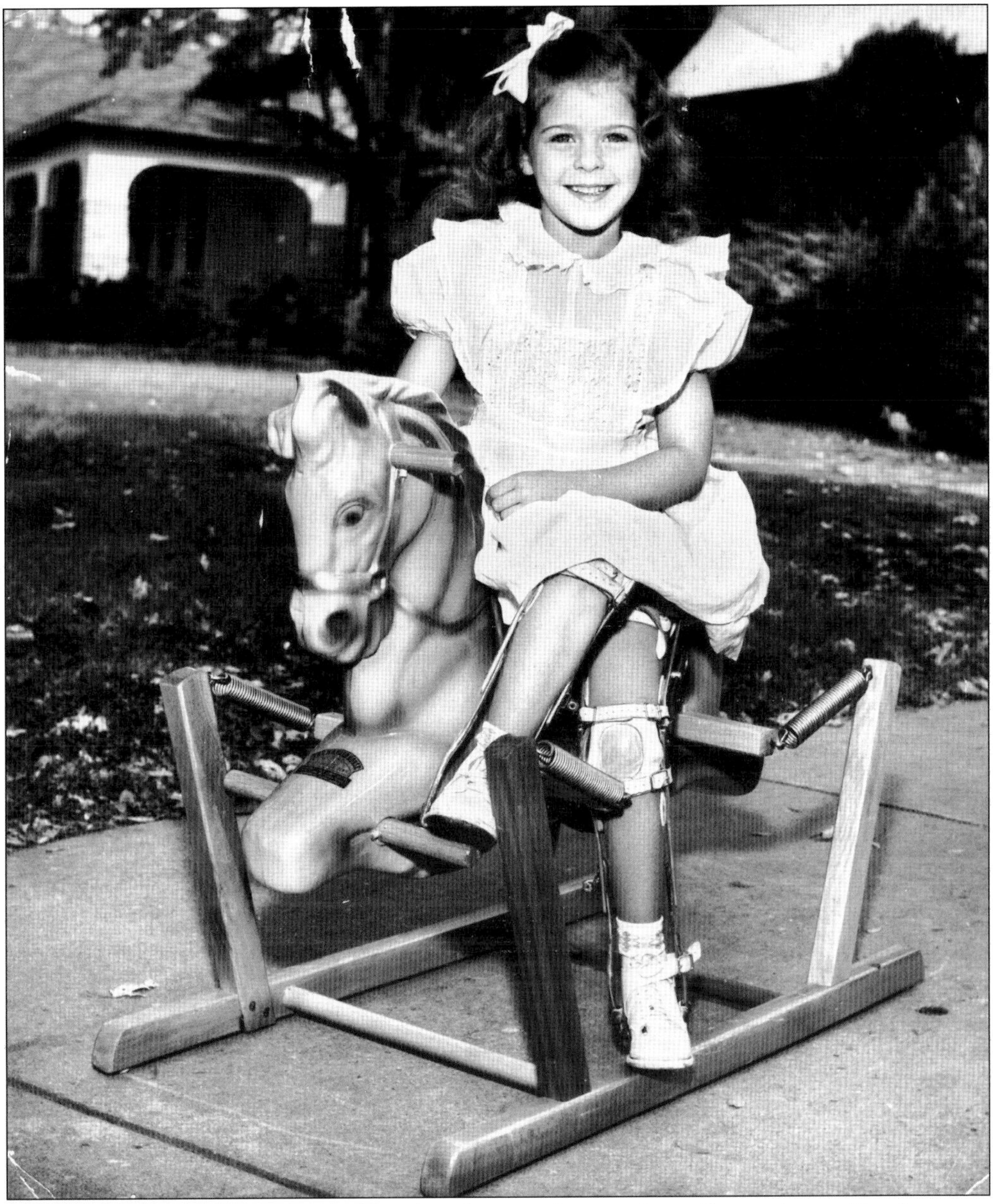

Mary Kosloski was five years old when this photograph was taken of her in front of her home on Walnut Street. She is sitting on a Wonder Horse that was manufactured in Collierville. Mary was selected as the national poster child for the Polio Foundation in 1955. She and her parents, Dorothy and Peter, traveled across the United States and into Cuba raising funds for the foundation and encouraging the public to be vaccinated against infantile paralysis. She visited the White House and presented Pres. Dwight D. Eisenhower a March of Dimes poster.

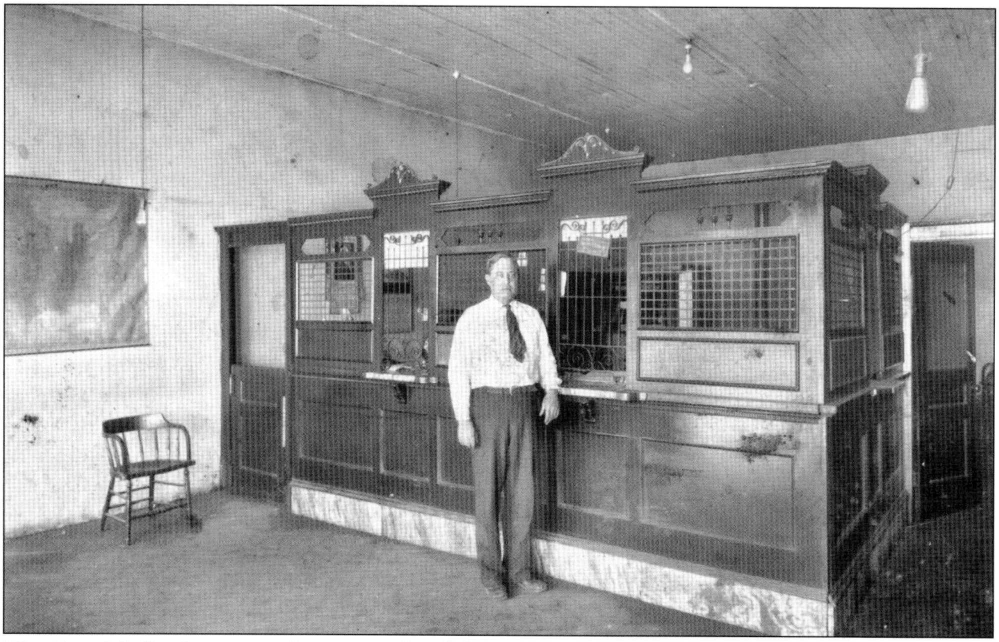

The People's Bank was on the west side of the square next to McGinnis Hardware. The Bank of Collierville was chartered in 1890. In 1908, the People's Bank was chartered, superseding the Bank of Collierville. The People's Bank has been robbed twice. In the 1920s, the safe was blown open, and again in 1930, the bank was robbed at gunpoint.

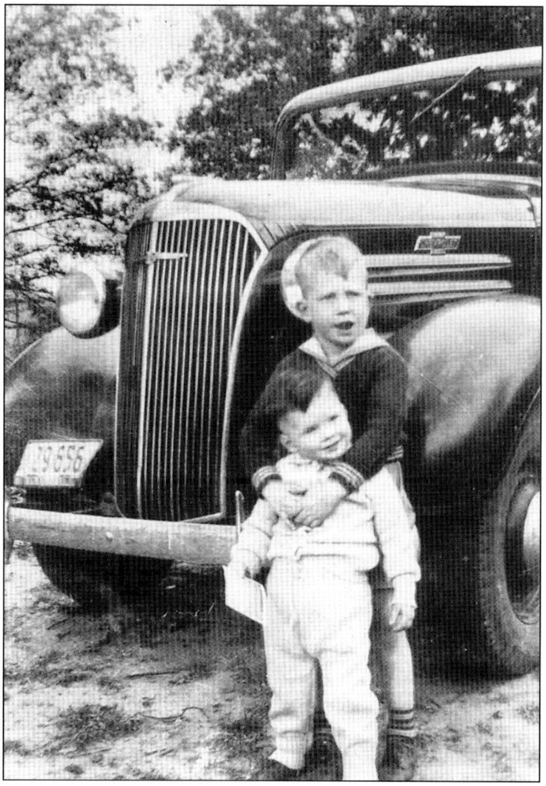

Buddy Wilson, age 5, and Cecil Wilson, age 2, and are shown in front of the family car in 1938. They were the children of Gail and Meady Wilson. The car was an early-model Chevrolet. Meady Wilson served as a law official.

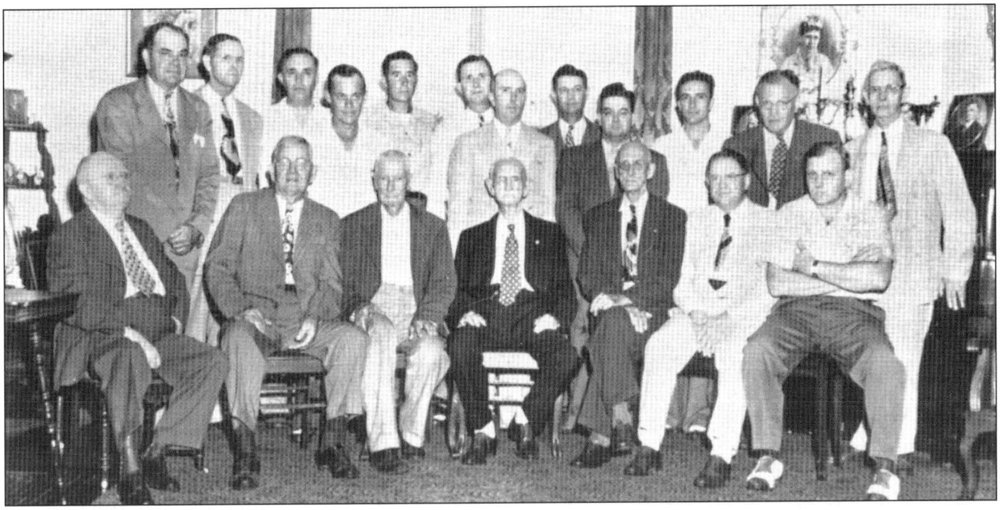

P. A. Perkins celebrated his 90th birthday in 1948. From left to right are (first row) Charles Dean, H. Franklin Kelsey, Tammy Hill, P. A. Perkins, Dr. S. W. McCall, Milton K. Mann Sr., and H. F. (Lin) Kelsey Jr.; (second row) Watson Kelsey, Lee Smith, J. C. Gilbert, Mark Wilkerson, Sam Cavaness, Thomas Hart, Dr. W. D. Parr, Mark Kirk, Dr. James Glenn, Joe Ridgeway, Herbert Lehmann, and unidentified.

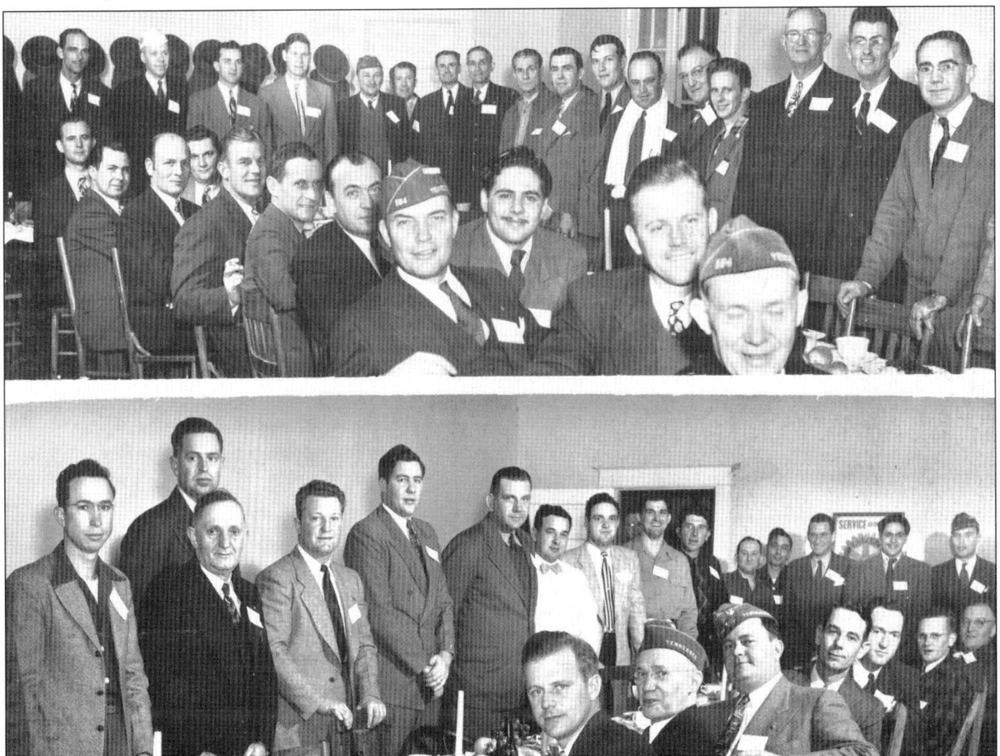

The Rotary Club is pictured at a gathering in the 1940s. The Rotary Club was first organized in Collierville in 1935 with a purpose of "service through growth of individuals through service." The organization remains active in the community today, assisting in youth projects and community improvements.

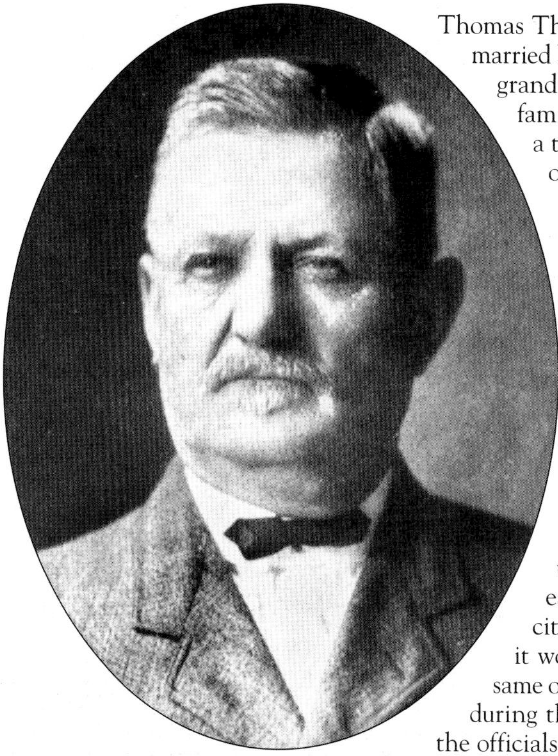

Thomas Theodore McDonald was born in 1846 and married Dora Virginia Moore from Collierville. Her grandfather, Thomas W. Moore Sr., moved the family to Collierville in 1836. McDonald was a three-term mayor of Collierville and served on the county quarterly court, later known as the Shelby County Commission. He was chairman of the court at the time of his death in 1922. Members of the Kelsey family are descendants of this marriage.

The privilege of voting has never been taken for granted in Collierville, as this early photograph indicates. But in 1939, the citizens voted against a new election because it would cost $200. They agreed to keep the same officials since $200 was a good deal of money during the Depression, and they were happy with the officials they had.

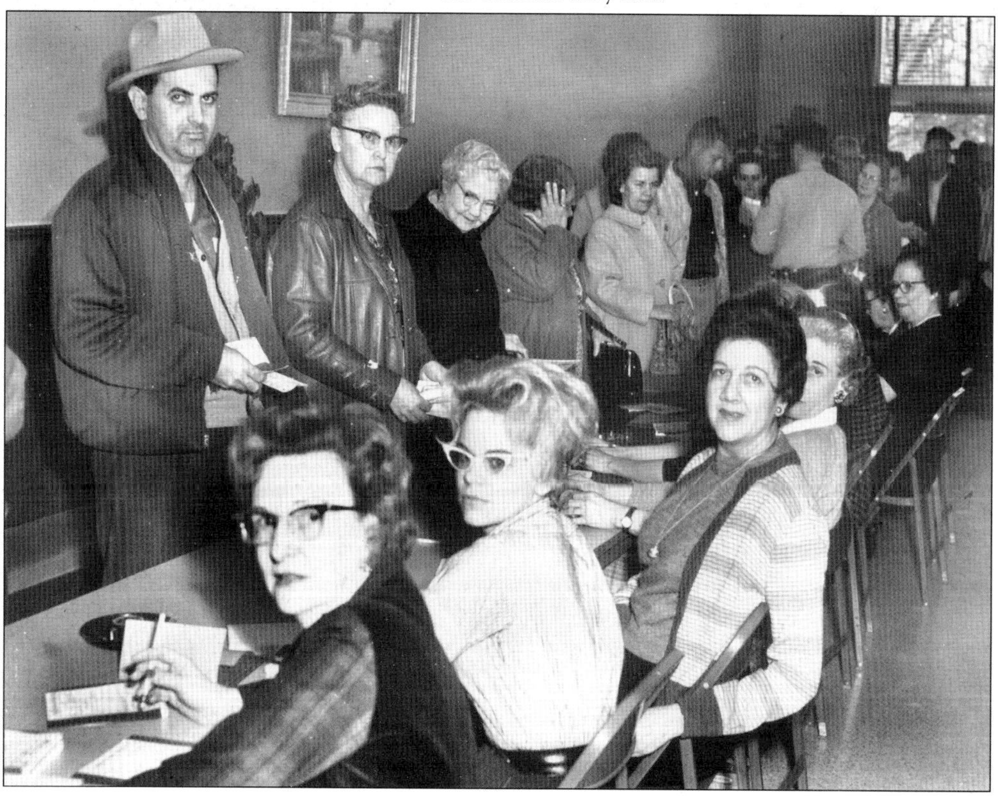

Wiley Washington McGinnis was the grandfather of Mayor Herman Wright Cox Jr. and owner of McGinnis Oil Company and McGinnis Lumber and Hardware Company on the square. He built his home on the corner of Mulberry Street and Walnut Street, just off the Town Square, in 1929. The chair in which he is seated remains in the family.

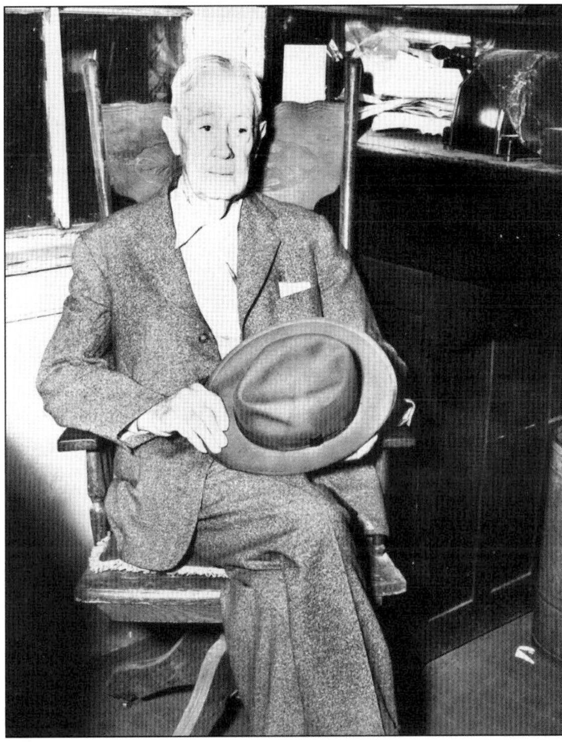

Herman W. Cox (left) and Wiley Washington McGinnis (center) are being presented a certificate for a distributorship with Sinclair Gasoline Company in 1939 by a Sinclair representative. The McGinnis family constructed the building, located on the corner of Washington Street and Main Street, in 1927, and the third and fourth generations continue to operate it.

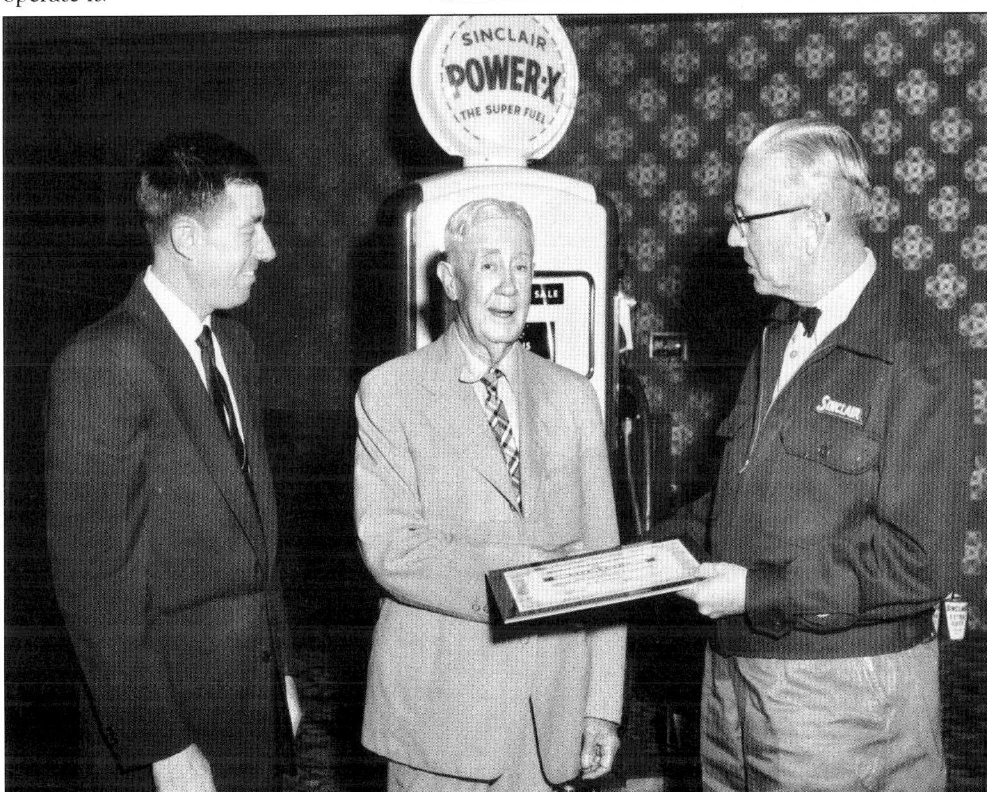

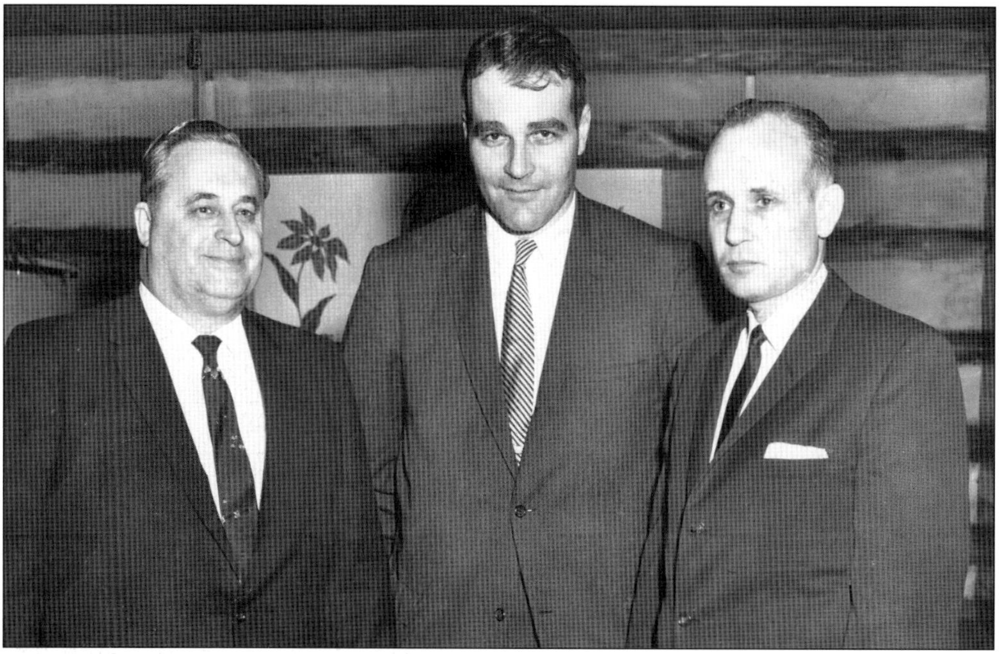

John E. Stamps, far left, and Tom Brooks, right, are pictured with Memphis mayor Henry Loeb. John Stamps was an Oldsmobile car dealer in Collierville for 30 years. He served as an alderman, mayor, and later president of the Citizens Bank. Tom Brooks, a local pharmacist, was an alderman and vice mayor.

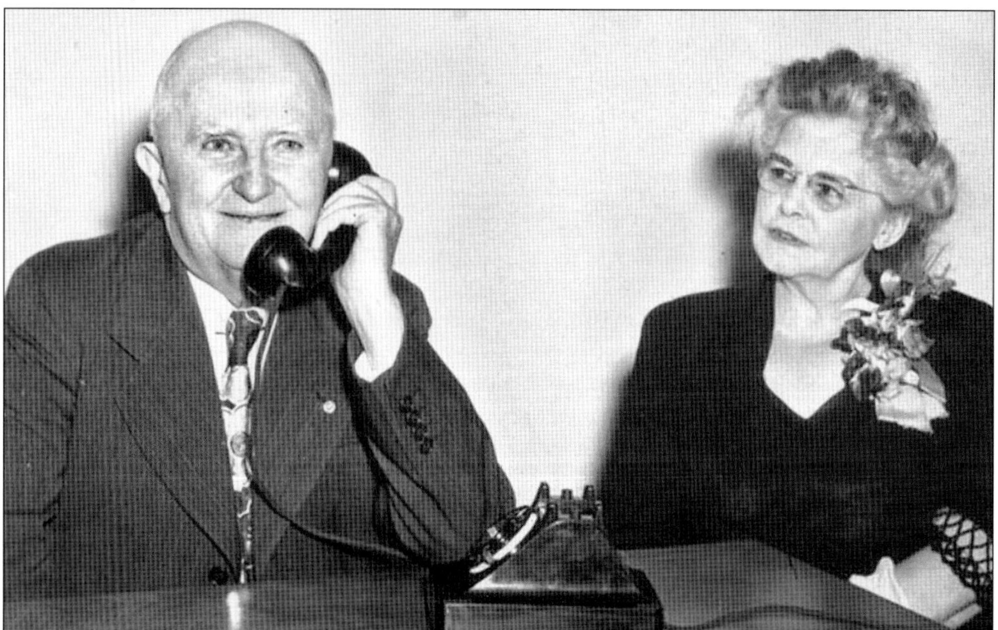

Mayor Charles Dean and his wife, Martha, are pictured making the first long-distance phone call soon after Collierville was connected to the Memphis Exchange. Mayor Dean called his oldest son, Robert Charles Dean, in Boston, Massachusetts. The date on the back of the photograph is April 1950.

John Pittman Humphreys was originally from Mississippi. He served in the Confederate army under Gen. Nathan Bedford Forrest. He and his family moved to Collierville in 1876 and opened a mercantile business. He was active in local politics, serving as alderman, vice mayor, and Shelby County justice of the peace, and he was elected chairman of the Shelby County Court in 1915. He was a member of the Collierville Presbyterian Church and the Collierville Masonic Lodge.

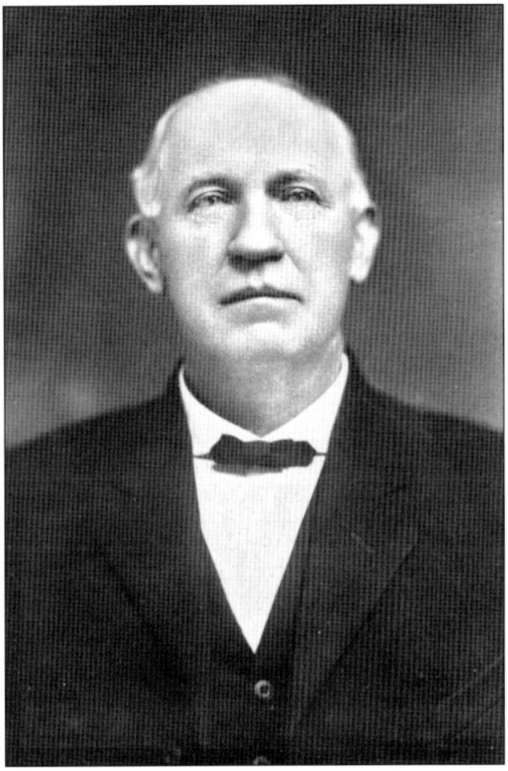

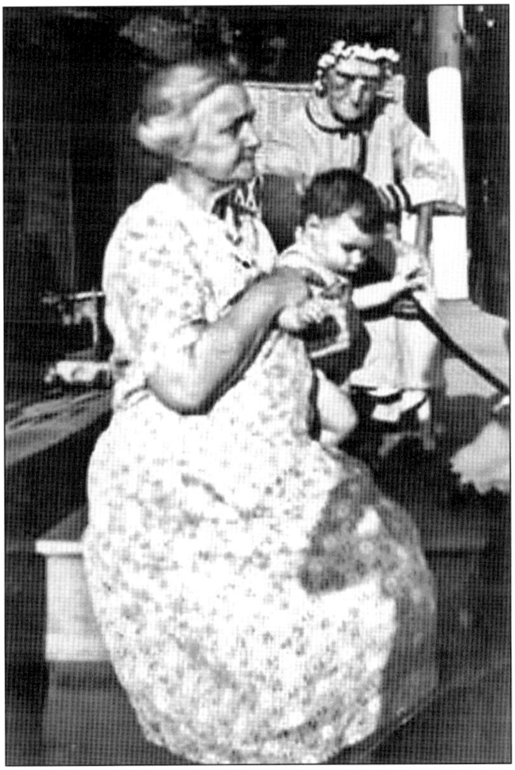

Martha Anne Dean (now Anne Babin) is pictured with her two great-grandmothers, Florence Jemima Stuart Dean (left) and Elizabeth Katherine Payne Little. They are on the porch of Florence Dean's home on North Rowlett Street, where Anne Babin and her husband, Alan, live today.

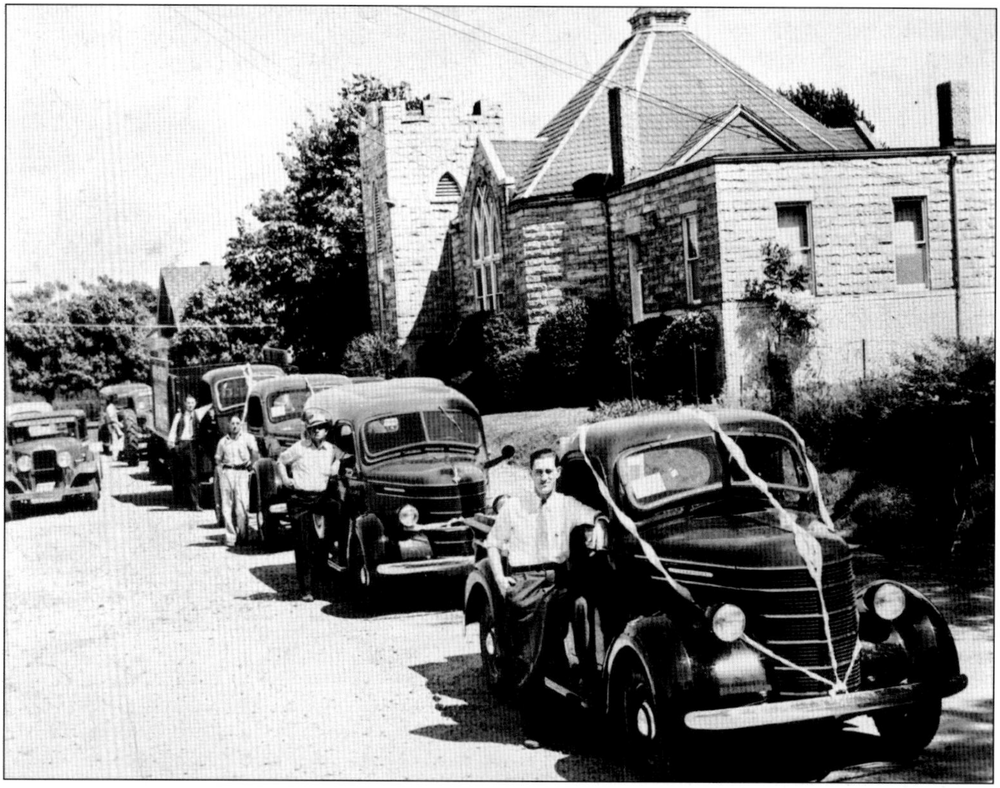

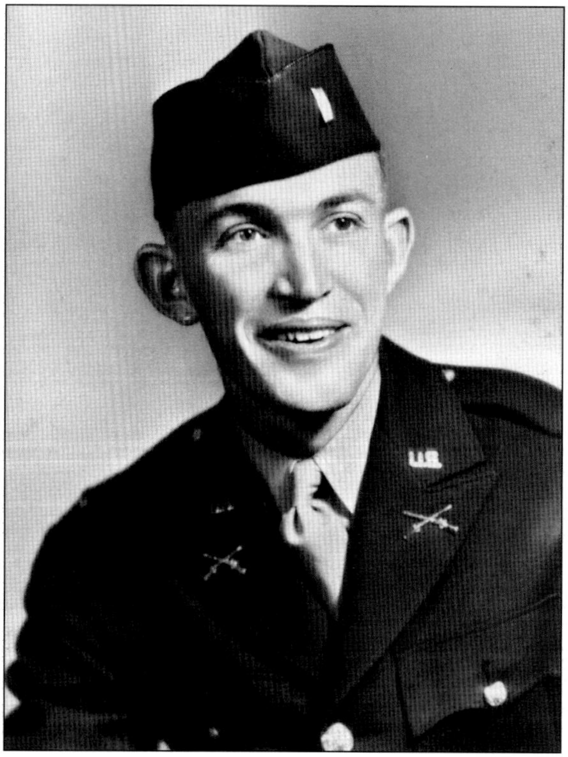

Cars line up on College Street for the beginning of the Cheese Carnival Parade. Earl Clayton (pictured beside the third car from the right) is the father of Joe Clayton. He worked for a local tractor company in Collierville and drove the parade car to advertise the business. The back of the photograph indicates that "Uncle Sherlock" is beside the first car, and John Williams stands beside the second.

James Milton Russell, captain, served with the 351st Infantry, 88th Blue Devil Division, in World War II. He was wounded in Italy and received the Purple Heart with an oak leaf cluster. After returning to Collierville, he married Clarene Pinkston, and they opened Russell's Farm Supply Company. He served on the Collierville Board of Alderman as registrar and was postmaster for 25 years.

World War I affected many Collierville residents. When Edgar Morton came home in 1919, he took a correspondence course in electricity and began work with Memphis Light, Gas and Water. He worked for them until his retirement. He brought the first light lines to Collierville and was their official rural representative. "Sorghum," as he was affectionately known, was active in the community until his death at 101 years of age.

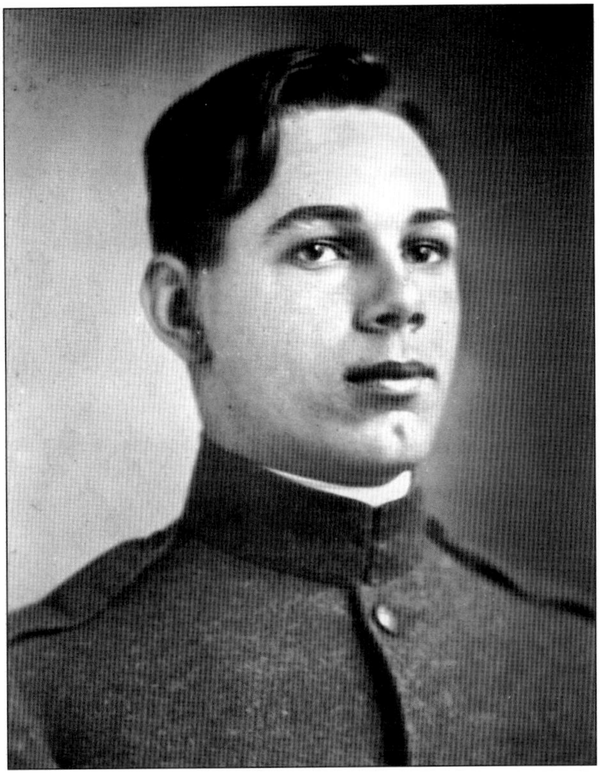

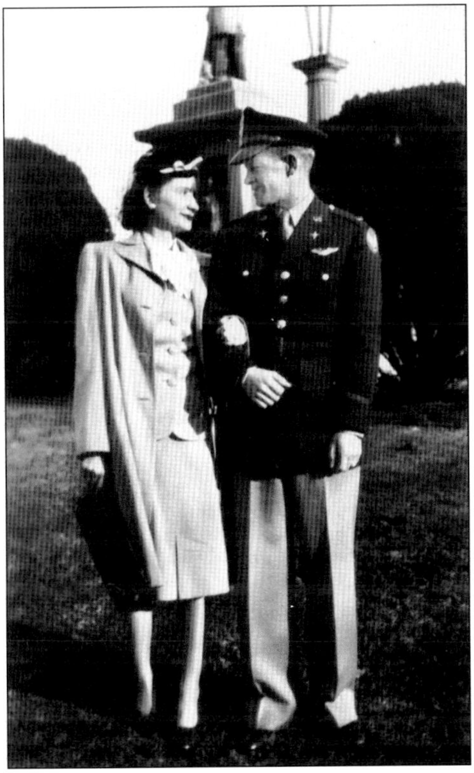

When Martha and Milton Mann married in February 1945, they only had enough gas ration stamps to honeymoon in Nashville. Milton was a lieutenant in the U.S. Air Force; they have been married over 60 years and are active in the community today.

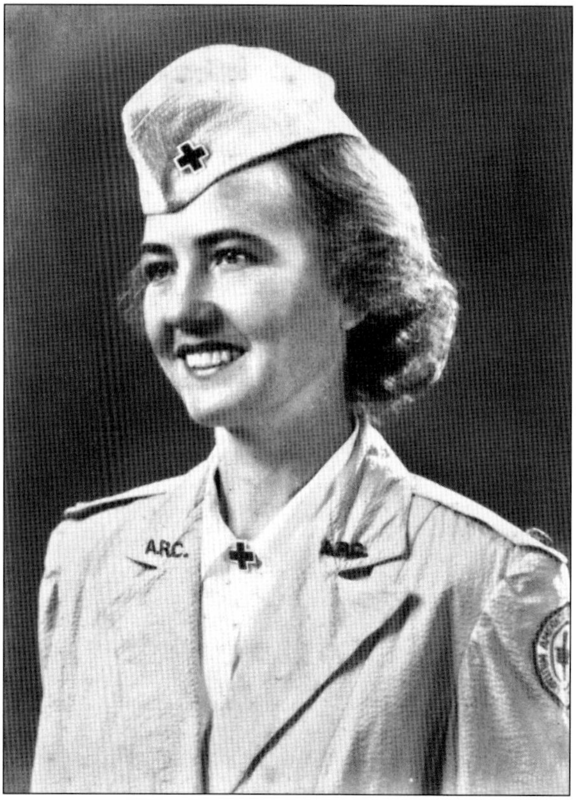

Twenty-six-year-old Margaret Treadwell joined the National Red Cross when she heard the news of the bombing of Pearl Harbor in 1941. She survived heavy bombing in Paris and London while working in the hospitals in Europe. Soon after VE Day, she returned to Collierville and married Lloyd Simpson. She lives in the home of her parents, Maude and Timmons Louis Treadwell Sr.

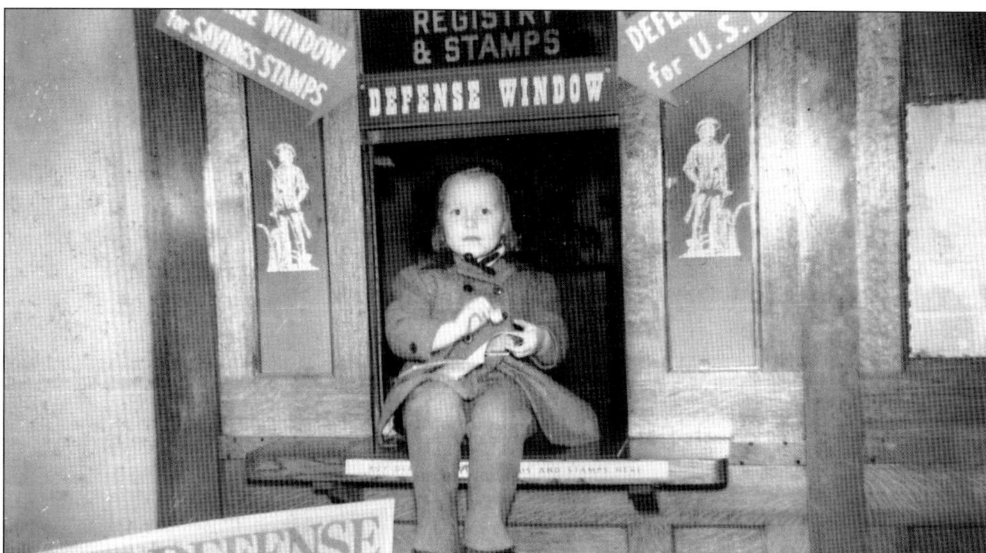

Little Mary Lou Cooper is pictured in front of the Collierville Post Office in 1942 to encourage patrons to buy World War II War Bonds. This photograph was run in the *Collierville Herald*, and copies of the paper were sent to servicemen from Collierville. From this, Mary Lou received dolls from around the world. Her mother, Lou Cooper, had taught many of these servicemen in school.

Three

SACRED PLACES

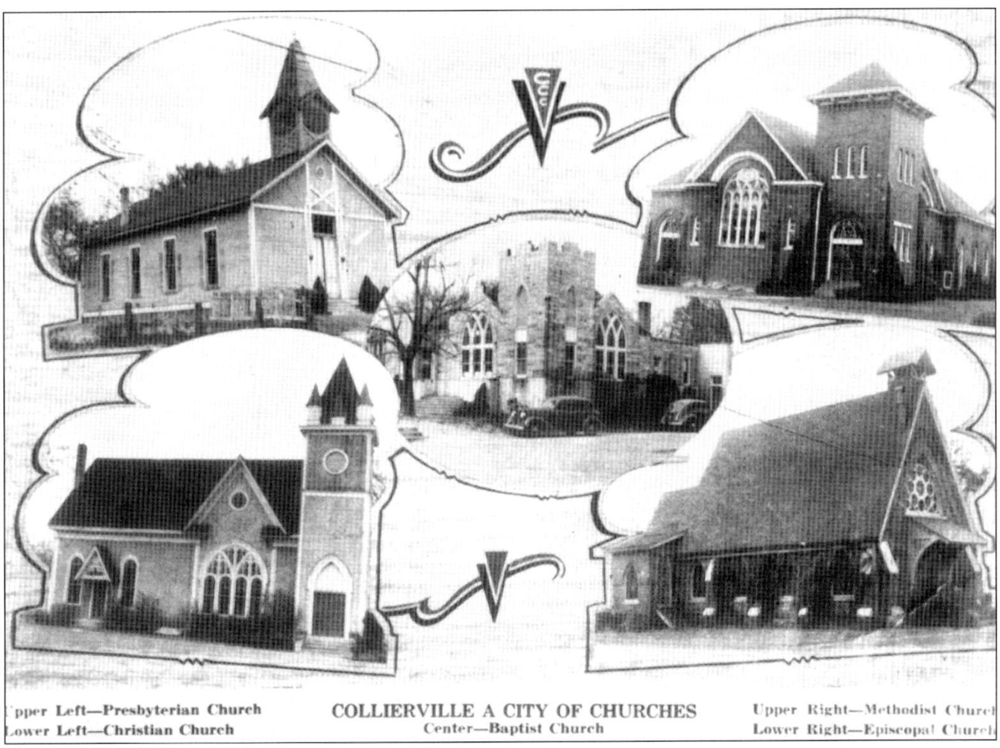

Early settlers in Collierville brought their religious heritage with them to face the starkness of frontier life. Settlers often met in homes before they were able to construct buildings. Churches were referred to in the earlier days as "meetinghouses," which were modest buildings that were often used as schoolhouses. Today these sacred places remind us of our rich religious heritage. Featured on this faded postcard are some of the earliest church buildings.

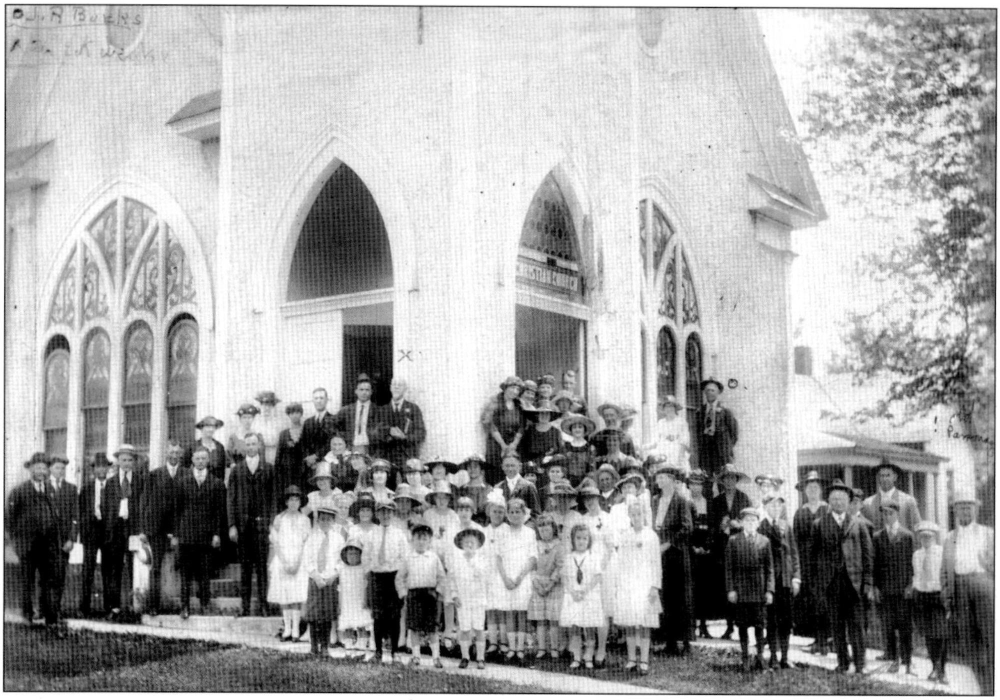

The congregation is gathered outside the Christian church building in 1909. This building was originally constructed in 1871–1873 and remodeled in 1906, with beautiful stained-glass windows and hardwood furnishings in the Gothic Revival style. Turned spindles decorate the choir alcove and front baptistery. One door faced State Line Road (Poplar Avenue) and one faced Main Street. The bell tower atop the west gable housed the 800-pound bell. The "White Church" was sold in the latter 1900s, has been used as an antique shop, and is presently a restaurant for fine dining. The photograph below is a faded image of the older building from the late 1800s.

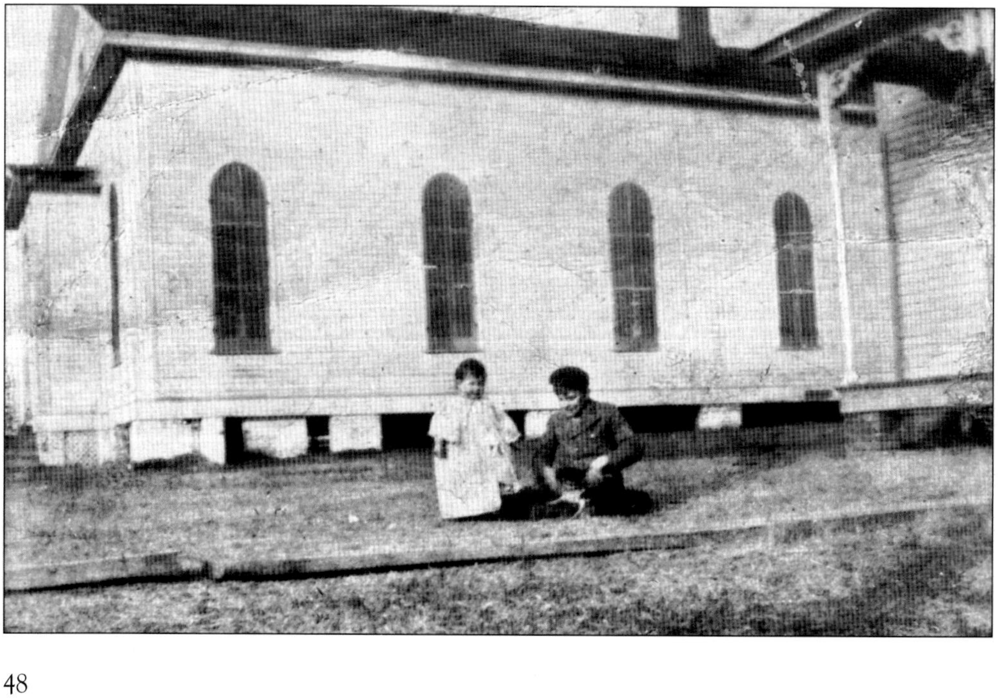

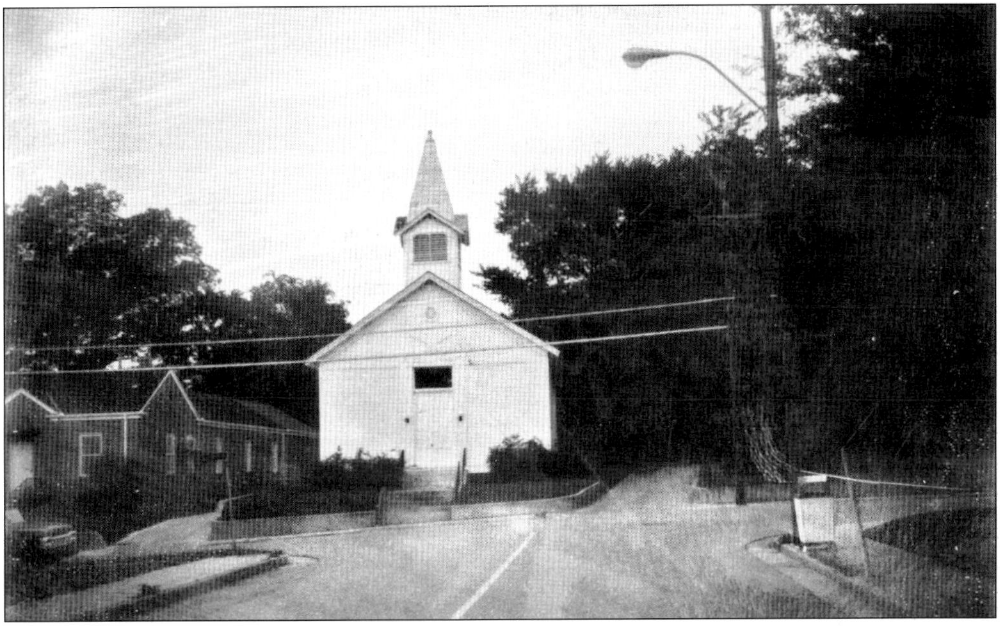

The Collierville Presbyterian Church was chartered in 1844 under the name of Salem, and when they moved to Collierville from Byhalia Road in 1872, the name changed to Collierville Presbyterian Church. The church was chartered with 17 members. A lot for the new church was purchased in 1885 for $100 and the building constructed in 1886. The congregation continued to worship at this location until 1965. The building has stained-glass windows and a stained-glass transom over the front double doors.

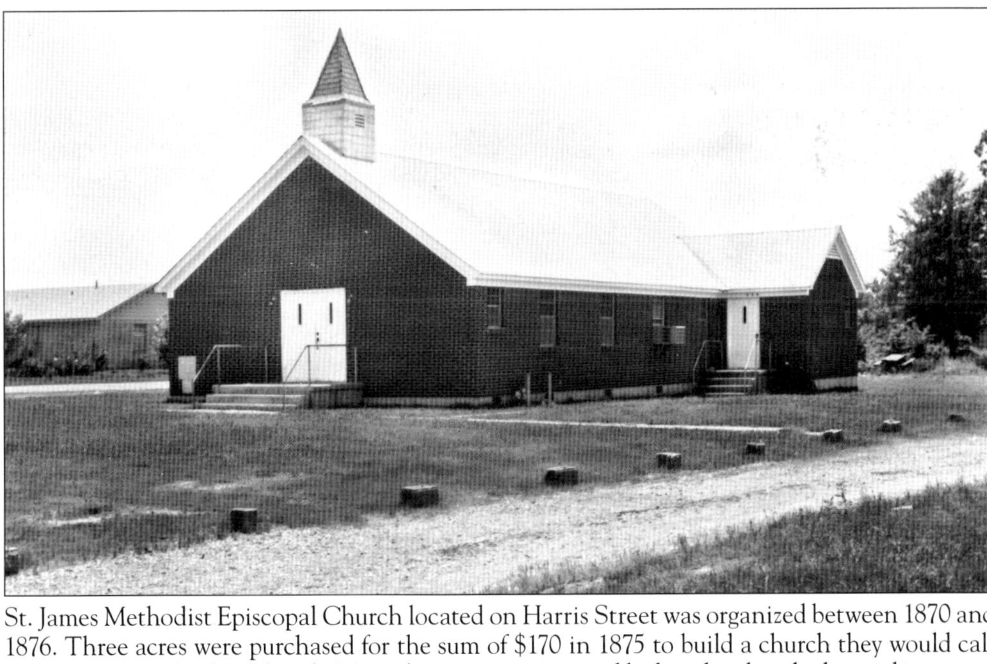

St. James Methodist Episcopal Church located on Harris Street was organized between 1870 and 1876. Three acres were purchased for the sum of $170 in 1875 to build a church they would call the Colored Methodist Church. More than a century passed before the church changed its name. The 1909 building in the photograph was originally a large frame building with 12 windows, a bell tower, and a large bell.

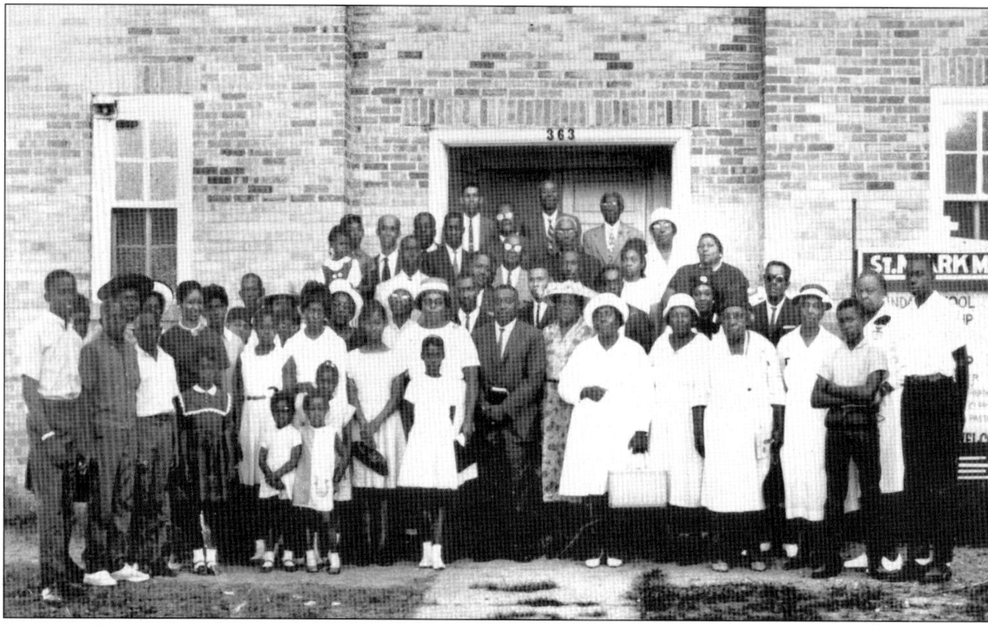

In 1860, the Abington family of Collierville owned a black slave named Abe Koens. The Koenses lived on the Abingtons' property. When Abe was a young man, he began holding prayer meetings in his home. In 1868, after the Civil War, the congregation secured a plot of ground from Margaretter Blain Abington for a meetinghouse. It is thought that the slaves were given the property in exchange for remaining in service with the family. After worshiping in a brush arbor, they completed a large brick building, St. Mark's, in 1873. The first pastor was Rev. John Williams. Koens served as secretary. Pictured in the two photographs are the congregation gathered outside the building that shows the exterior and the Sunday school class inside. St. Mark's has been an active congregation for more than 138 years.

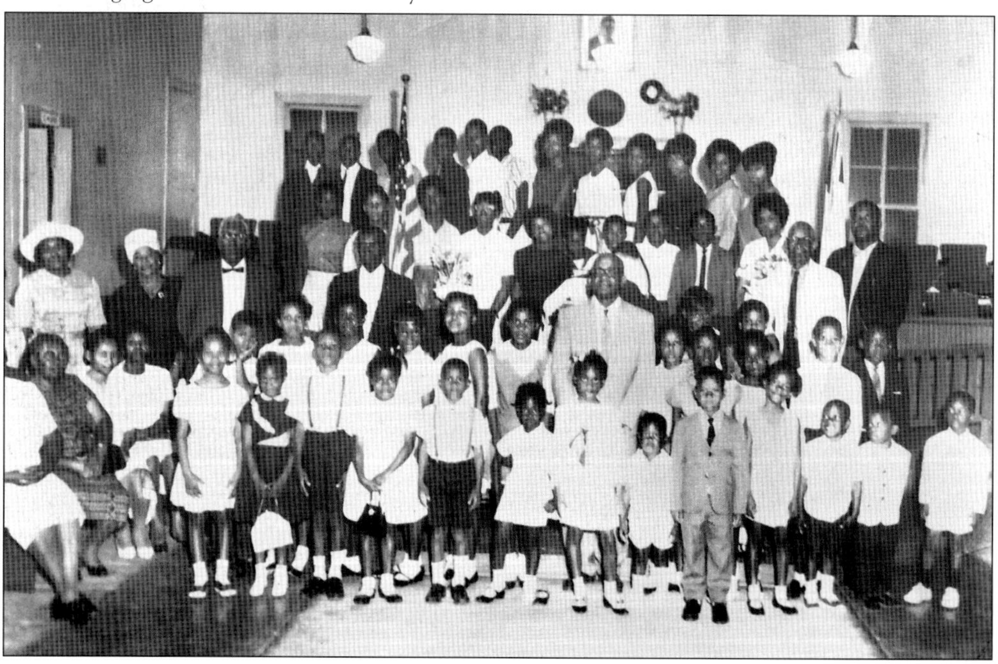

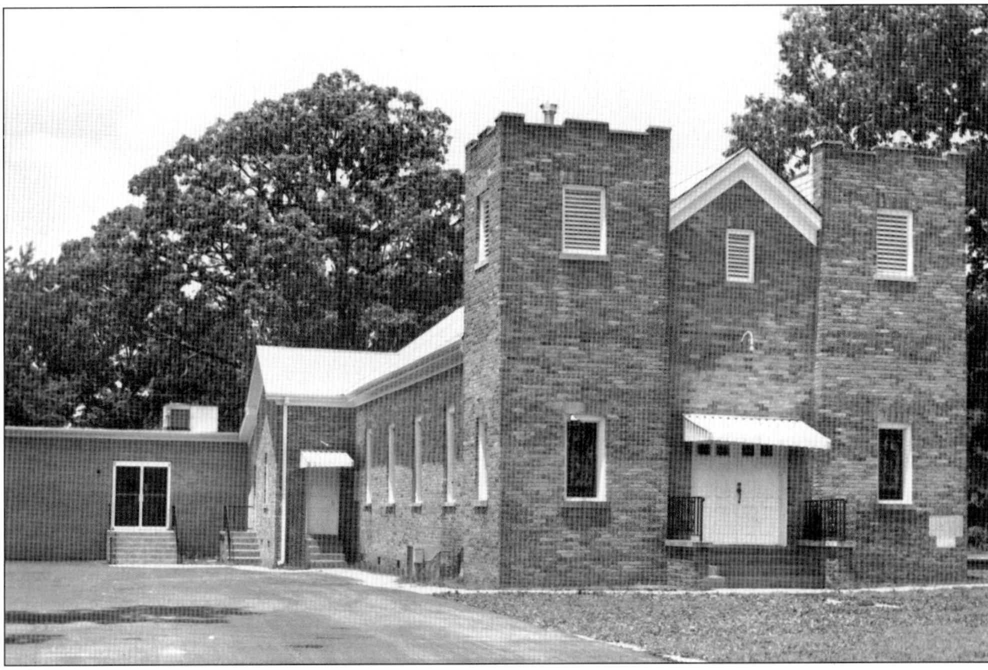

This is an early picture of St. Mark's Missionary Baptist Church Building located on Highway 72 at Sycamore Road. The church grew from the small gathering in Abe Koens's home and now has a large attendance. Members of the early congregation are buried adjacent to Mount Olive No. 2 Missionary Baptist Church east of Mount Pleasant Road on Keough Road.

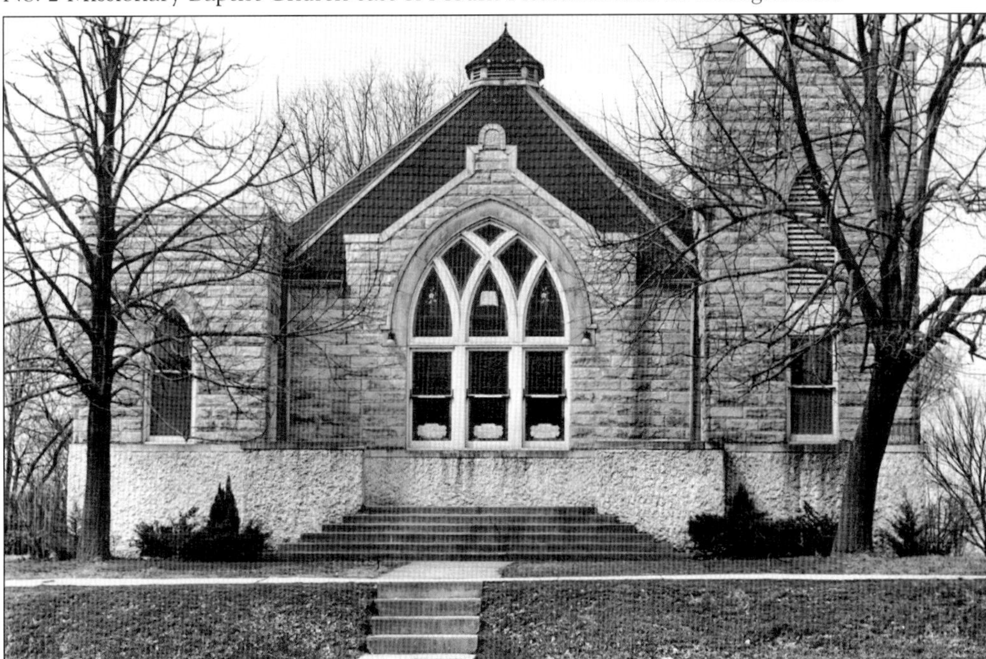

An early photograph shows the old Baptist church before it burned in 1944. An earlier white clapboard building had been built in 1875 on property purchased for $225. This 1909 building was located to the south of the corner of College Street and Walnut Street.

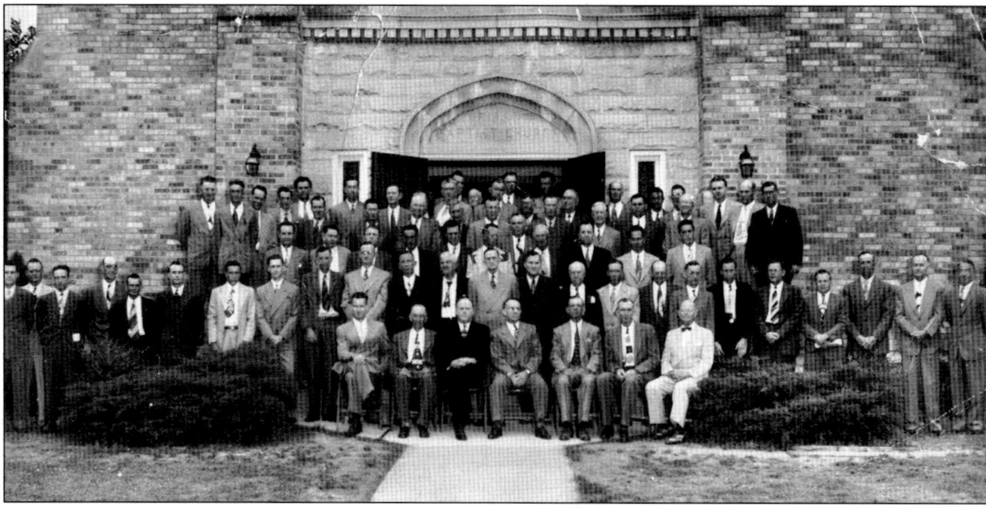

This photograph, entitled "Baptist Men," is taken in front of the Baptist church on Walnut Street. The congregation had begun as Shiloh Baptist Church prior to 1836. In 1856, the church maintained a membership of 38, with 24 whites and 14 blacks, before it moved to Collierville and was renamed Collierville Baptist Church. By the time this photograph was taken in the 1940s, attendance was well in the hundreds.

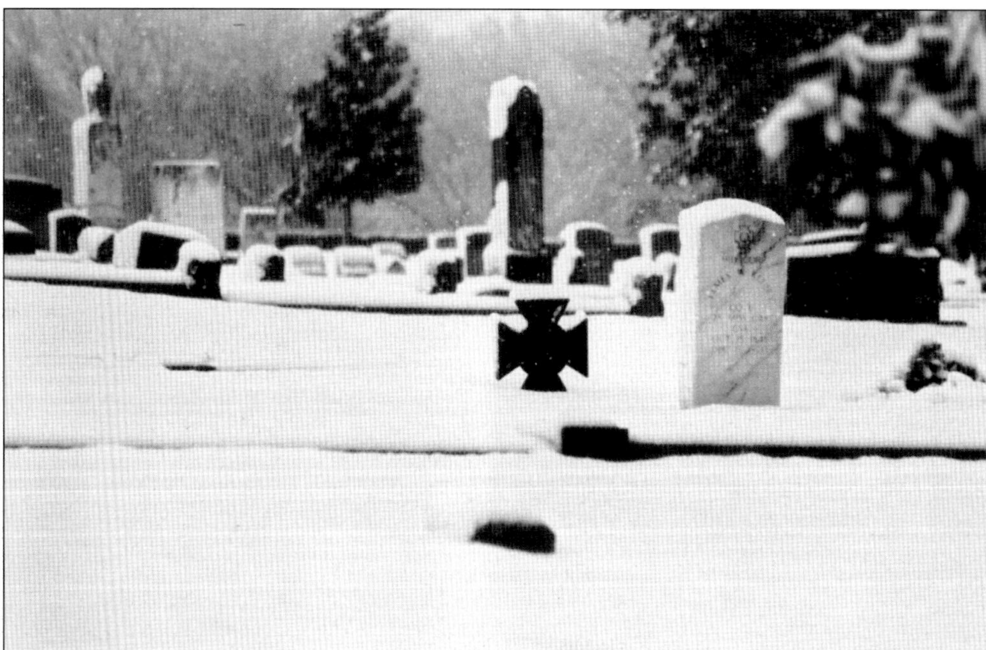

Many of Collierville's former citizens are buried in Magnolia Cemetery. The Southern Cross of Honor is on the grave of James Watson Kelsey Sr. and other Confederate soldiers. The cross is made of cast iron and is identical to pins given to the soldiers by the United Daughters of the Confederacy.

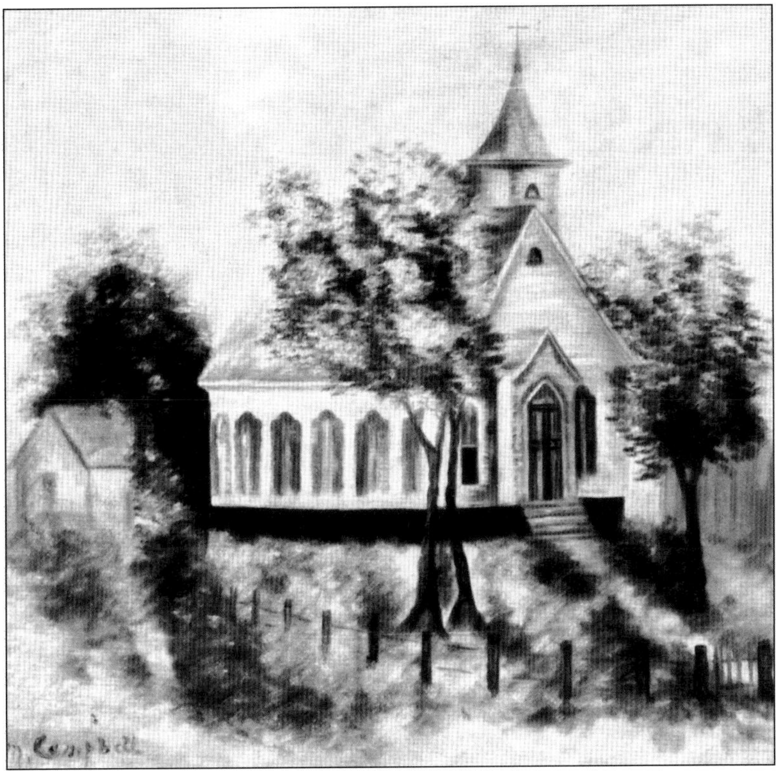

The drawing is of the early United Methodist church that was located at the corner of Highway 57 and North Main Street until 1899. Most of the early churches relied on circuit riders for their preaching services well into the 20th century. After the Battle of Shiloh in 1862, wounded soldiers arrived by train and were taken to the Methodist church and to the J. K. Waddy home on Walnut Street.

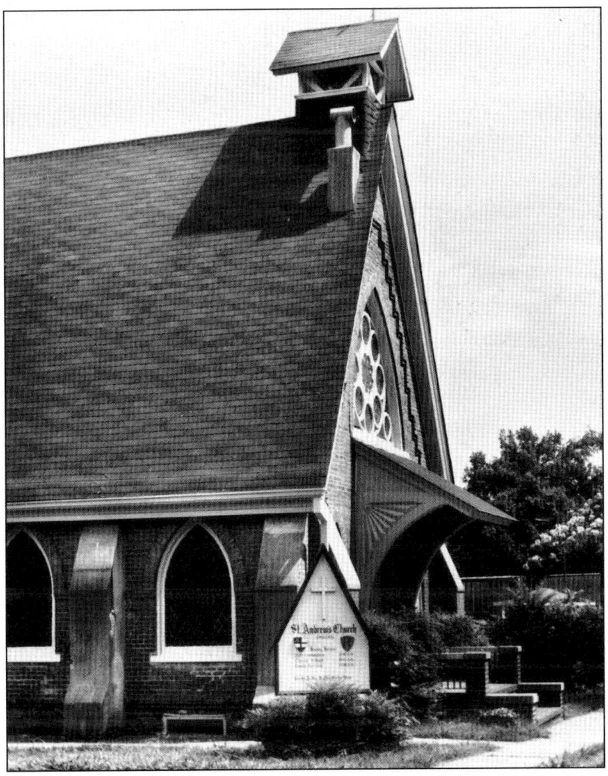

In 1890, the cornerstone was laid for St. Andrew's Episcopal Church. The red-brick church was constructed in the form of a cross, with painted arches and beautiful, mellow woods. The cost of the church was $3,000. The original eight stained-glass windows feature medallions of French origin. St. Andrew's is the only church in Collierville with an active congregation that remains at its original site near the square.

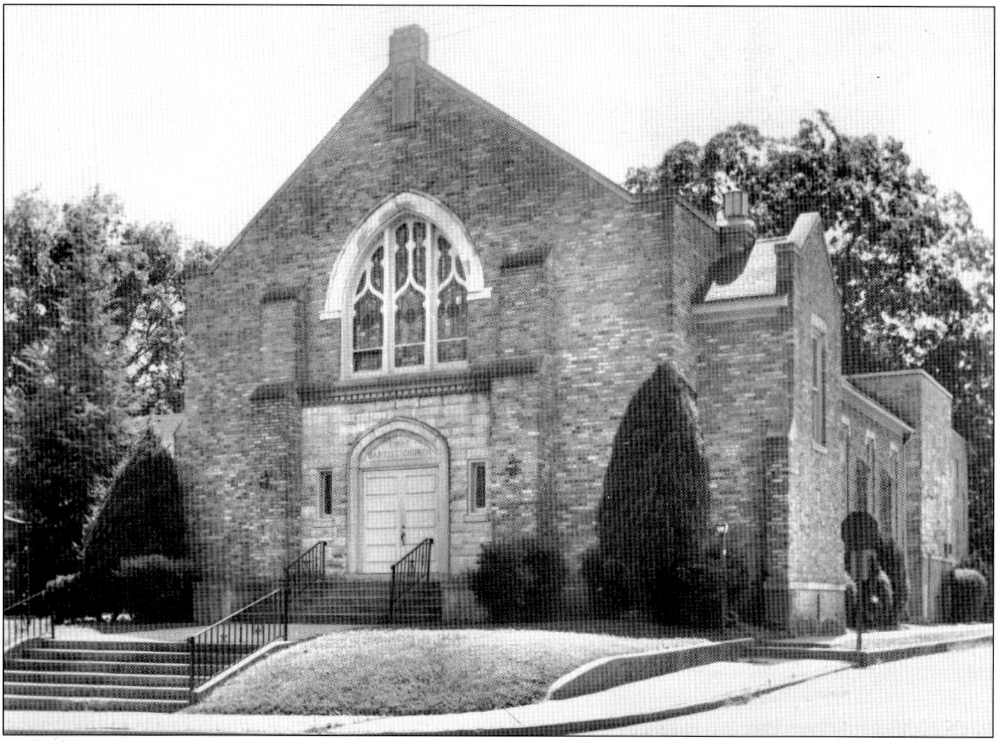

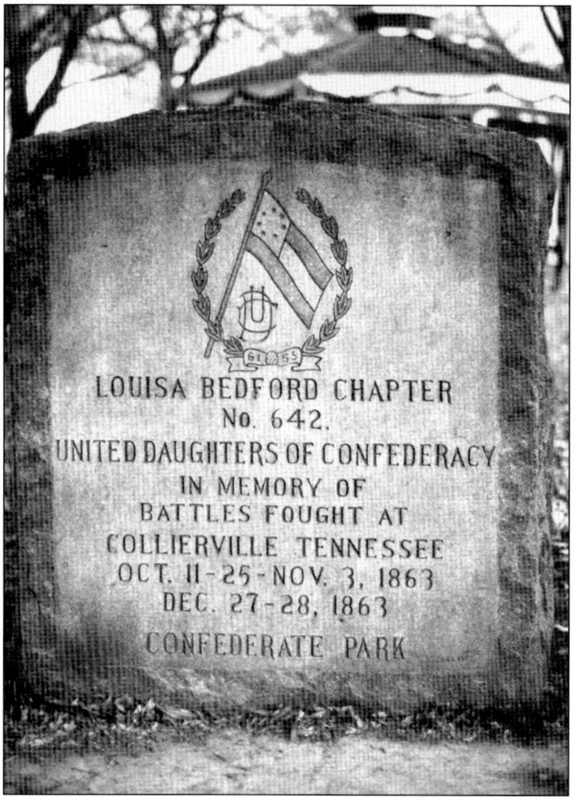

The Collierville Baptist Church is pictured after a total loss from a fire in 1944. The new building had a seating capacity of 400, including the balcony, and was dedicated in 1946, debt free. Beautiful stained-glass windows and new furnishings completed the new church building.

The marker in the Confederate Park on the Town Square was dedicated in memory of the battles fought at Collierville on October 11–25, 1863; November 3, 1863; and December 27–28, 1863. The United Daughters of the Confederacy, Louise Bedford Chapter No. 642 placed the marker.

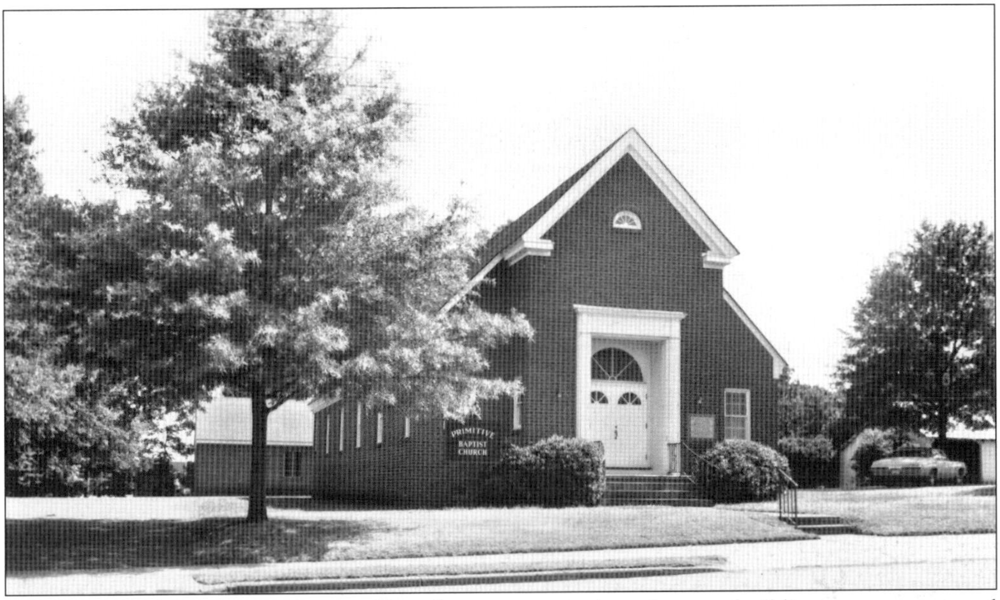

The Collierville Primitive Baptist Church was organized, and a new building was constructed in 1949 on Highway 57. Elder Wiley Sammons and his wife, Elizabeth, donated the building for the new congregation of nine charter members. This congregation has grown in number and remains active in the community.

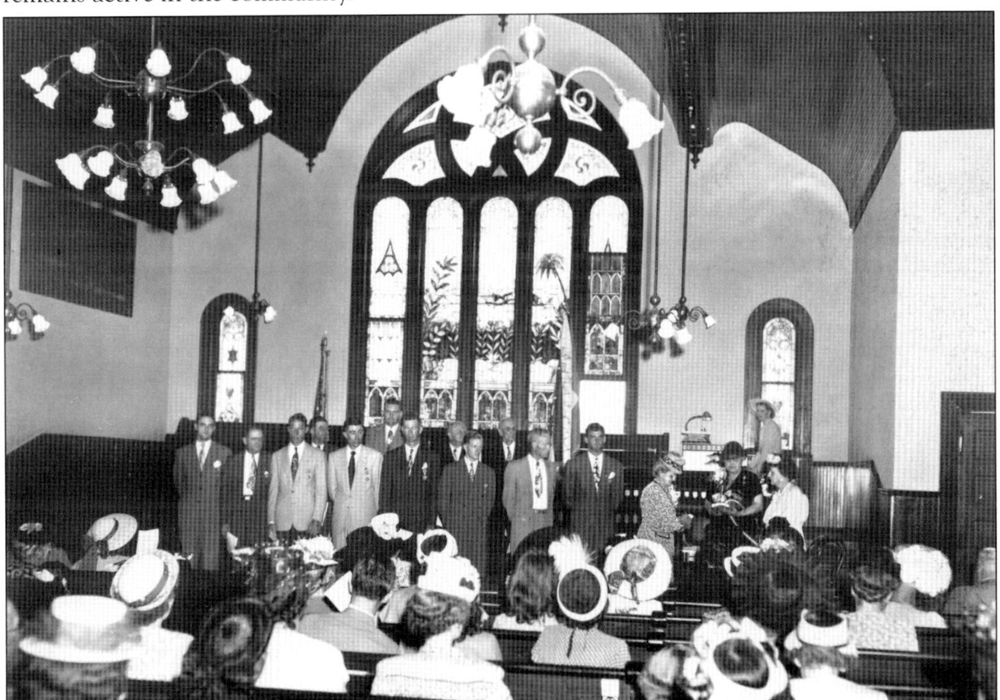

On June 1, 1947, Collierville veterans from World War I and World War II gathered in the sanctuary of the United Methodist Church for a ceremony honoring their service to our country. The Military Cross of Honor was presented to each of the veterans by the United Daughters of the Confederacy. Presiding was Mrs. Bettie Craig from the Louise Bedford Chapter.

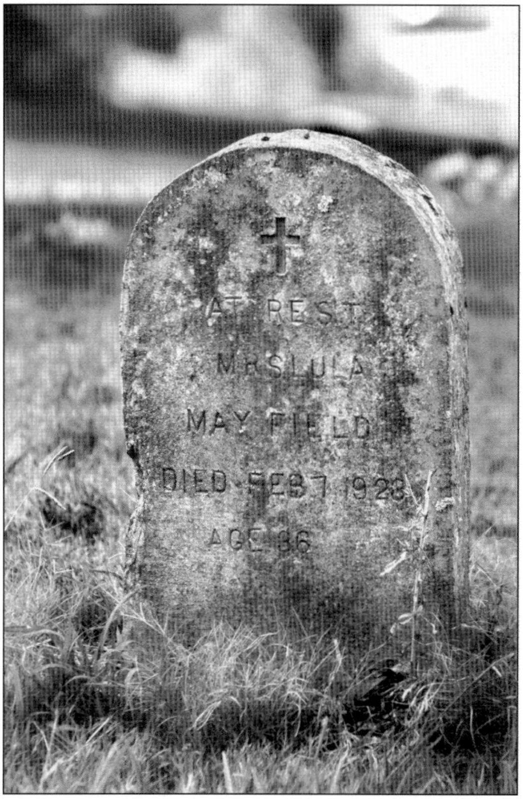

The simple headstone is in the cemetery of Mount Olive No. 2 Missionary Baptist Church. Mount Olive No. 1 is located outside of town. Rev. John Crutcher organized this congregation in 1865. The land was donated, and a small wooden church was built. Services were the first Sunday of each month. From 1942 through 1944, Mount Olive's offering was $4 to $5 per month and the pastor was paid $2 monthly.

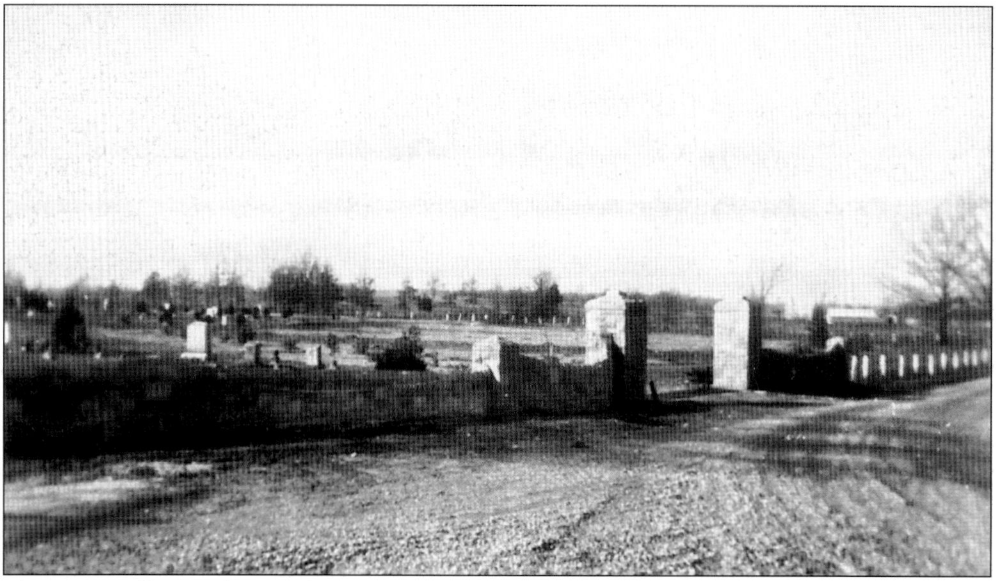

The stone wall around Magnolia Cemetery was completed in 1940. Odie H. Bishop, who built the wall, was a well-known stonemason. He worked at Memphis Memorial Park and also constructed the wall around Graceland in Memphis, the home of Elvis Presley. Donor plaques are on the inside of the wall.

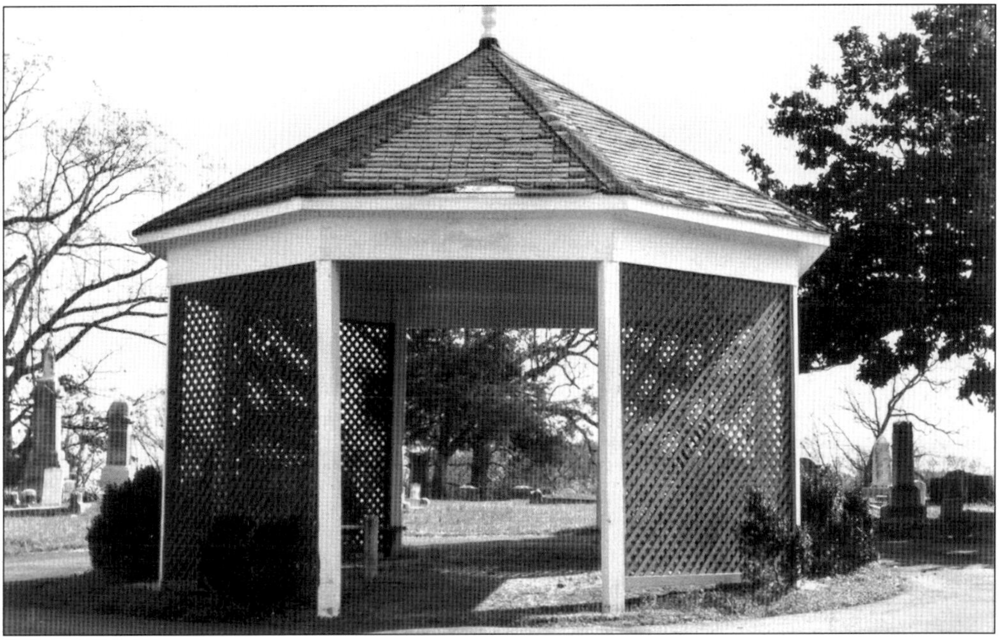

The Summer House is pictured at Collierville's Magnolia Cemetery, which was established in 1878. Before the establishment of the cemetery, people were buried in family or church cemeteries. Magnolia Cemetery was originally the burying ground for the William J. Brown family. One of the earliest structures was the summer house or gazebo, pictured. The earliest burials, from the Brown family, are located close to this structure. Also buried here is an unknown Confederate soldier.

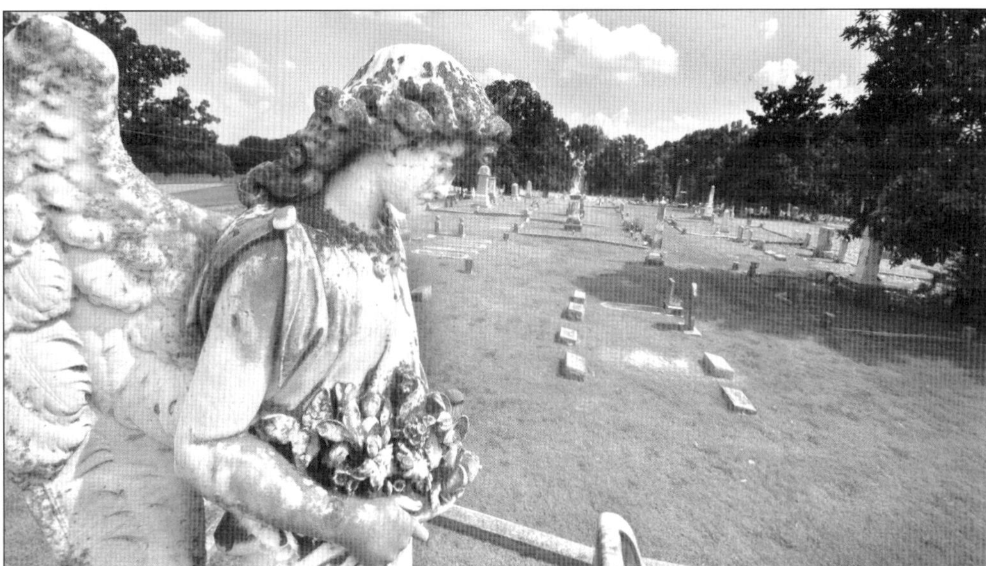

The towering statue of an angel in Magnolia Cemetery serves as a reminder to those left behind that their loved one is in the watchful care of God. The angel is over the grave of Harrison Irby, born in 1818 in Halifax County, Virginia, who died April 1, 1893, and his wife, Marina J. Moore Irby, who was born March 31, 1818, in Anson County, North Carolina, and died October 20, 1893.

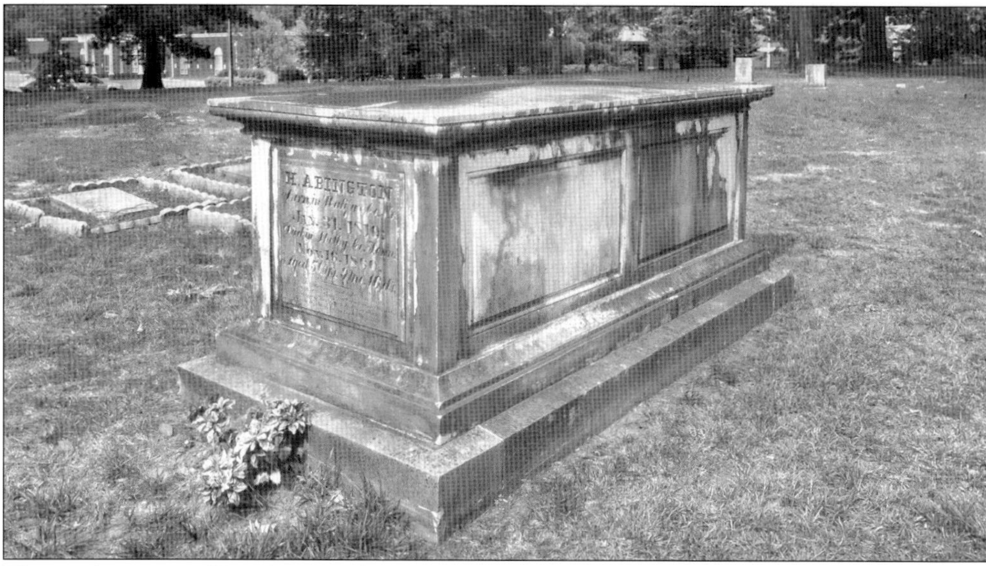

This is the grave of Hardeman Abington, son of Littleberry and Sarah Moore, who died on November 16, 1860. He was buried in the Lowry Cemetery, located on Poplar Avenue, under the upright vault by his first wife and daughter. The vault was ordered at the time of his death but, due to the Civil War, was not delivered until 1865. When the vault did arrive, it was placed over his grave site. He and his wife, Betsy Biggs, were the parents of Collierville's first mayor, James B. Abington.

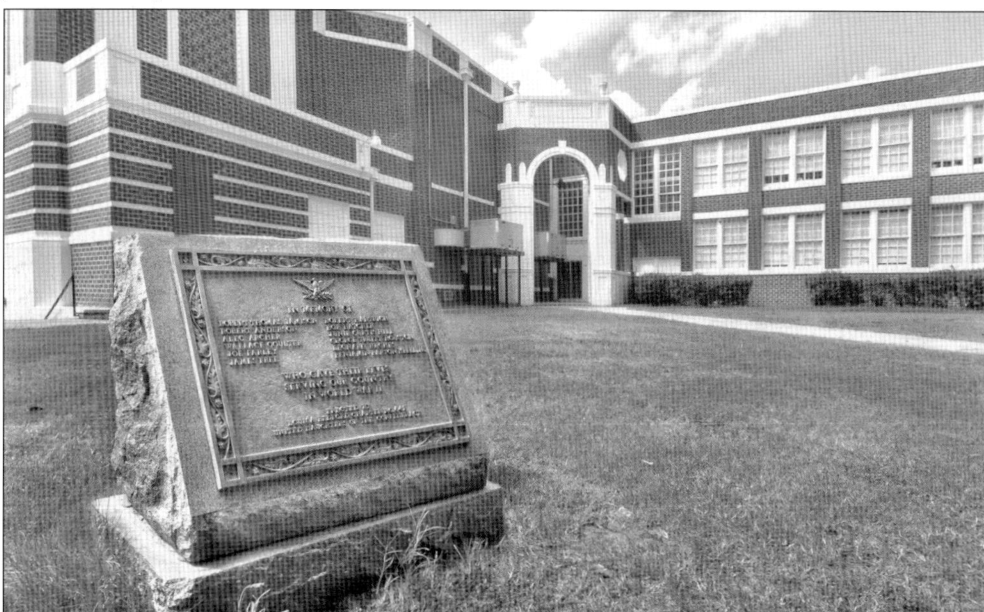

The lone marker on the grounds of the Collierville Middle School was erected by the Louise Bedord Chapter No. 642, United Daughters of the Confederacy, to commemorate the World War II soldiers who "gave their lives serving our country." The names listed are Robert Thomas Jamison, Robert Anderson, Alec Archer, Wallace Coulter, Joe Farly, James Free, Robert Hartrich, Bob Hatcher, Junie Curtis Hill, George Truitt Houston, Leonard Hughes, and Benjamin Barton Isabell Jr.

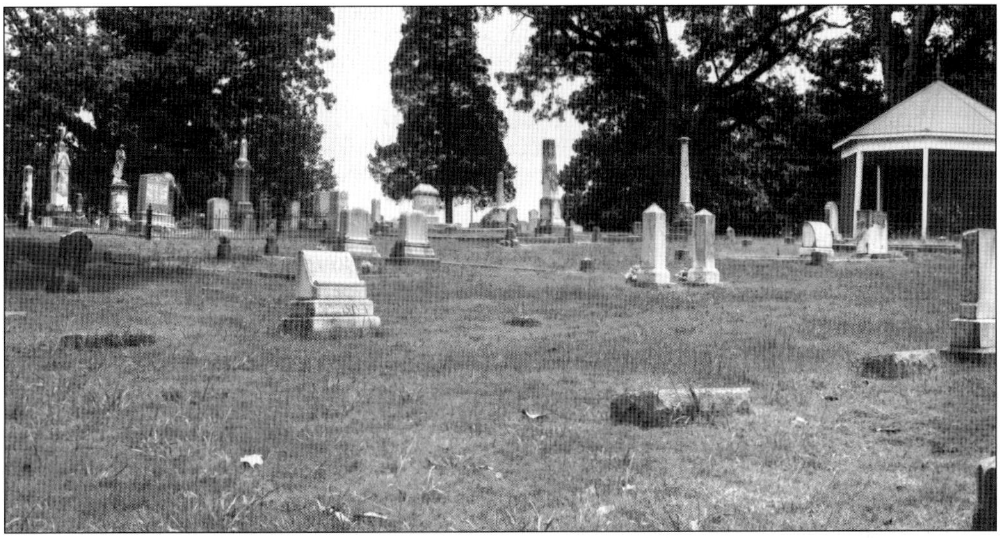

There is little today to remind Collierville citizens of the yellow fever epidemic that struck the community in 1878. Even though the small town had prepared by lining the streets with lime and carbolic acid and enforcing quarantine, they were faced with panic, confusion, and turmoil. Many fled Collierville as they had Memphis. Despite valiant efforts, by October 4, 1878, there were 60–70 cases and 30 deaths, including the mayor, the marshal, and a noted physician. Of the 200 left in the community, half were ill. Some of the victims were buried in Magnolia Cemetery, and some are buried in unknown graves.

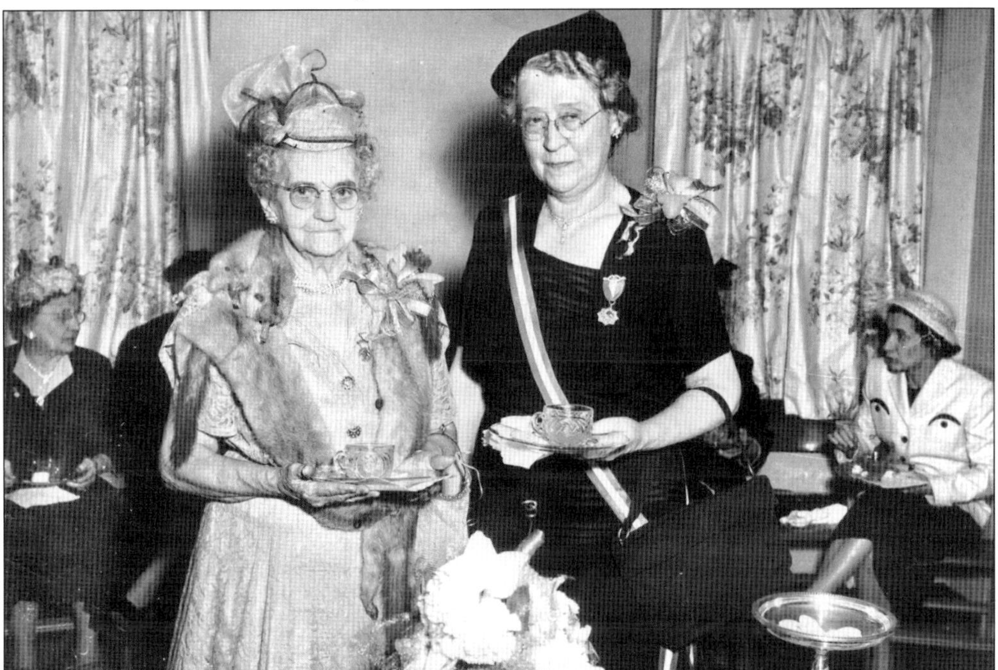

Mrs. Bettie Craig, on the left, is seen entertaining guests at a United Daughters of the Confederacy Reception in Collierville. Craig was a member of the organization for over 50 years and served as president of the Louise Bedford Chapter for 35 years. She was also vice president of the Tennessee Division of the United Daughters of the Confederacy.

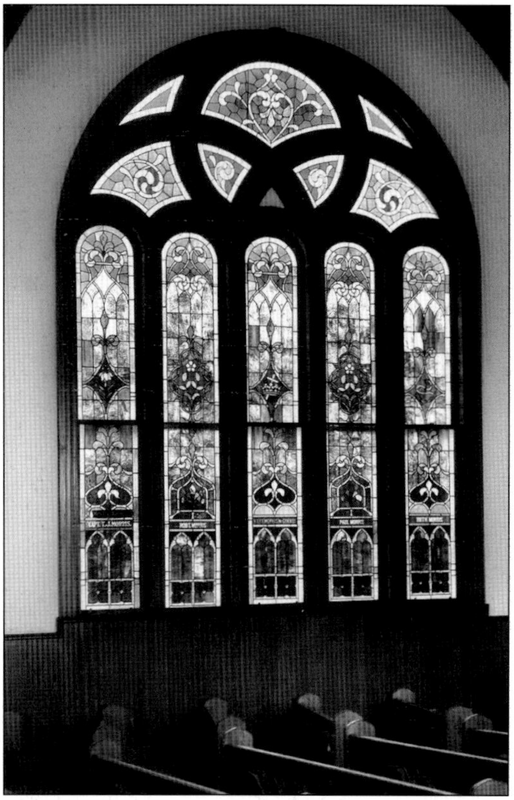

The stained-glass windows at the Collierville United Methodist Church also reflect the rich heritage of the congregation. The windows bear names in memory of families who contributed to the development of the congregation and the community. The windows were purchased in the 1930s from Venice and are noted for their unique vibrant colors, especially the color blue.

The Collierville United Methodist Church moved to the corner of Rowlett and Center Streets in 1900, with the first service held in 1901. The original entrance to the building was on North Rowlett Street. In 1948, an annex was added. The beautiful windows, high vaulted ceilings, and two-story bell tower are the church's outstanding features. The building is still in use by the Methodist church congregation for early traditional Sunday morning services and special programs.

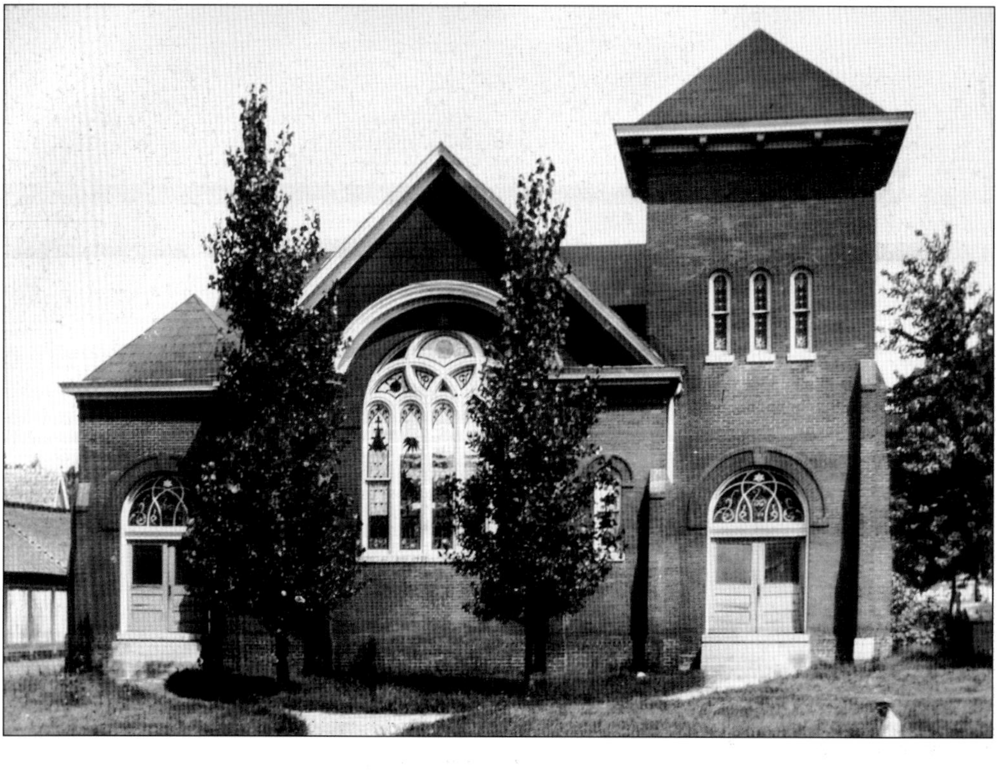

Four

PLACES OF LEARNING

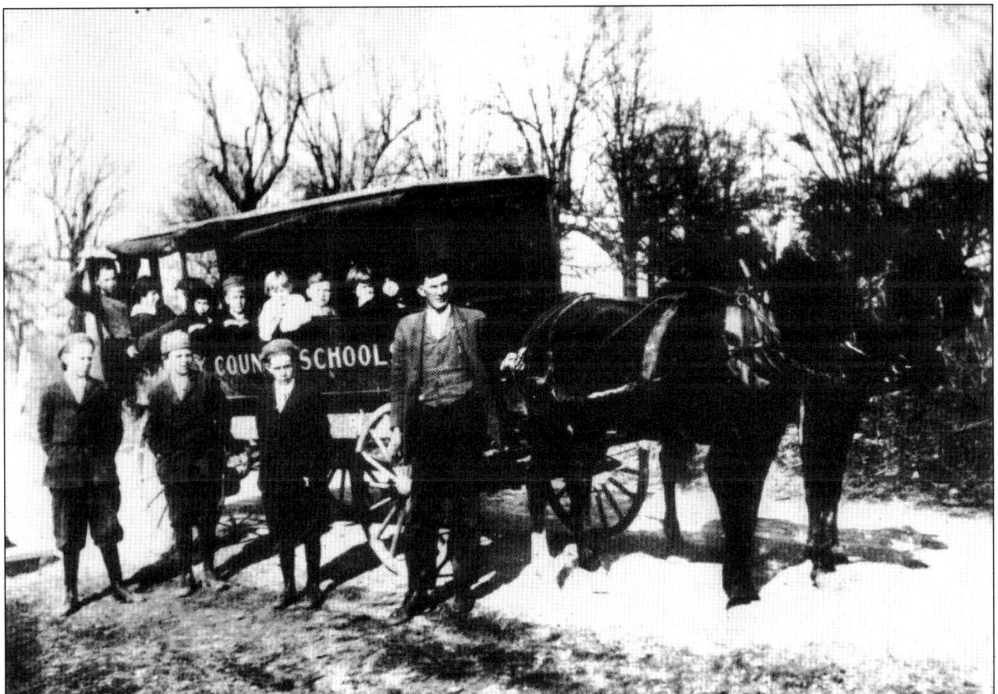

Before the modern school bus, children rode a wagonette pulled by either mules or horses. During the cold winter months, the wagons were enclosed, and heated bricks were kept on the floor. The first wagonettes were introduced in 1908 and eventually were replaced by motorized buses in the 1920s. Collierville was fortunate to have civic leaders who recognized the importance of educational institutions. By 1842, the Collierville community had common schools along with private schools. The Collierville Female Academy, incorporated in 1856, was the most prominent in the early days to be located in the town limits.

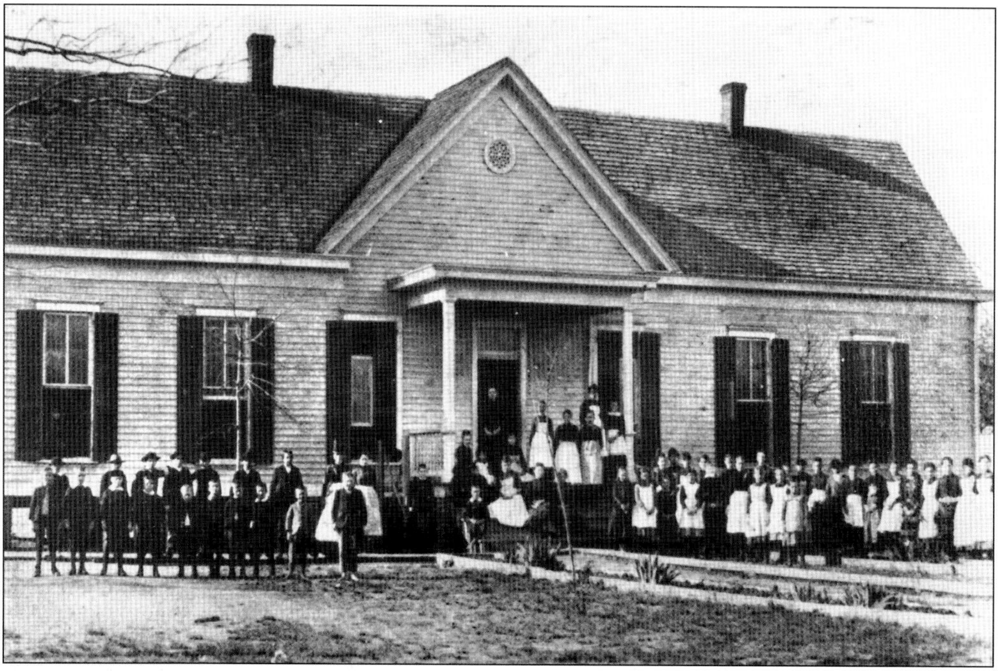

In 1881, Miss Holden's Seminary opened in Collierville on present-day South Rowlett Street. The school was considered ahead of its time. Anna Holden had graduated in 1859 from the LaGrange Institute and, with the help of her two brothers, established her school in Collierville. In 1893, it was purchased by the board of education and opened as a boy's school in 1895.

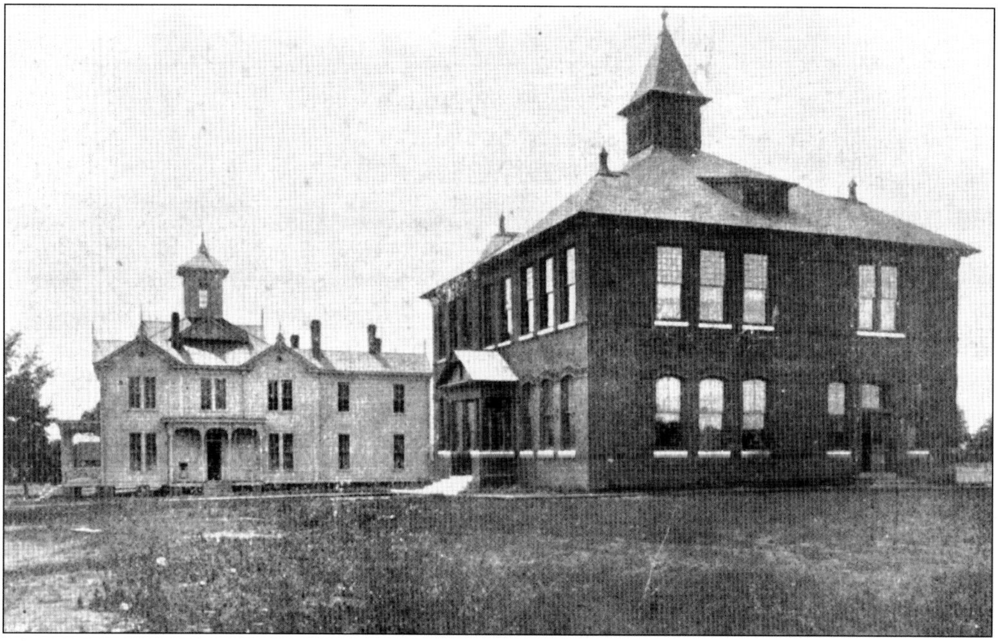

The Bellevue Female College was founded in 1872 and located on College Street and Walnut Street. The school, on the right, was built in 1871; the boarding house is seen in the background. High school tuition was $3 per month, with an additional $13.50 for boarding. The school operated until 1904. An institute of learning has remained at this location for more than 138 years.

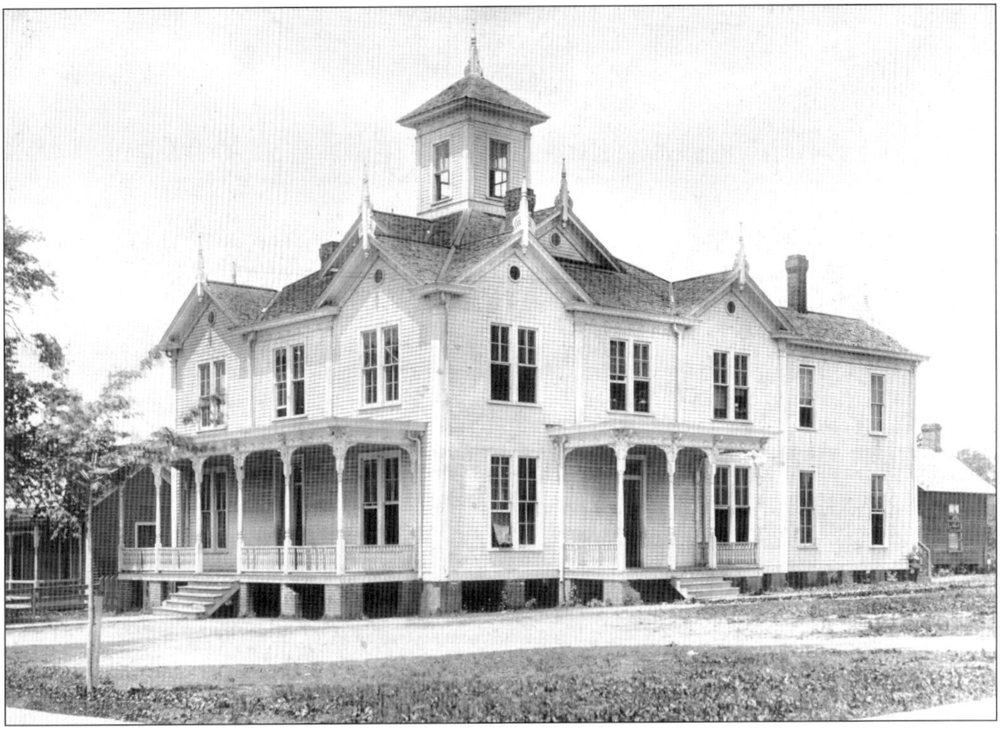

The boarding house for the Bellevue Female College, built in 1872, was an impressive two-story house for young ladies attending the school from a distance. In 1886, Bellevue and Anna Holden's school had a combined enrollment of over 300 students.

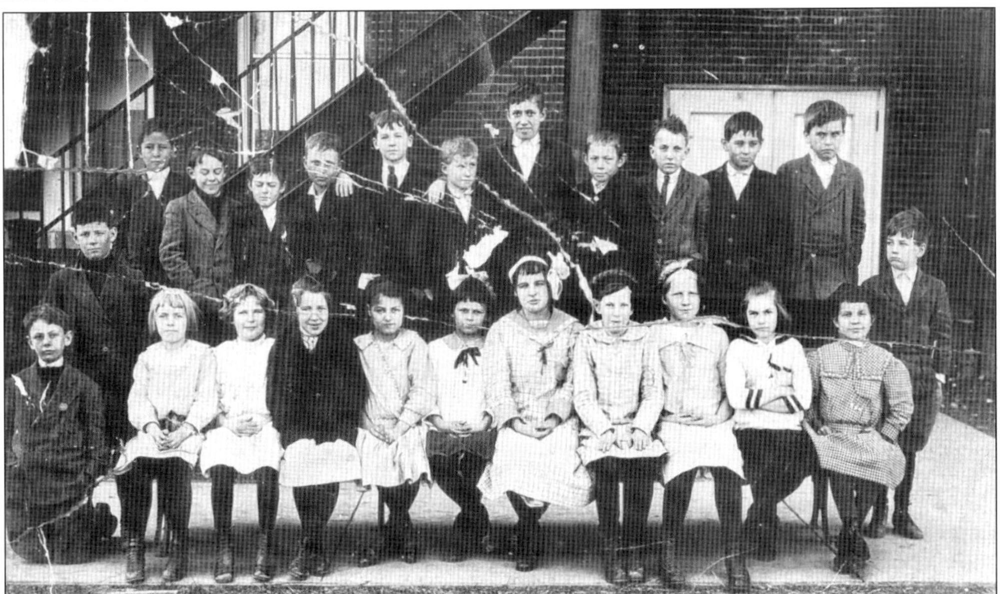

The fourth-grade class is gathered at the Collierville High School in 1913. Little Ivy Garland, the mother of Gene Morton, is the third child from the right in the first row. She would marry Edgar J. Morton in 1920. They first lived on Powell Road, then bought a home at 243 East Poplar Street, and later moved next door to 253 East Poplar Street.

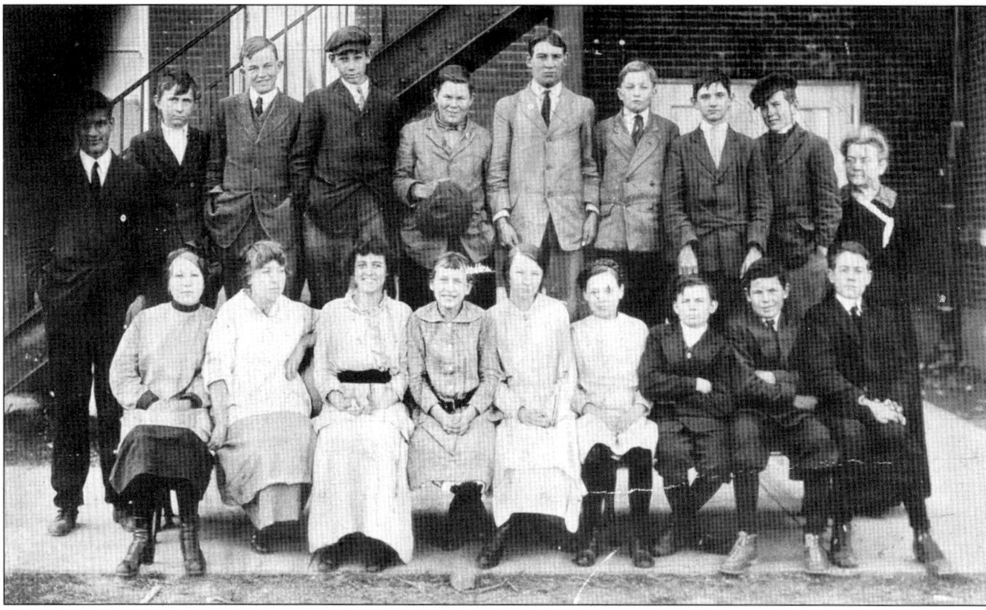

In 1915, the seventh grade posed outside the Collierville High School wearing their Sunday best. All of the young men have on coats, and most are wearing ties. The young ladies were wearing modest dresses with black stockings and shoes.

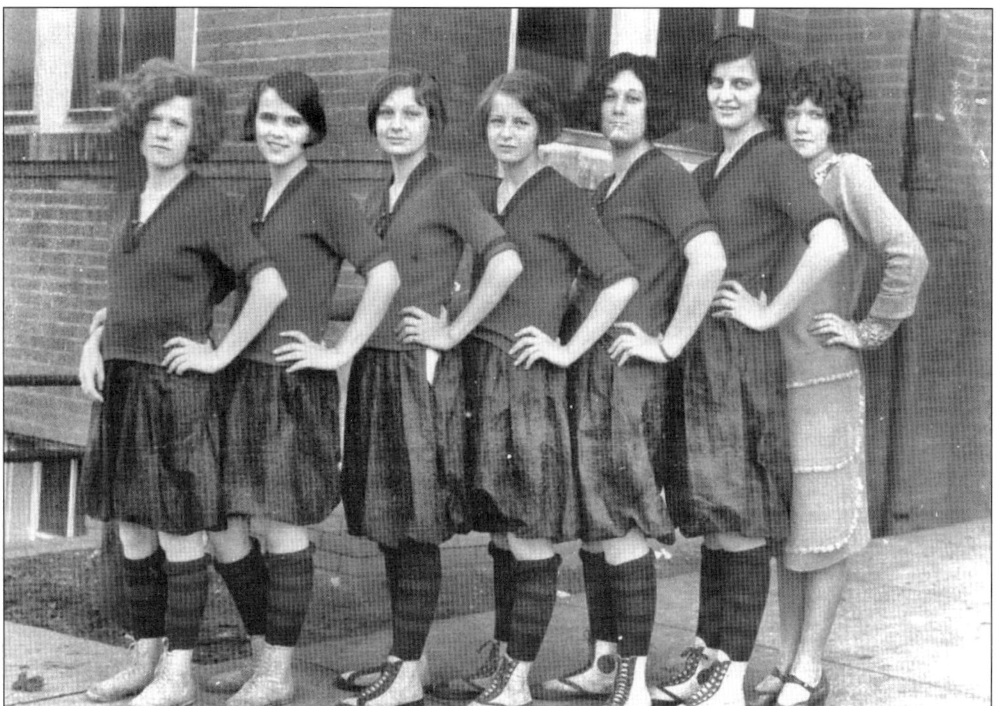

Collierville High School girls' basketball team of 1926–1928 is pictured here. Collierville had a girls' basketball team as early as 1922. The uniforms, with black stockings, were restrictive on the court during the game, but modest for the girls to wear in public games.

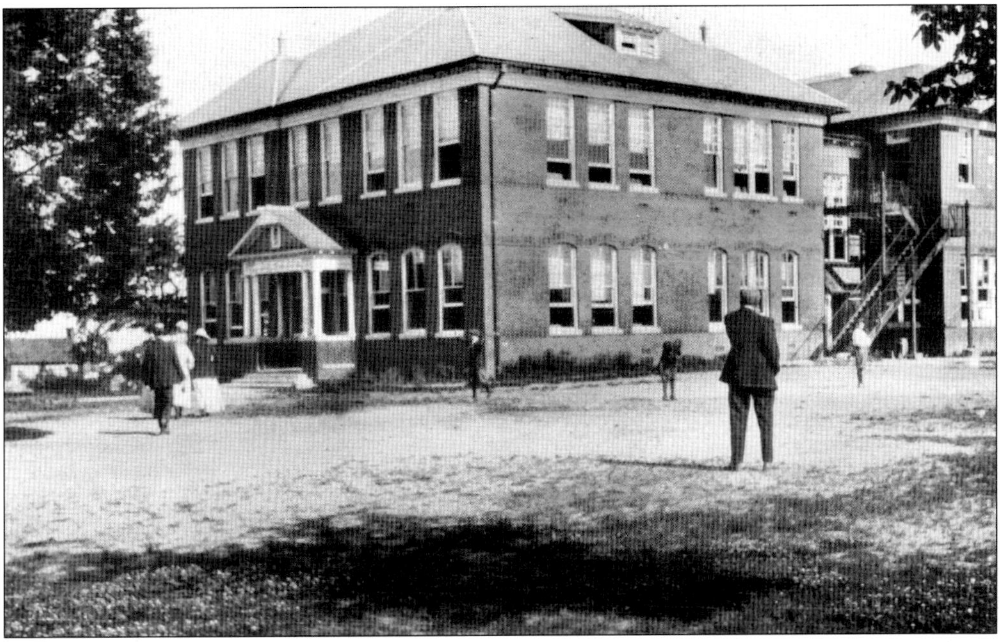

The high school was built in the early 1900s with additions made in 1911, 1924, and 1933. A large gymnasium was added in 1926. In 1903, a teacher's salary averaged $40.85 per month. Many of the teachers boarded with local families.

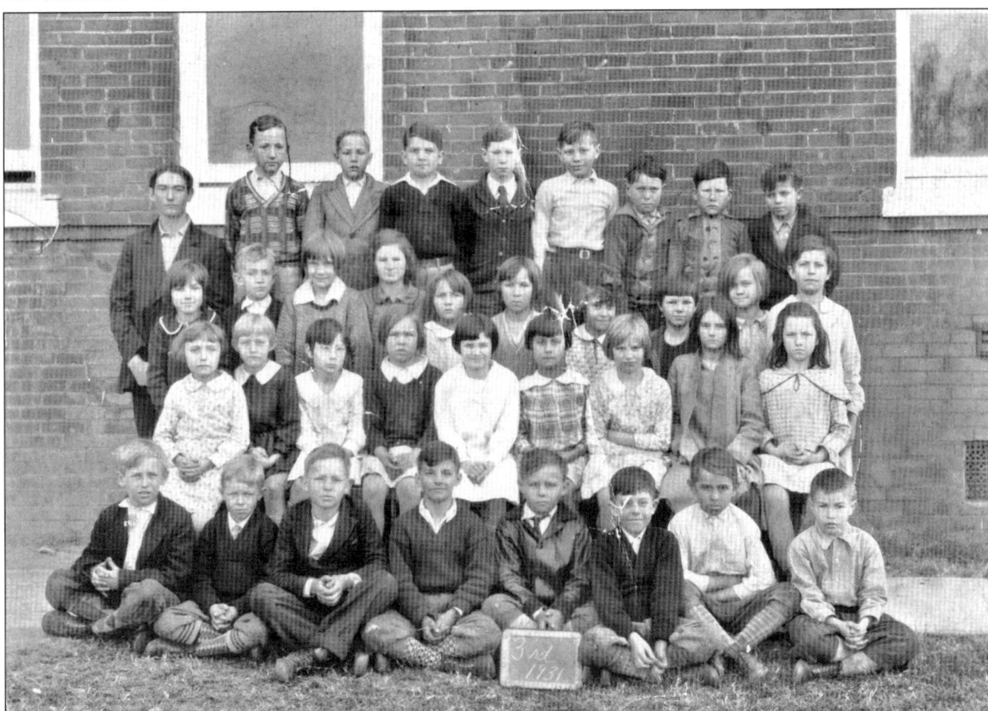

Third-grade students are pictured in 1931. Students in the first row are, from left to right, Homer Lee Vaughn, Milton Mann, Eugene O'Neil, Vance Carrington, Ralph Suggs, Herman Wright Cox, Finley Russell, and Elgin Rutledge.

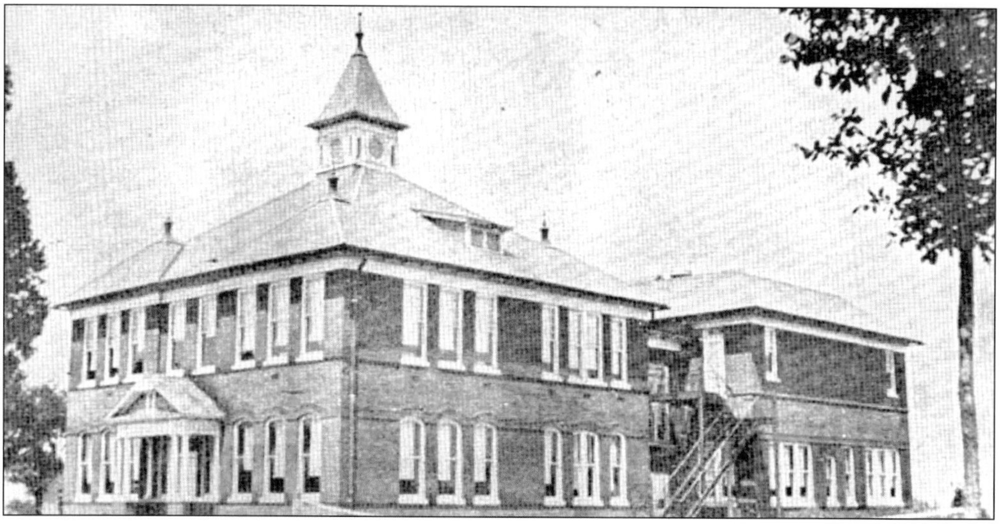

The Collierville High School is shown here in 1916. This building was built in 1897 on the same location as the Bellevue Female College. Columns were on the front of the building. By this date, all boys and girls attended the same school, as the county could not afford to maintain two public schools in Collierville.

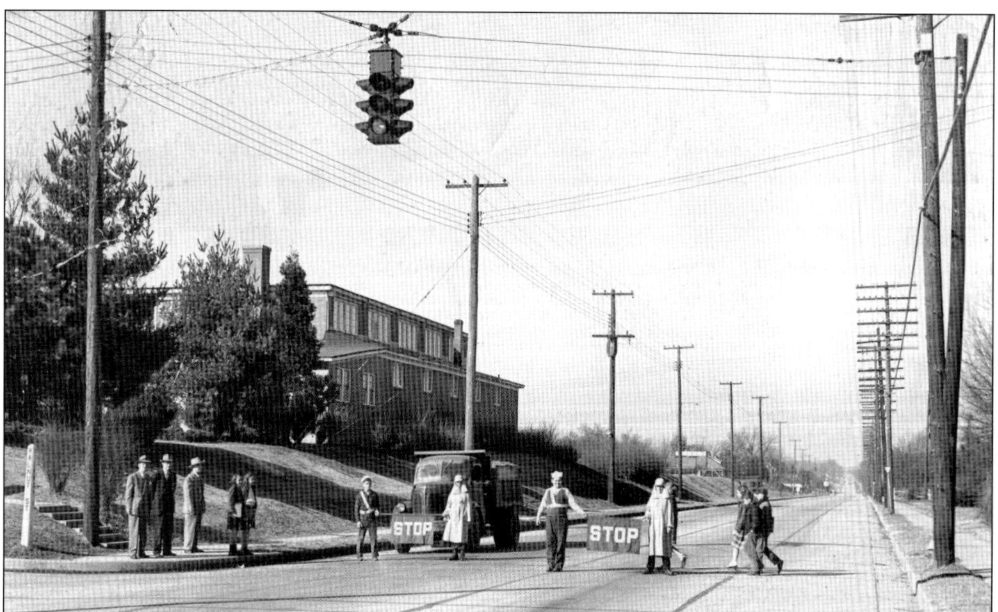

Students serve as school crossing guards. The crossing at Walnut Street and State Line Highway 57 (present-day Poplar Avenue) is almost deserted in the 1940s. Notice the suits and hats worn by the adults.

Nine students from the black community make up this class in August 1925 at the Collierville School. The original frame building was located close to today's overpass at Byhalia Road. Prof. O. L. Armour, who served as a teacher, was known for his leadership ability with the young people. The young girl seated on the right in the front row was the daughter of Mitchell Spears, who taught music to her and Velma Garmon in the 1940s.

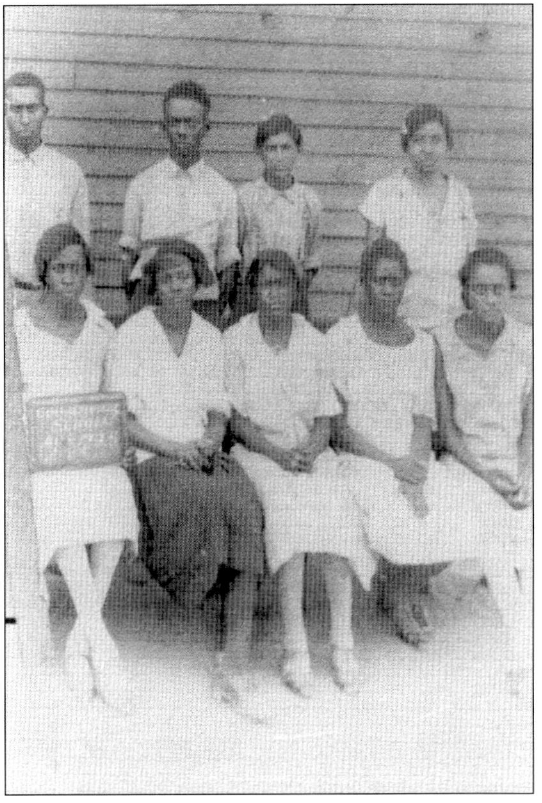

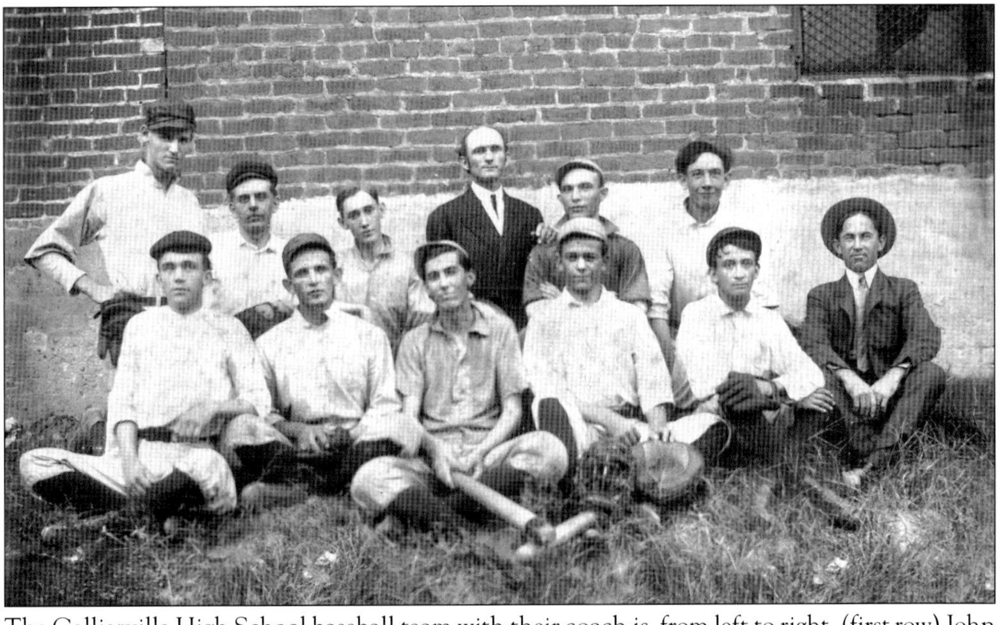

The Collierville High School baseball team with their coach is, from left to right, (first row) John Walker, Sam McDonald, Sidney Humphreys, Jim Hester, Ray Roach, and John Lynch; (second row) Jim Fleming, Franklin Kelsey, Turner Humphreys, Dr. Eugene Johnson, Emmet Williford, and Noland Leake.

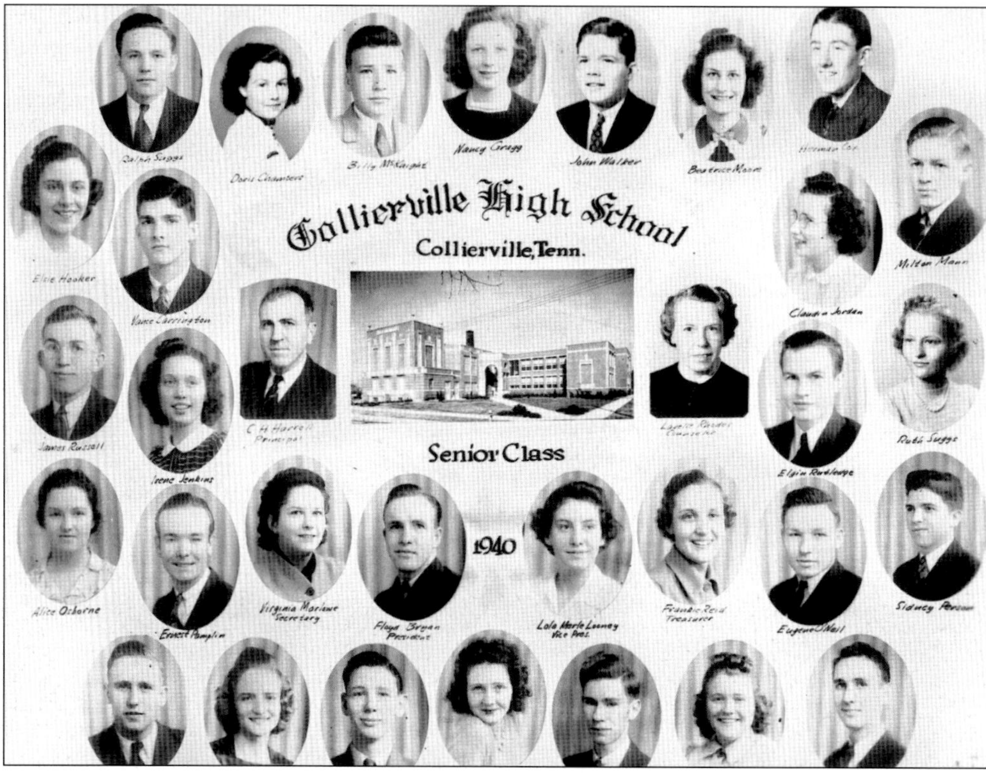

The Collierville High School graduating class of 1940 will scarcely have begun their post–high school careers before the United States enters World War II, and they are called on to face grave peril and accept heavy responsibility as members of America's "Greatest Generation."

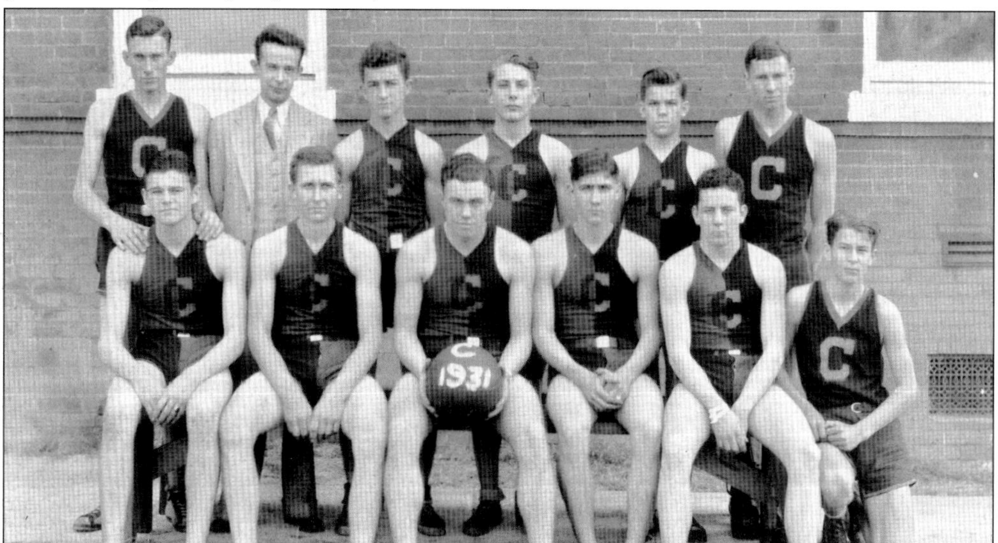

The Collierville High School basketball team is pictured in 1931. From left to right are (first row) Aubrey Guy, Thomas P. Hart, Ray Seward, Gordon Baxter, Davis Leake, and Howard Clayton; (second row) Orville Duscoe, Coach Eddie B. Hudgens, Lawrence Parsons, unidentified, Howard Carrington, and Robert Shelton.

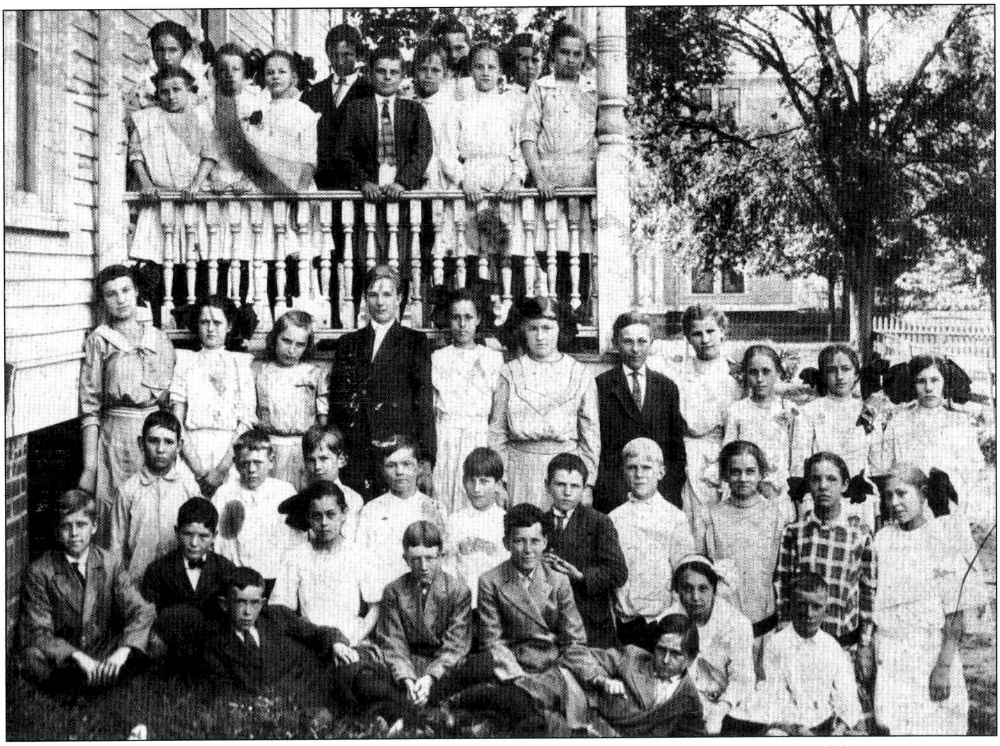

This is an early photograph of a class at Anna Holden's school, known as "Miss Holden's Seminary." Holden had the reputation of being an excellent educator and disciplinarian and in the front rank of her profession. The seminary became one of the best schools in the state. Herman Wright Cox Sr. is in the middle of the first row of this photograph, and Lydelle McGinnis is on the third row, far right, with a large bow in her hair. The two later became husband and wife.

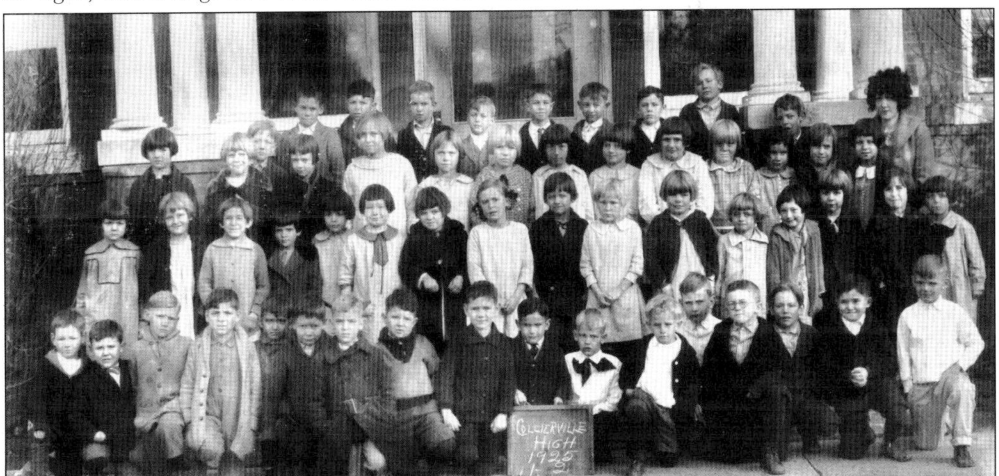

Grades one and two pose outside the Collierville School in 1925. Annexes had been added to the school building the previous year to accommodate the growth. The following year, 1926, a gymnasium would be built for the students. Two pot-bellied stoves warmed the new gym. In 1924, the high school was one of only three schools accepted in Tennessee for membership in the Southern Association of Schools and Colleges.

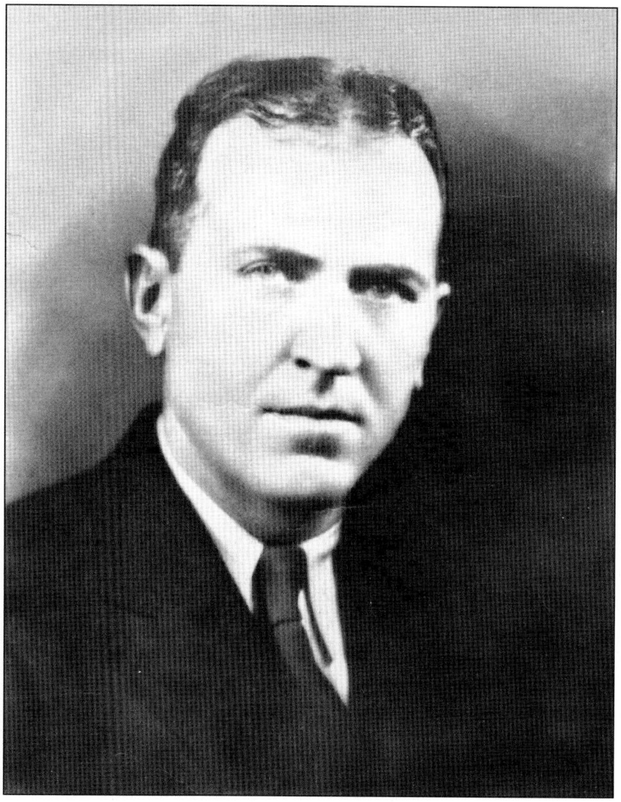

Charles H. Harrell was the beloved principal of Collierville High School from 1932 to 1945. He has been described as a "good person and one who would strive to bring out the best in each student." Principal Harrell and his wife, Hopsie, and their family lived adjacent to the school building in a home that faced College Street. Harrell Theater at the Collierville Community Center is named in his honor.

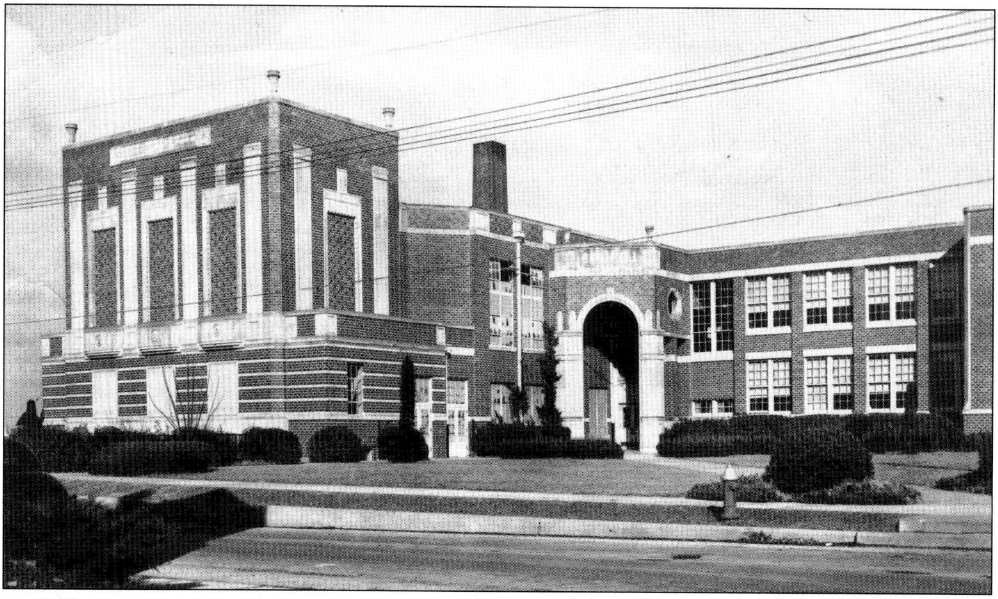

In 1933, Pres. Franklin D. Roosevelt's Works Projects Administration provided a much-needed addition for the school in Collierville as a project in Shelby County. The new building was built on the same location as the female college and the 1900 building. The two annexes from 1911 and 1924 were salvaged. The new school was completed in three years and today serves as the Collierville Middle School.

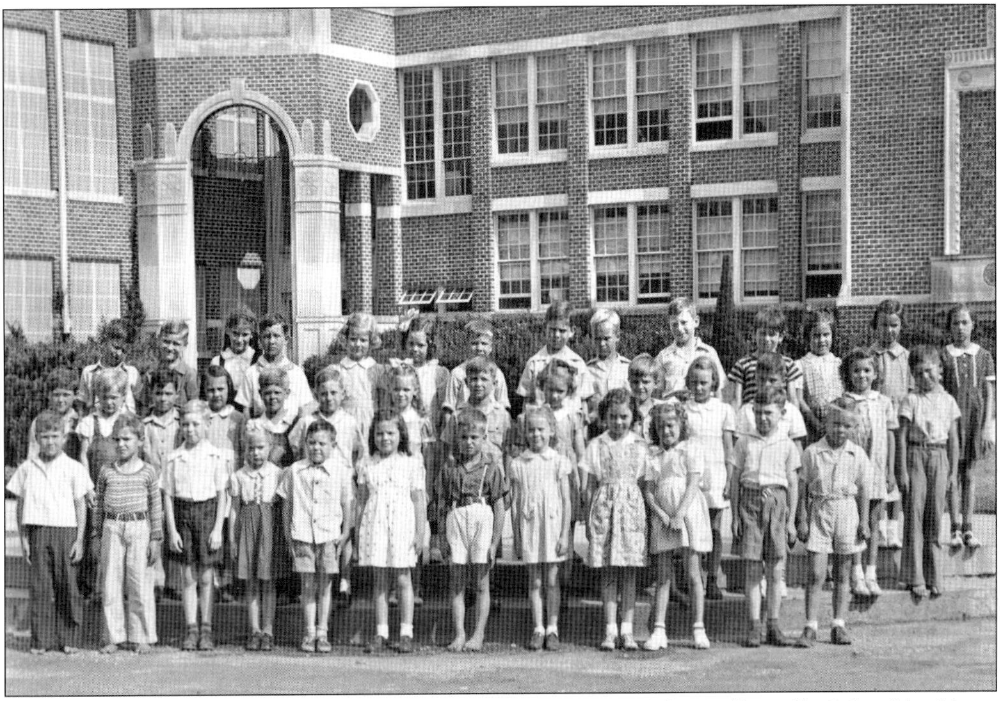

A Collierville elementary class of 1942 is pictured in front of the Collierville School building. Girls always wore dresses to school, and most of them had a sash that tied in the back. Ribbons or barrettes in the hair were also common. Boys wore button shirts and were allowed to wear cut-off pants in the warmer months. Note that some of the boys in the photograph are barefoot.

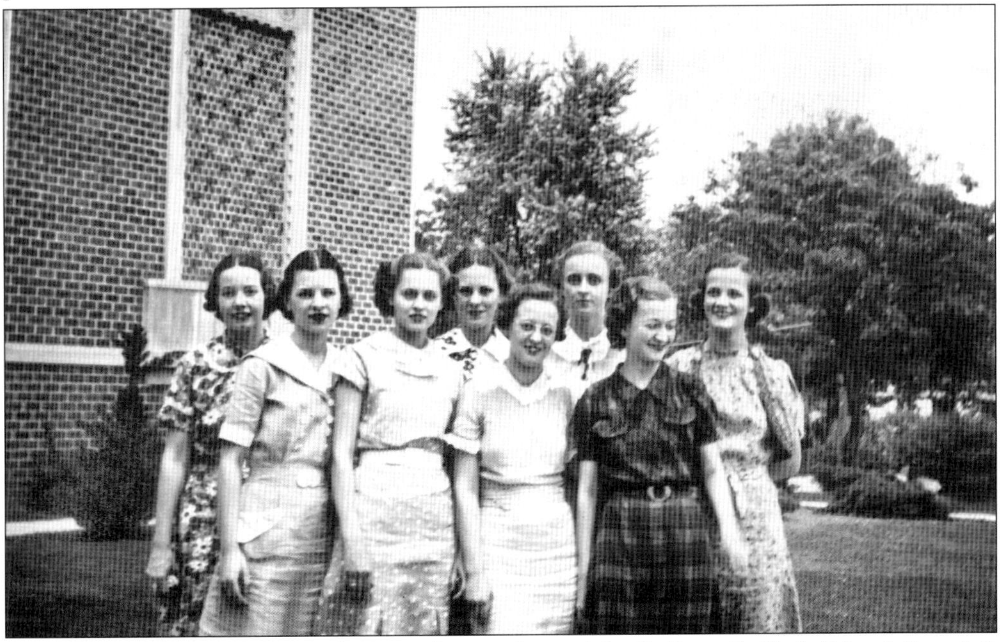

A group of girls from the class of 1937 gathers in front of the Collierville High School. From left to right are Doris Kirk, Ruth Rives, Dorothy Higgs, Dorothy Farley, Oneida Reid, Sara Hinton, Alice Montgomery, and Elizabeth Carrington.

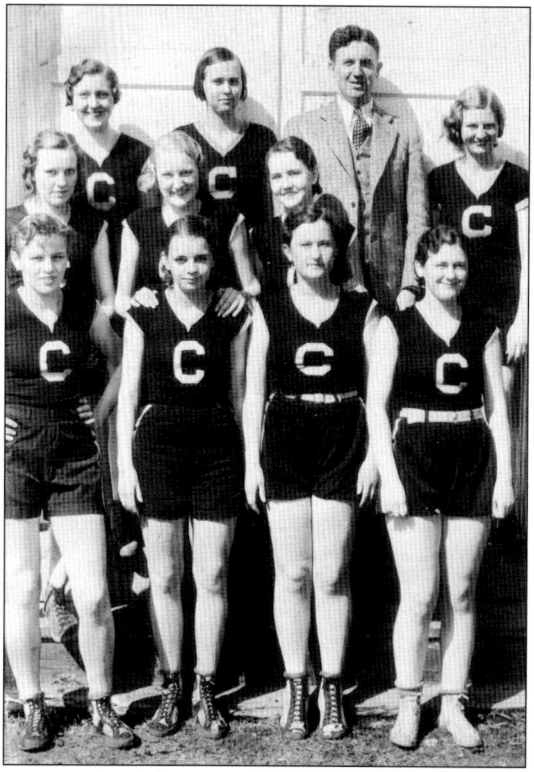

The girls' basketball team at Collierville High School in 1930–1932 are, from left to right, (first row) Sally Priddy, Grace Duscoe, Martha Hughes, and Ruby Crawford. Coach John Hall Jacobs is pictured with the girls. In 1934 and 1935, the girls' team won the district championship, and in 1936, they won the regional championship.

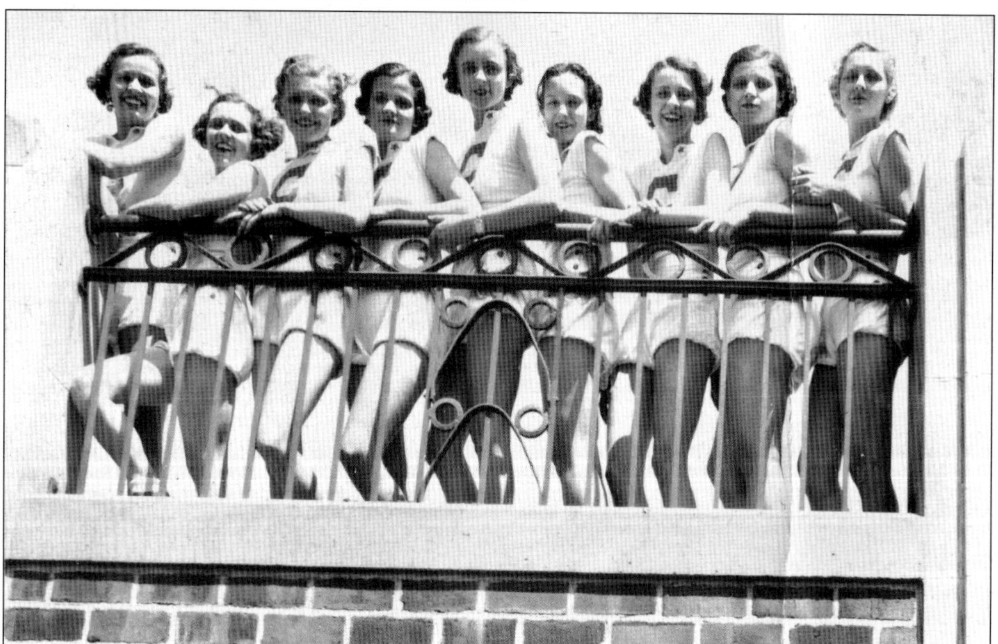

Posing outside the Collierville High School is the 1936 girls' basketball team. This team won the West Tennessee Regional Championship. The team members are, from left to right, Mary Grace Priddy, Marie Neely, Camille Baxter, Elizabeth Carrington, Sara Hinton, Elizabeth Martin, Dorothy Hinton, Janie Carrington, and Cecilia Morris.

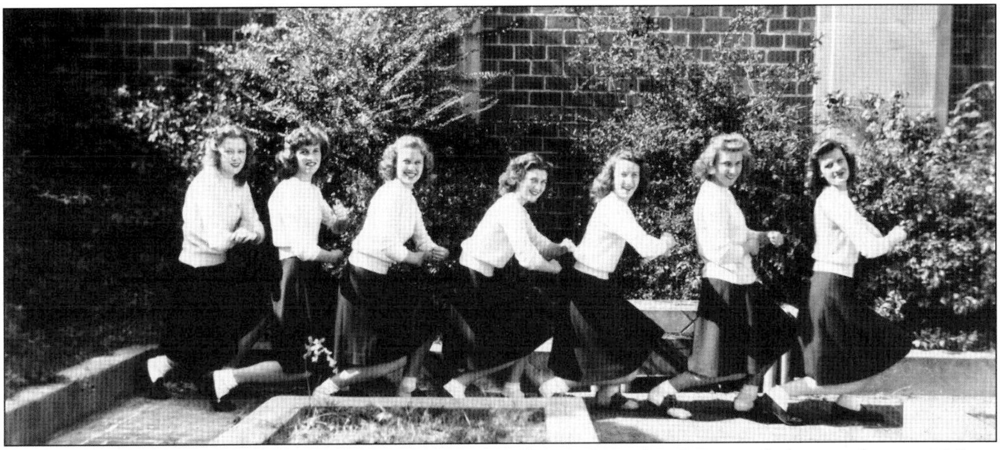

The 1946 cheerleaders pose outside the Collierville High School. From left to right are Kelsey Ann Jones, Lois Farley, Betty Jo Bulle, Donnie Sue Hill, Virginia Pulliam, Mary Sue Ballard, and Jean Crawford. The school colors were originally black and gold and later changed to maroon and white.

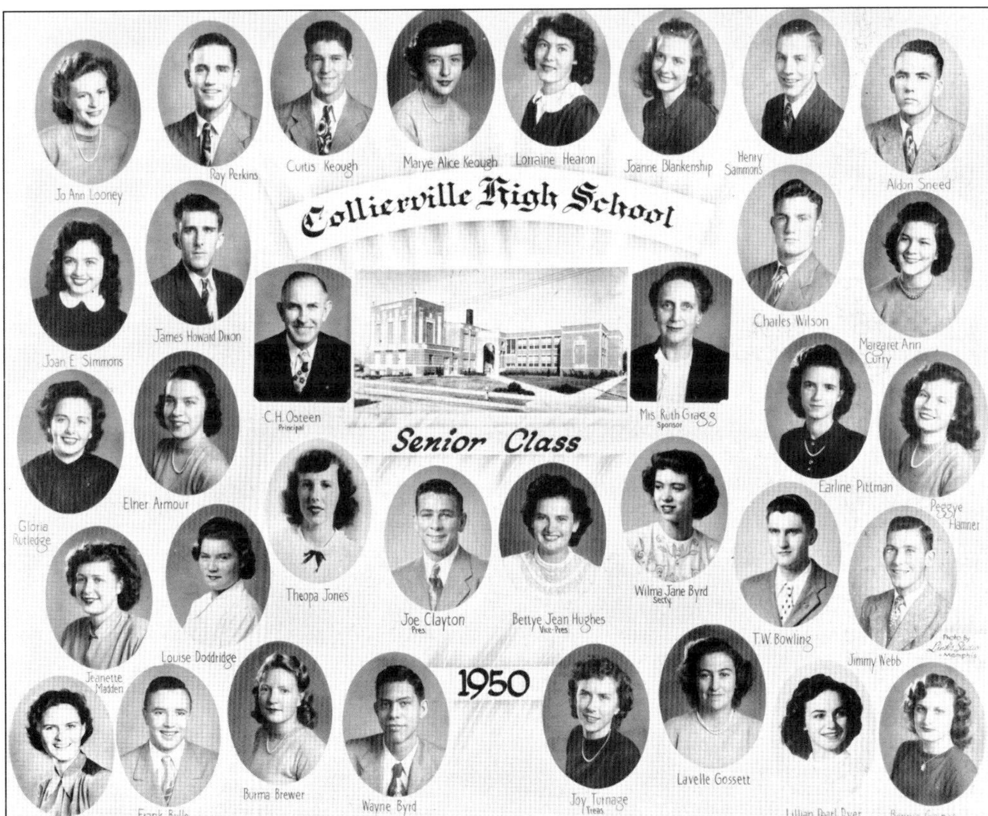

The graduating class of 1950 benefited from much of Collierville's growth. The future looked bright for these seniors. Clifton Herman Osteen (left, center) was the principal and served from 1945 to 1971. Joe Clayton (lower center), class president and captain of the football team, continued his education at Memphis State. He spent his professional career in the educational field as coach, teacher, principal, and a member of the Shelby County School Board.

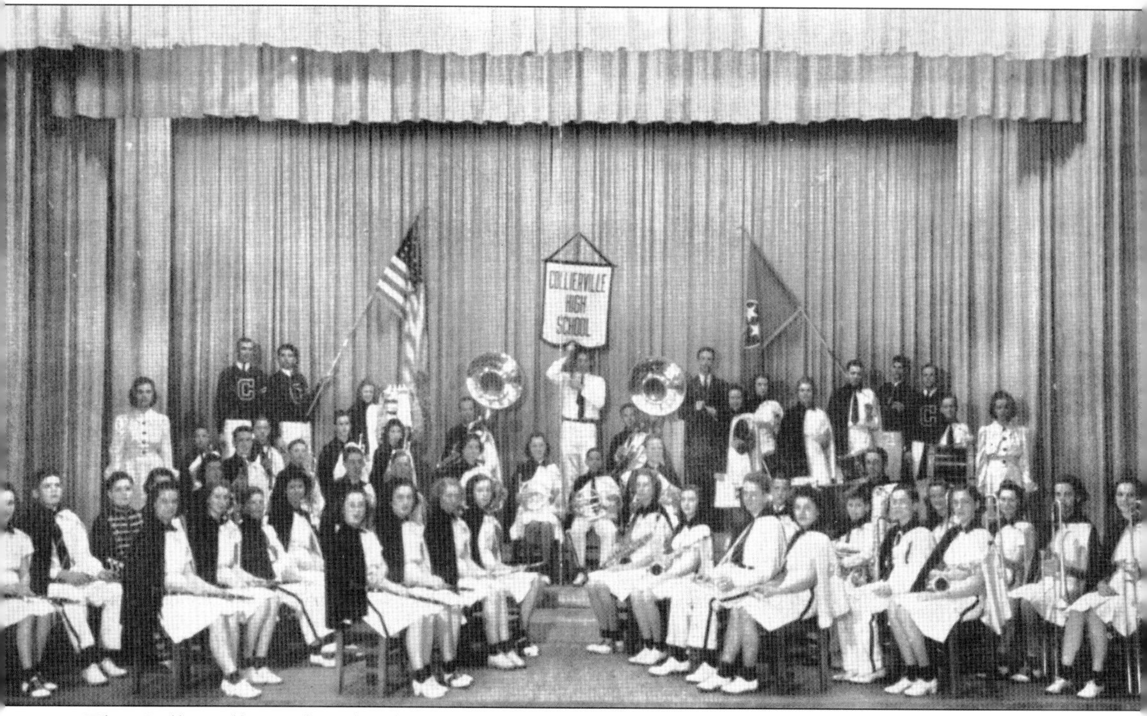

The Collierville High School Band of 1939–1940 is featured in a souvenir program that was published by the Collierville High School music department for their annual concert that was held on May 23, 1940. The program states that "new instruments have been added to the band and we have been able to do a much higher type music in both the band and chorus." The band was First Division Winner of the concert and marching band contest in West Tennessee. Lowrey Haynie was the director of the music department.

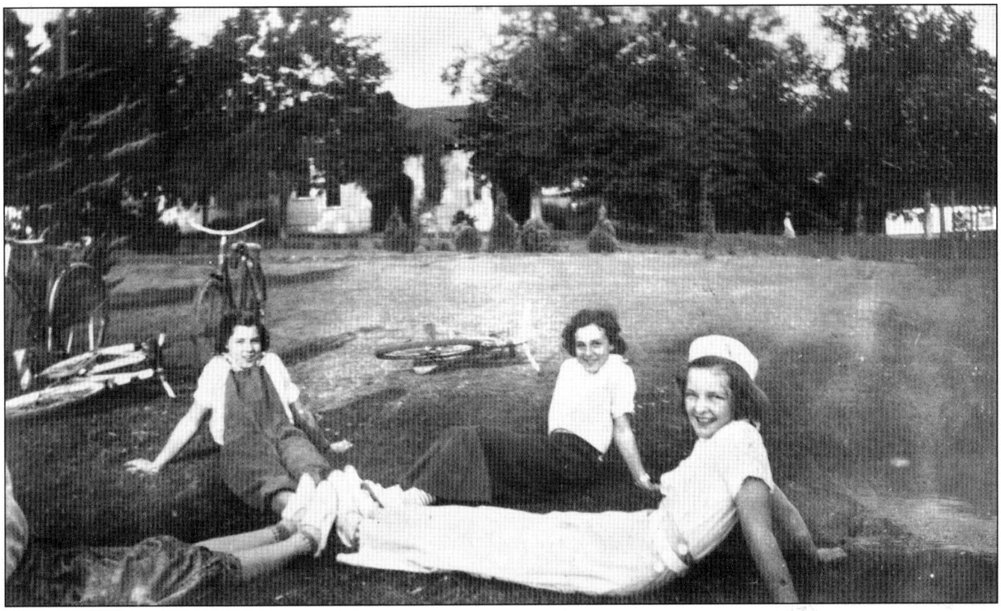

Grace Ward McFerrin (in the white cap) is pictured on the lawn with her girlfriends from Collierville High School. The date on the photograph from her scrapbook is 1934. Grace Ward was raised in the McFerrin home, located on Poplar Avenue (State Line Road). She married Howard Jamison.

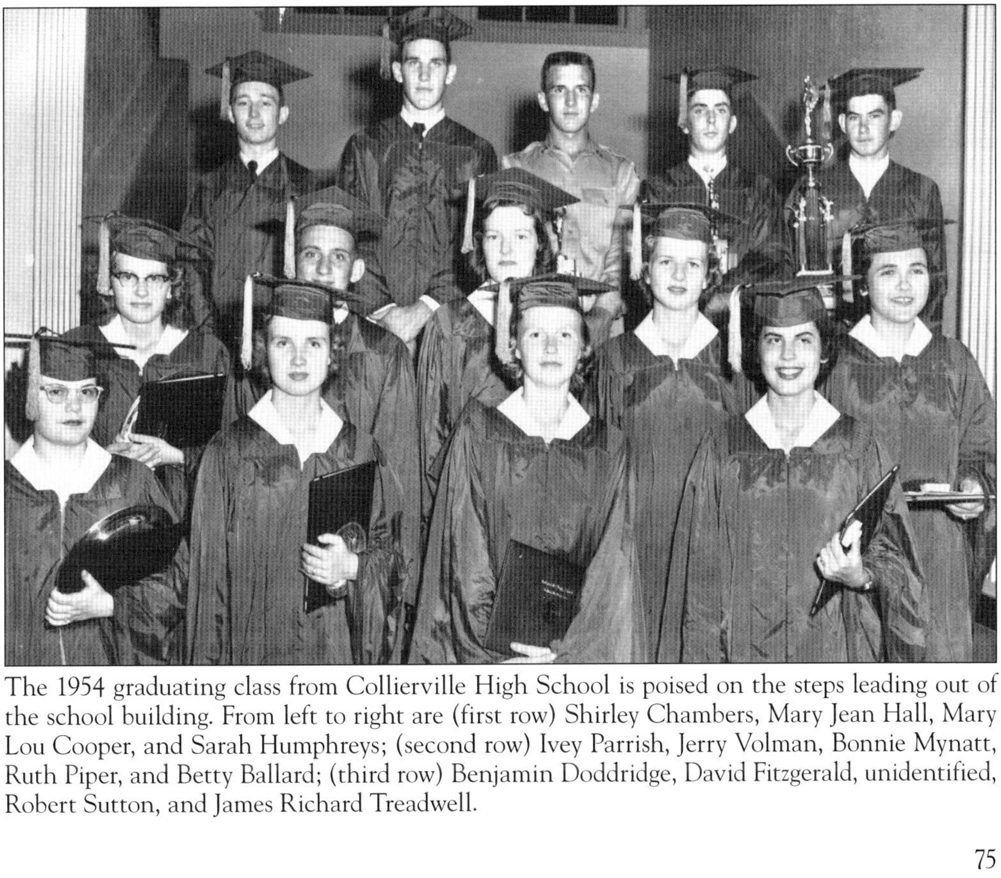

The 1954 graduating class from Collierville High School is poised on the steps leading out of the school building. From left to right are (first row) Shirley Chambers, Mary Jean Hall, Mary Lou Cooper, and Sarah Humphreys; (second row) Ivey Parrish, Jerry Volman, Bonnie Mynatt, Ruth Piper, and Betty Ballard; (third row) Benjamin Doddridge, David Fitzgerald, unidentified, Robert Sutton, and James Richard Treadwell.

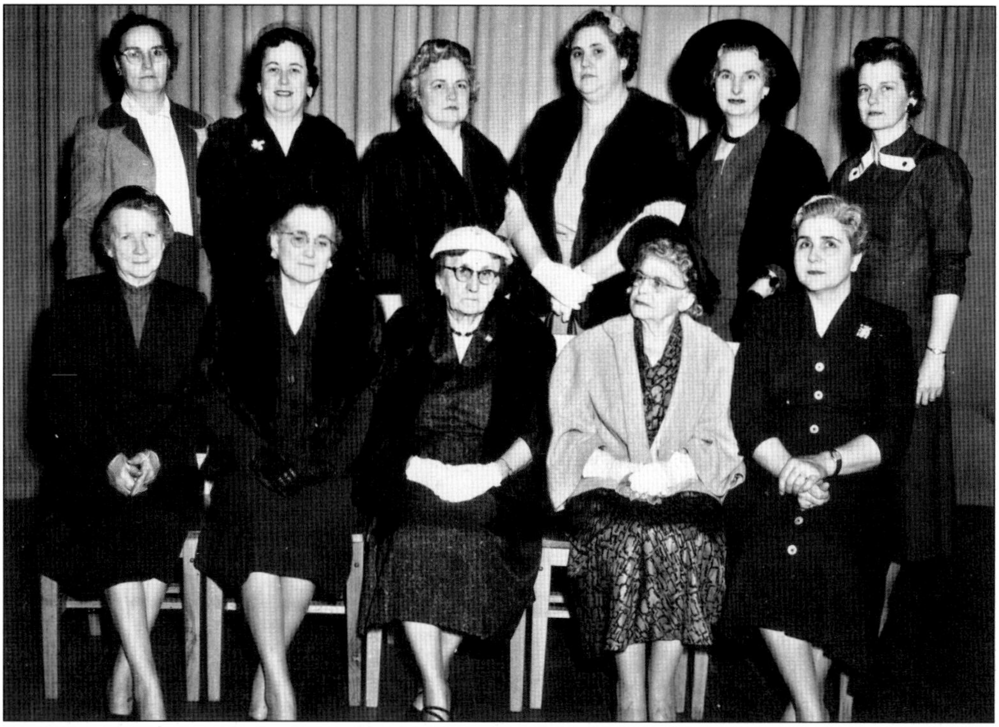

The Parent-Teacher Association (PTA) supported the Collierville school while adhering to principles set forth by the national organization. Meetings were held in the auditorium after school on the first Thursday of each month. This photograph was taken in the early 1940s and includes present and past presidents of the organization.

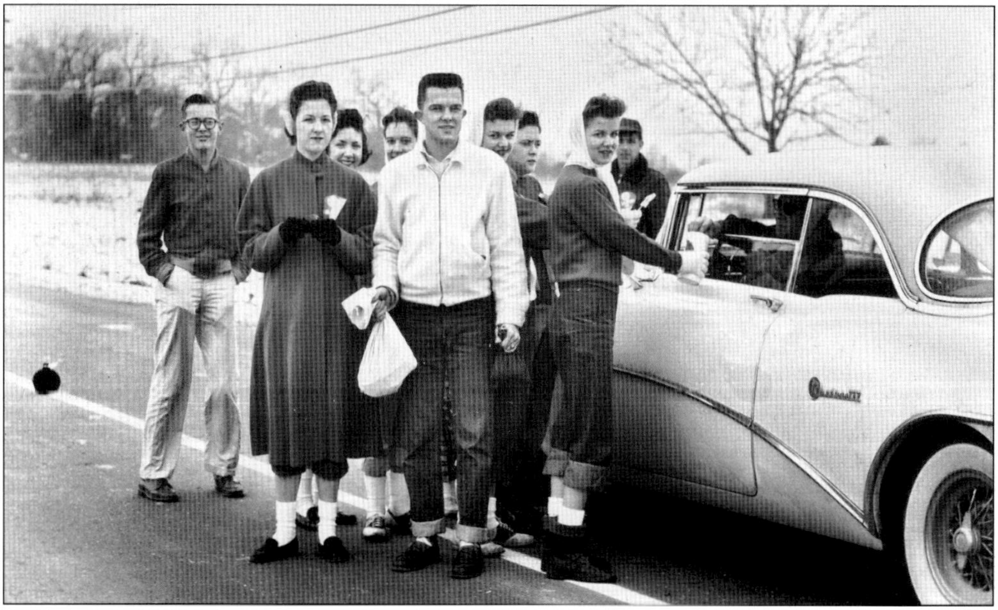

Collierville High School students have always been supportive of community fund-raisers. As the "happy days" of the 1950s approach, this group of young people is stopping cars to raise funds for a worthy cause. Blue jeans with the cuffs rolled up were the fashion rage.

Five

Places of Work

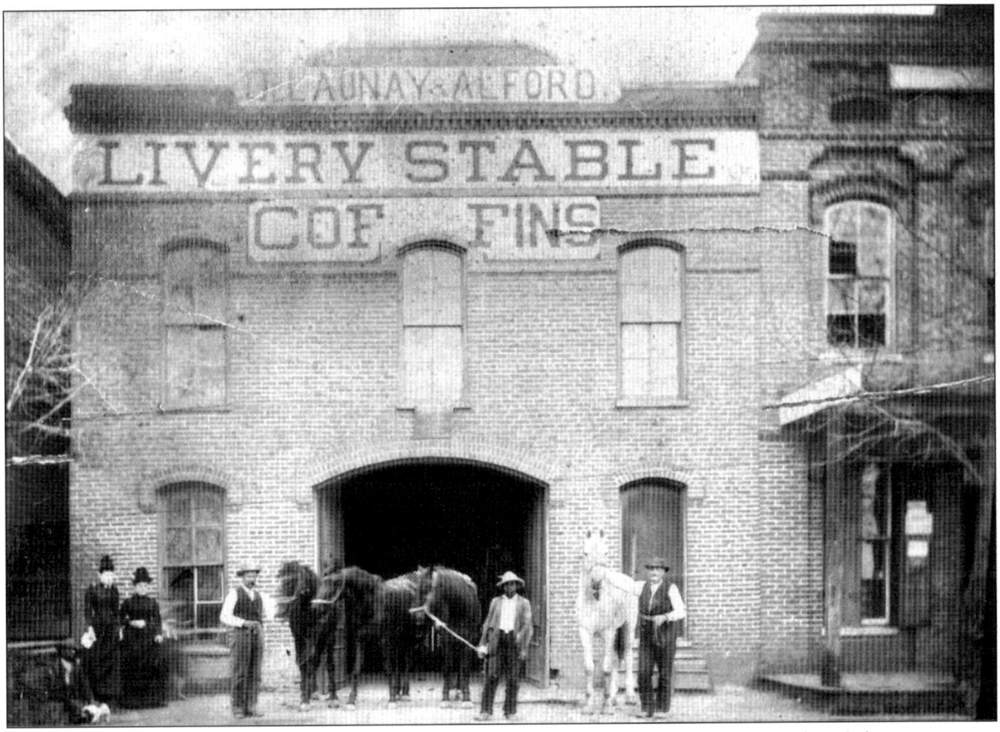

DeLaunay and Alford Livery Stable and Coffins was located on the east side of the square on Main Street. Coffins were kept upstairs. It was not unusual for businesses to use their buildings for several trades. James R. DeLaunay, one of the owners, was a Civil War veteran. His fellow officers, who were captured with him as prisoners of war and detained at Johnson Island during the war, signed a small autograph book. A copy of the book is now located in the collection at the Tennessee State Museum.

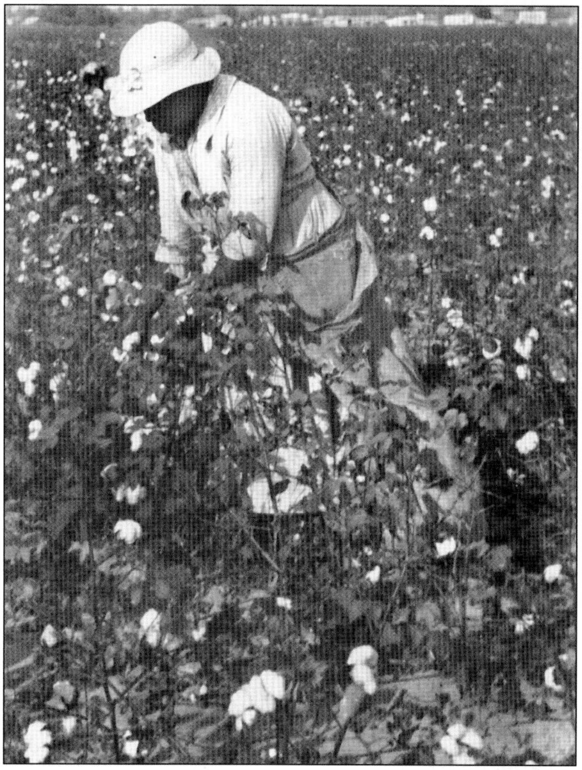

Cotton has always reigned king in the South. Since cotton grows in warm climates, Tennessee was one of the major cotton-producing states. Slave labor was used earlier on large plantations. Small farmers harvested their own crops or used hired help. Picking cotton was difficult work, and the heat could become very oppressive in the fields. In addition to picking the cotton, the pickers must drag the "cotton bag" with them as they pick. This bag would be slung over the shoulder, allowing the arms to move more freely. The mechanical cotton picker replaced the men and women who spent long hours working in the cotton fields for a living. Tractors and later mechanical cotton pickers changed cotton production and the lives of those who picked cotton. Cotton remains popular today and is used more than any other fiber in the world.

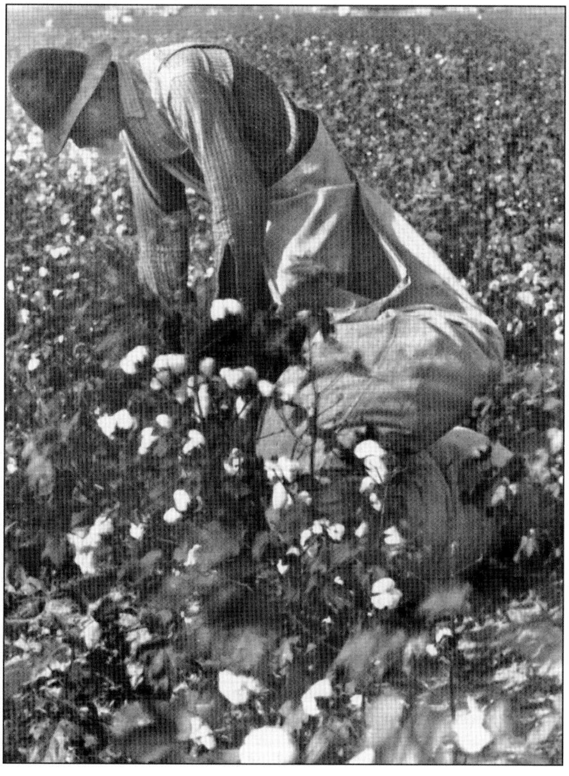

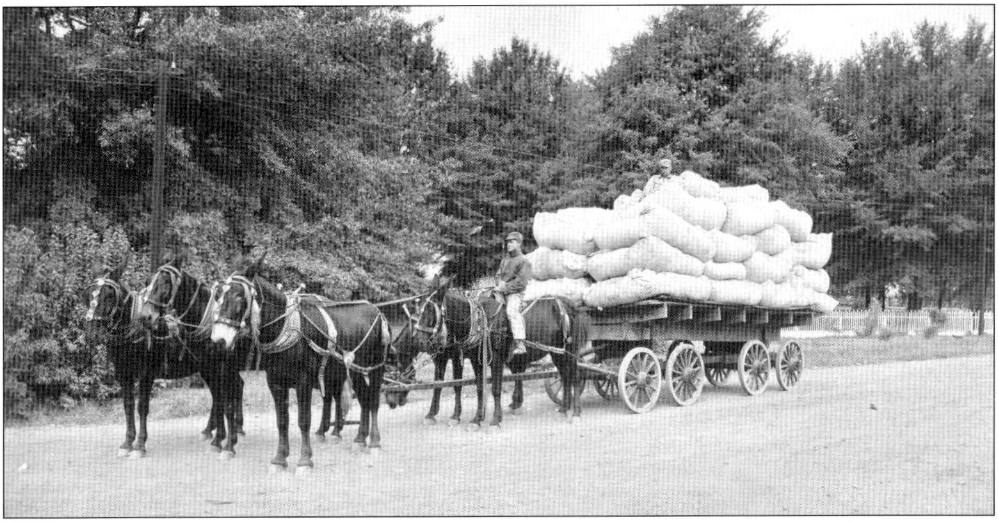

Farmers brought their cotton to Collierville in the early days by mule-drawn wagons to be shipped by rail to designated destinations. Before the railroad, the trip could take days to reach the Memphis market. The depot platform was used for selling cotton during the fall and winter months and occasionally for dancing during the summer. Rows of cotton bales sitting on the Collierville depot were common as late as the 1950s.

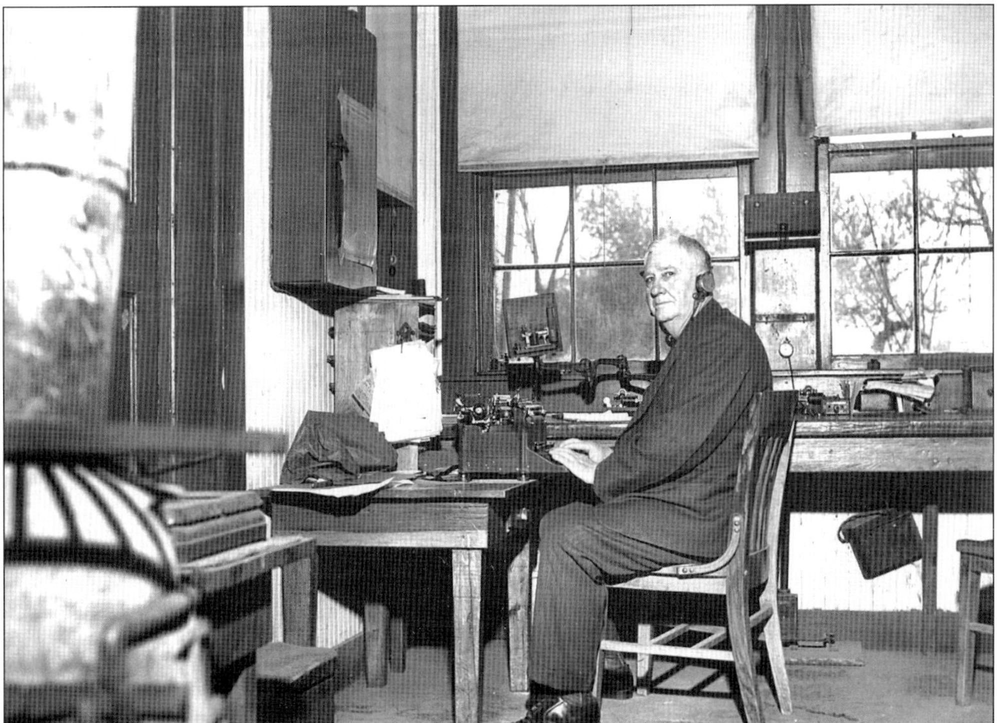

George Crawford worked with the Southern Railroad as an agent. This photograph was taken in 1948. Many of the furnishings and fixtures in this picture remain in the depot today. The depot now houses the Main Street Collierville offices. Graham Clayton, president of Southern Railroad, donated the depot to the Town of Collierville in 1976.

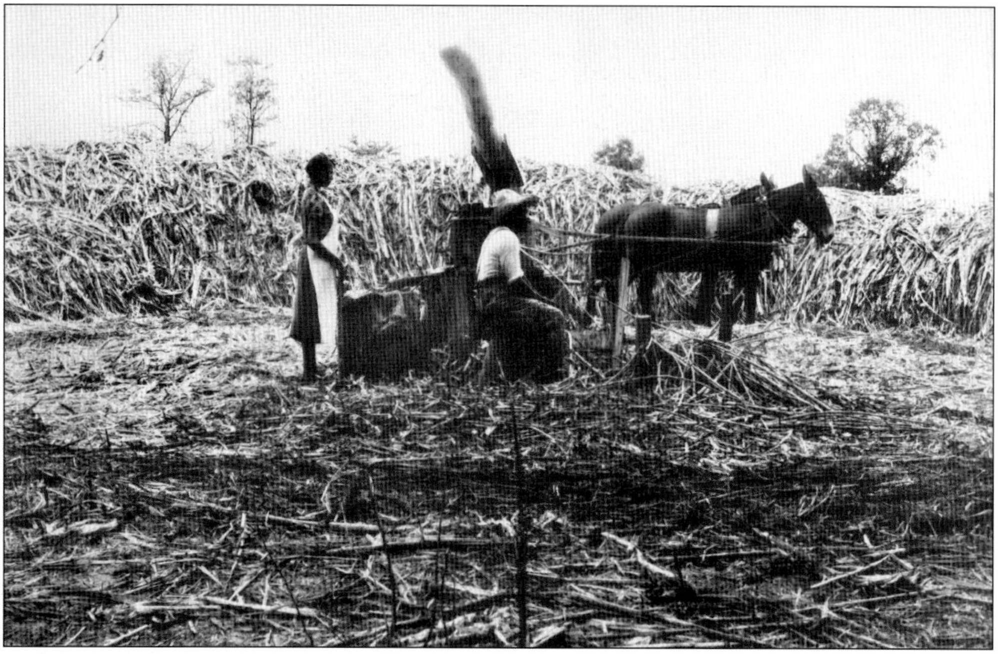

Making sorghum or sugar cane molasses was a common sight on many of the farms in and around Collierville. The cane was cut and stripped of all its leaves. The bare stalks of cane would then be fed into a grinder or mill that was powered by a mule. As the mule walked, the mill would press the stalks of cane and the juice would be collected in a wooden barrel. It was necessary to stand near the mill to feed the stalks but also to keep a watchful eye for the mule and the extended pole. A shed would be set up nearby for the final preparation. As the juice was cooked over a fire and began to boil, the impurities would be skimmed off. When the molasses was ready, clean and shining jars and bottles were lined up, ready to be filled.

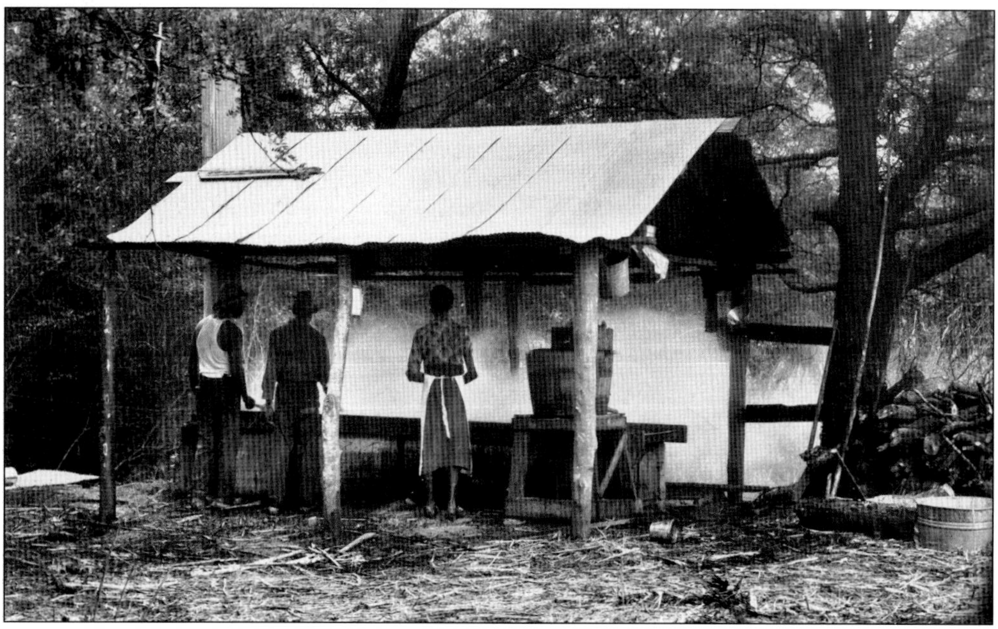

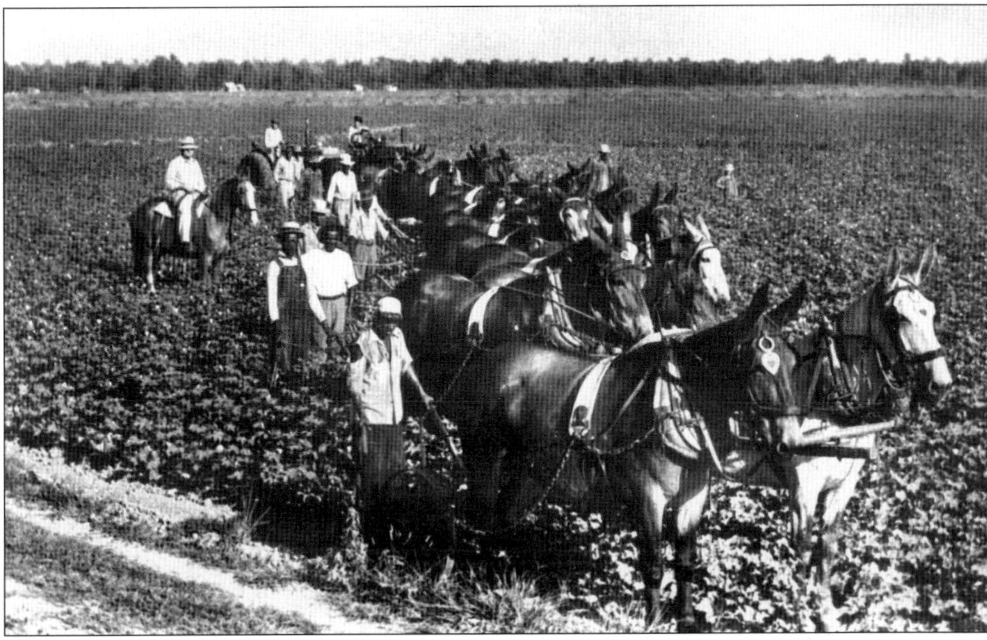

Farmers in and around Collierville used mules for heavy-duty work. They were the right animals for pulling wagons, like this one seen coming out of the cotton fields. It was not uncommon to see wagons pulled by mules around the town as late as the mid-1940s.

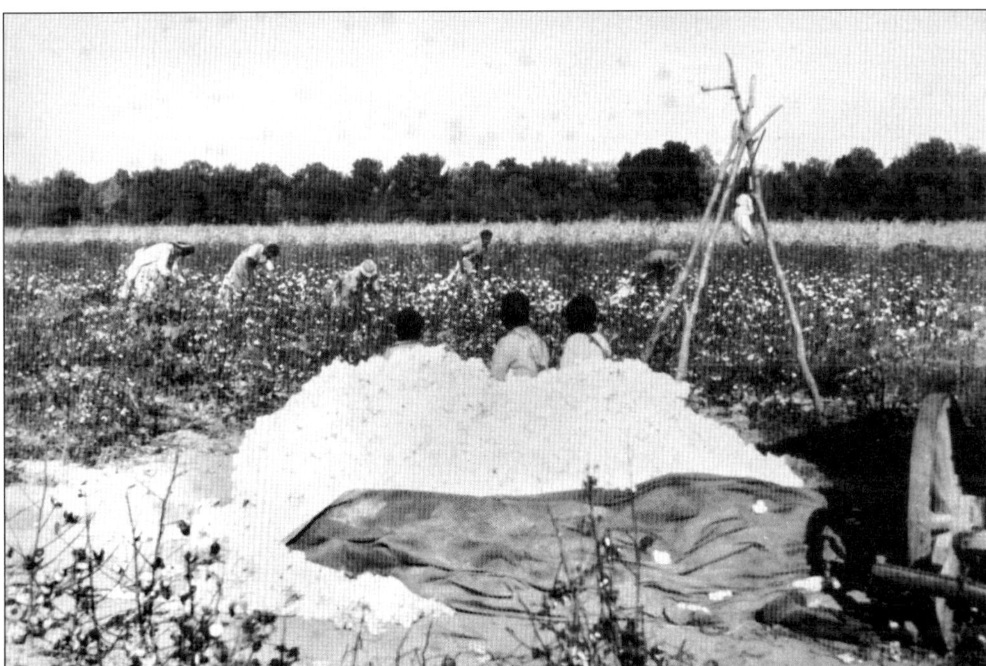

The children sitting on top of the cotton are in sight of their parents, who are busy picking cotton in the fields. It was necessary for women working in the fields to bring their young children with them while they worked. As soon as a child was old enough, they would be required to help with water buckets or however they were needed.

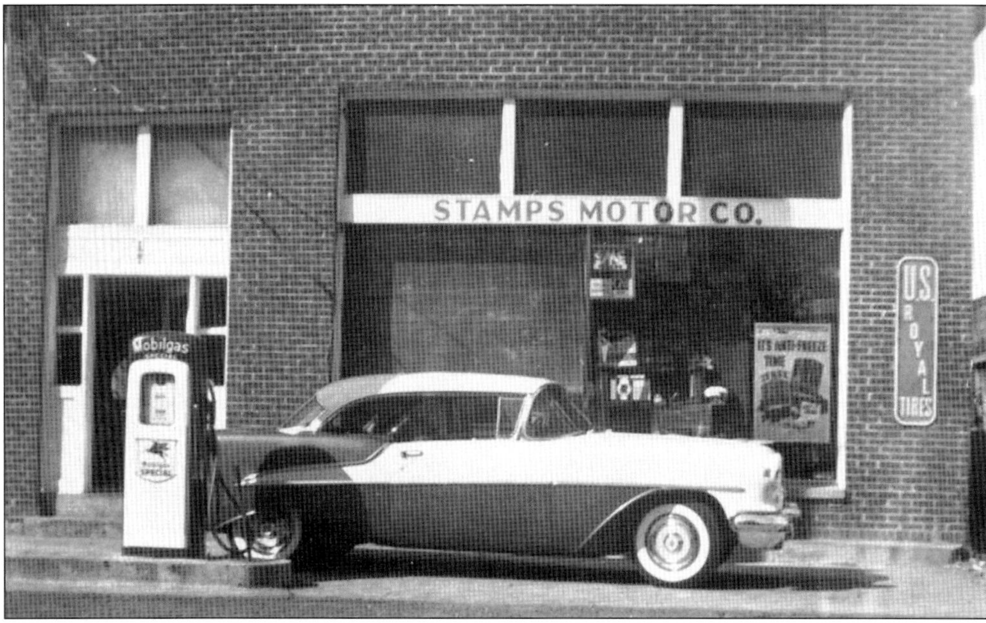

Stamps Motor Company was just off the square on the west side of Main Street, across from the fire station. The Stamps family lived over their business until a fire in 1944 damaged their building. Four other businesses on the north side of the Town Square were damaged.

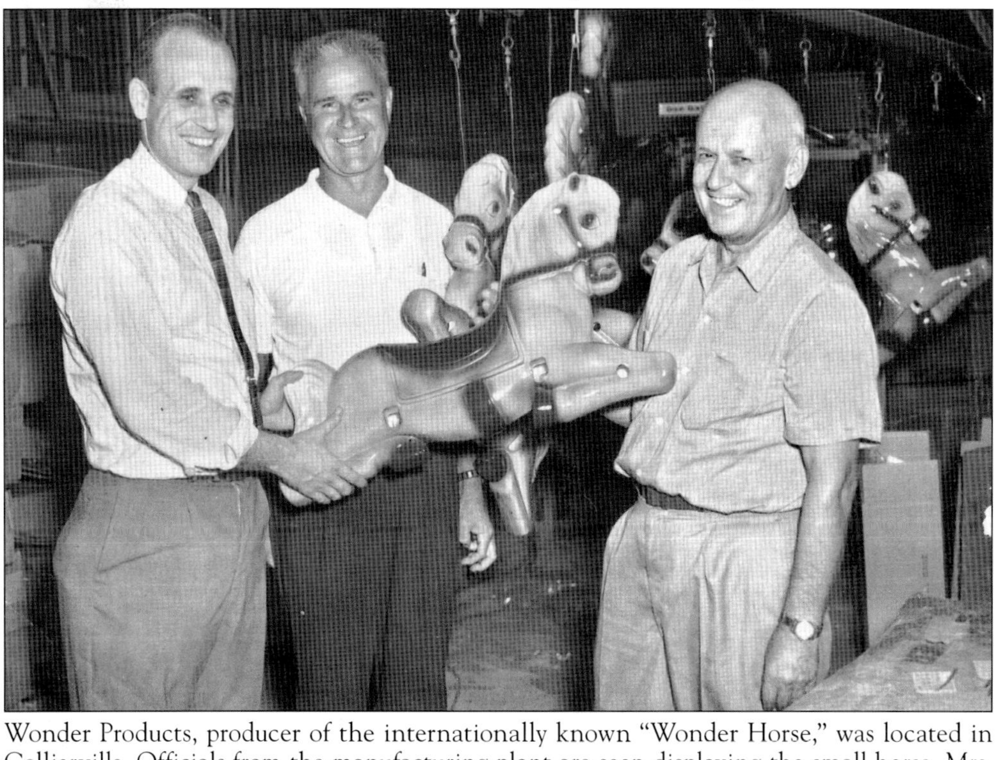
Wonder Products, producer of the internationally known "Wonder Horse," was located in Collierville. Officials from the manufacturing plant are seen displaying the small horse. Mrs. Minnie Bishop Smith designed many of the Wonder Horses and was noted for her artwork in the area. She was the daughter of Odie Bishop, who built the stone wall at Magnolia Cemetery.

The "Coolerator" from H. W. Mann Ice Company was advertised in the *Herald Newspaper* in the 1930s. The icehouse was located on Mill Street and furnished ice for the town of Collierville until the 1950s. It was also here that the children found a place to swim. Ice deliveries were made on a regular basis to local residents, similar to the milk delivery.

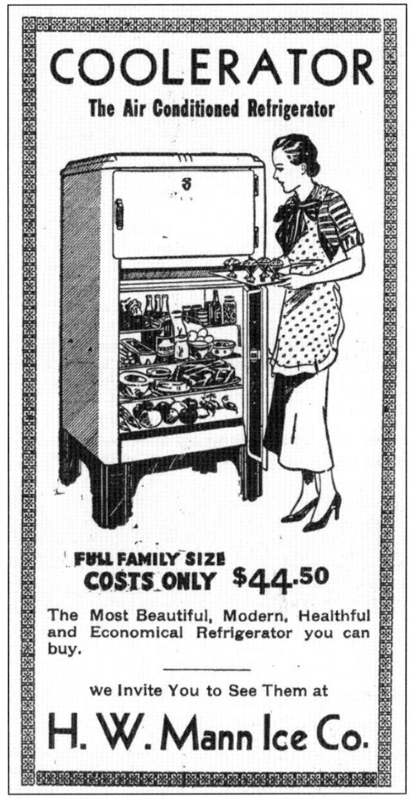

Kroger Grocery Store was located on the Town Square on Mulberry Street. The store gave many of the young students an opportunity to work after school and on Saturdays. Joe Clayton worked here as a delivery and stock boy.

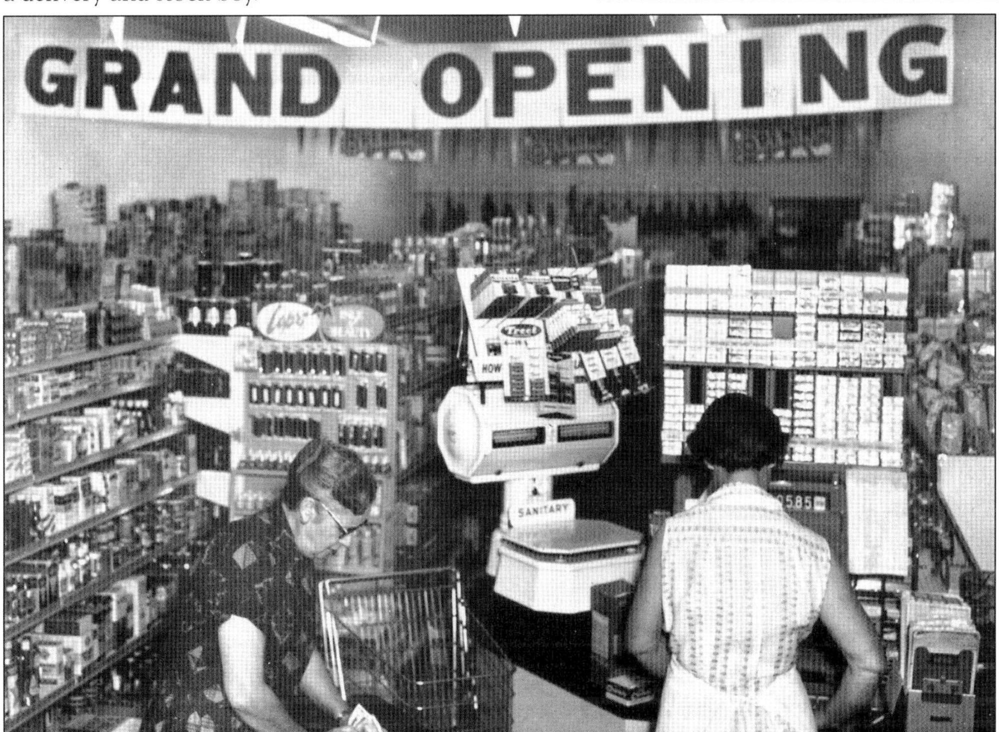

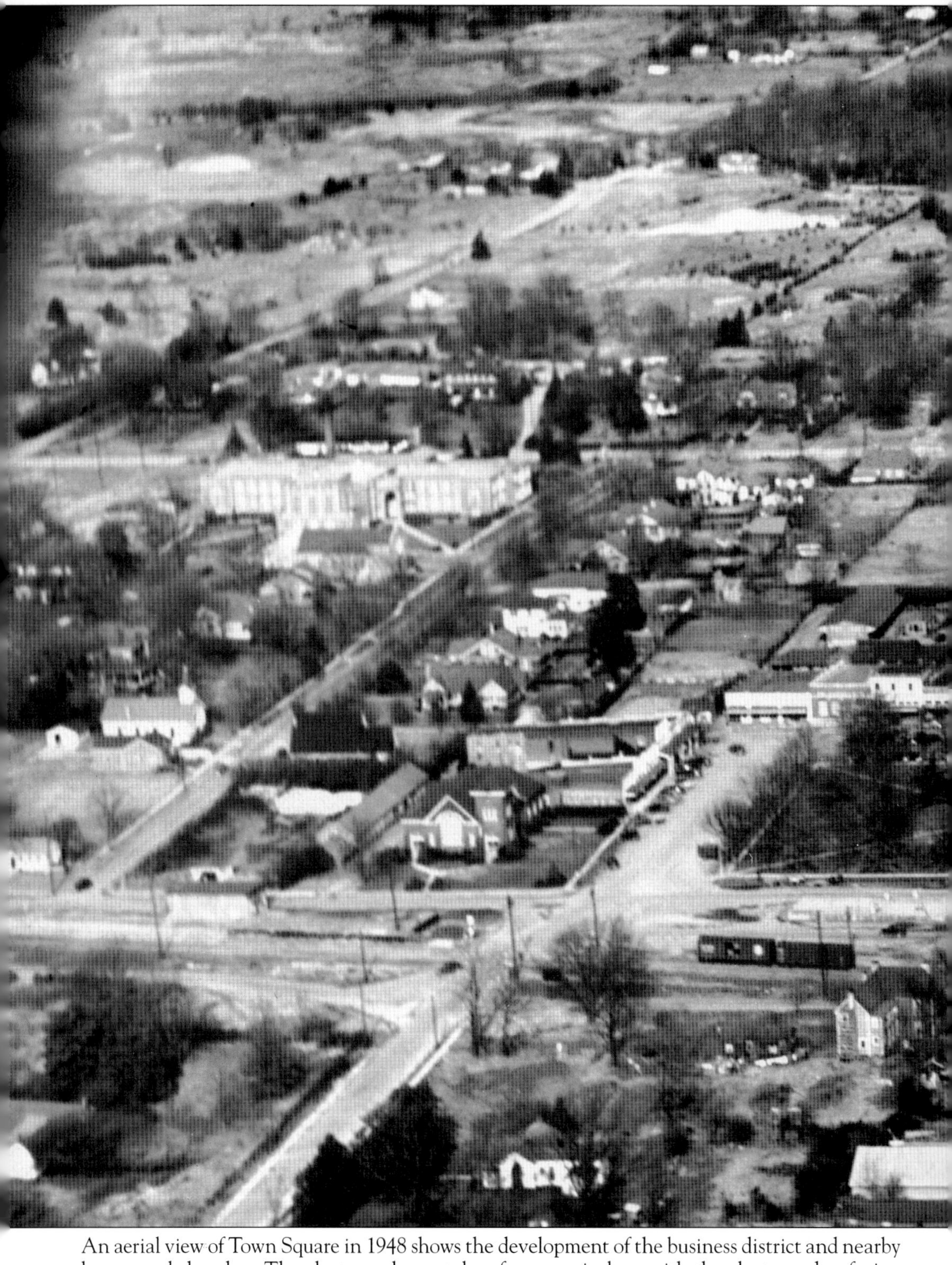

An aerial view of Town Square in 1948 shows the development of the business district and nearby homes and churches. The photograph was taken from an airplane with the photographer facing

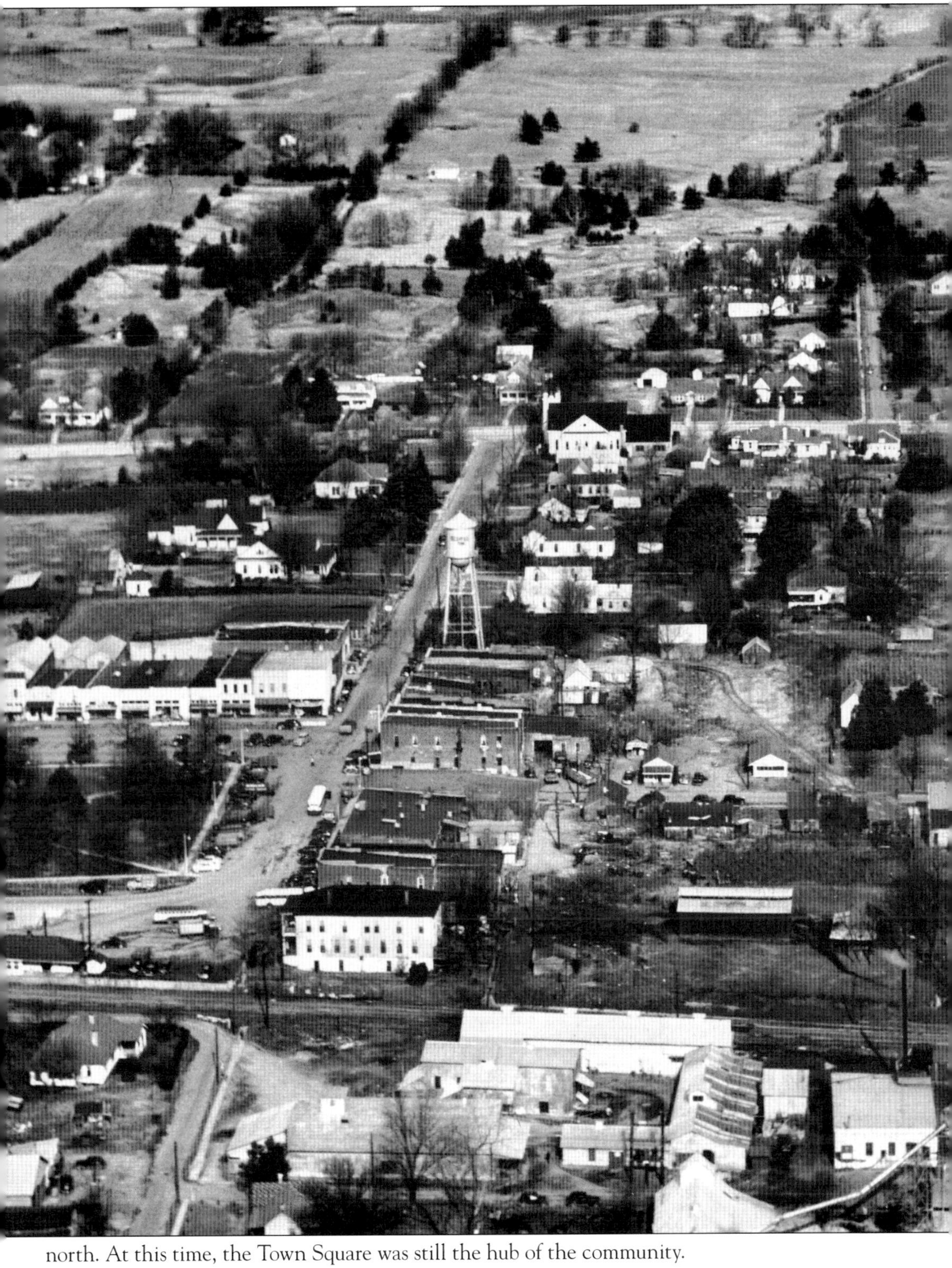

north. At this time, the Town Square was still the hub of the community.

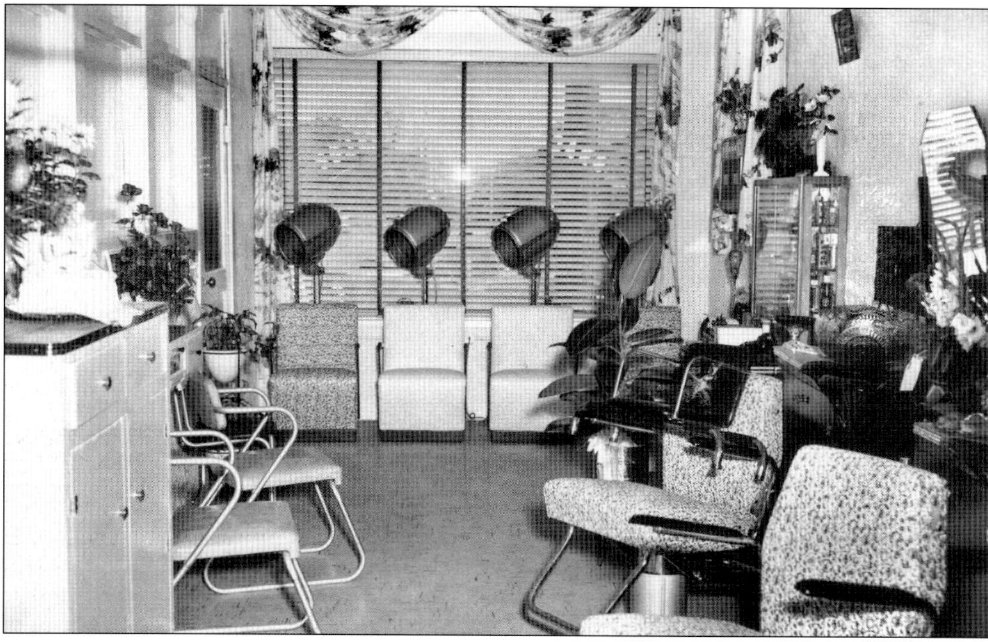

Grace's Beauty Shop was located on the northwest corner of Mulberry Street on the Town Square. The beauty shop was in the front part of the building, and Dr. Lee Pearce's was in the back. Access to Dr. Pearce's office was down a long narrow hall. Grace Piper Jamison Duscoe opened the beauty shop after World War II, and today there remains a shop at this location.

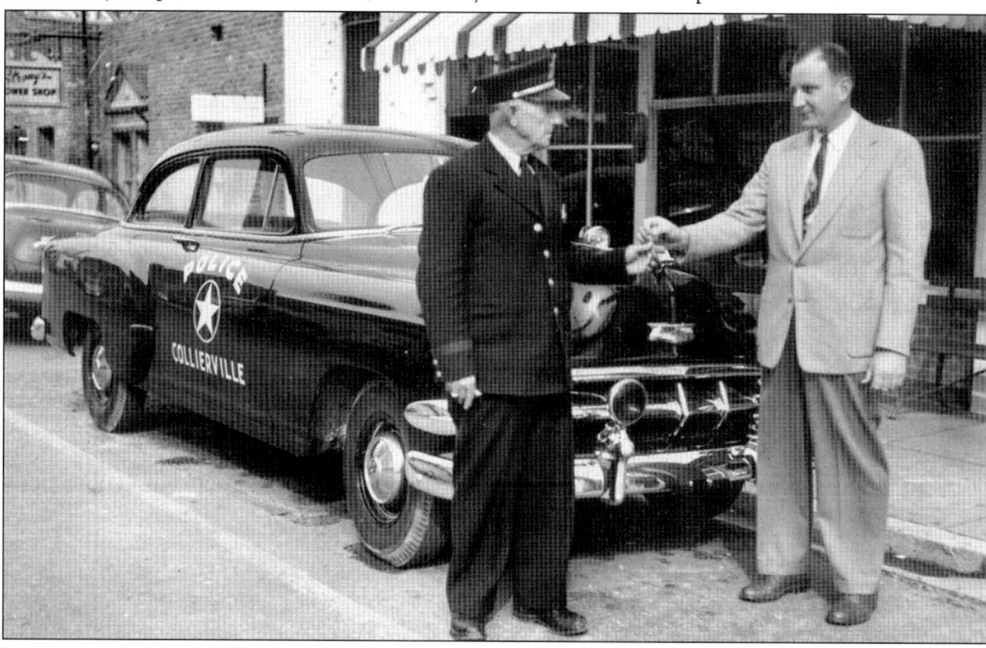

Town marshal and first chief of police Jesse Low is pictured in the early 1950s, accepting the keys to Collierville's first police car from James Kelsey of Kelsey Chevrolet Motors. The cost of the car was $875. When Chief Lowe needed to use the car, someone else had to drive because he never drove. Before he had the police car, he would stop vehicles on the road and have the driver take him to his destination.

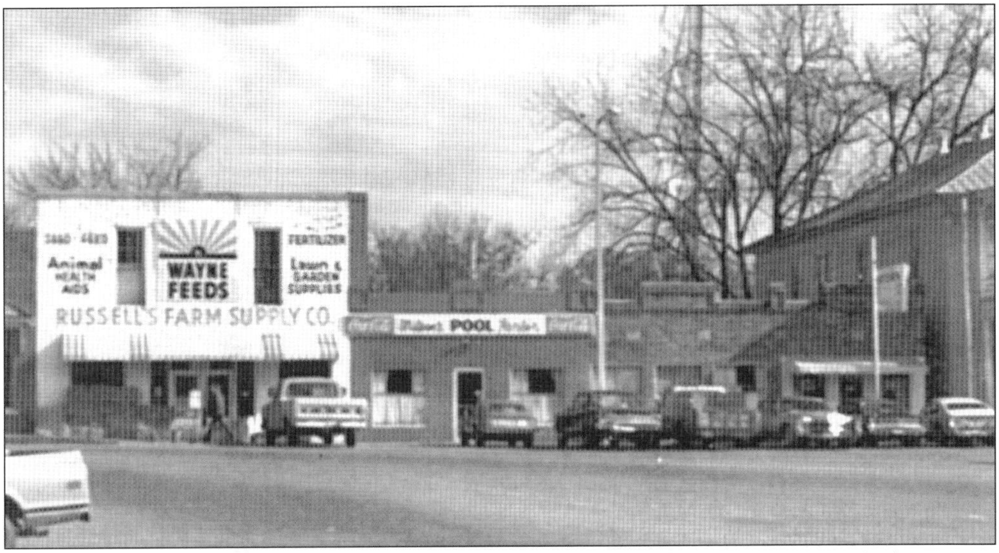

Russell's Farm Supply Company was established by James and Clarene Russell in the late 1940s on Poplar Pike. In the early 1950s, they moved to the east side of the square into a building that had been used for a livery stable, feed store, and International Harvester. In April 1976, the store burned, and they moved across the railroad on Center Street.

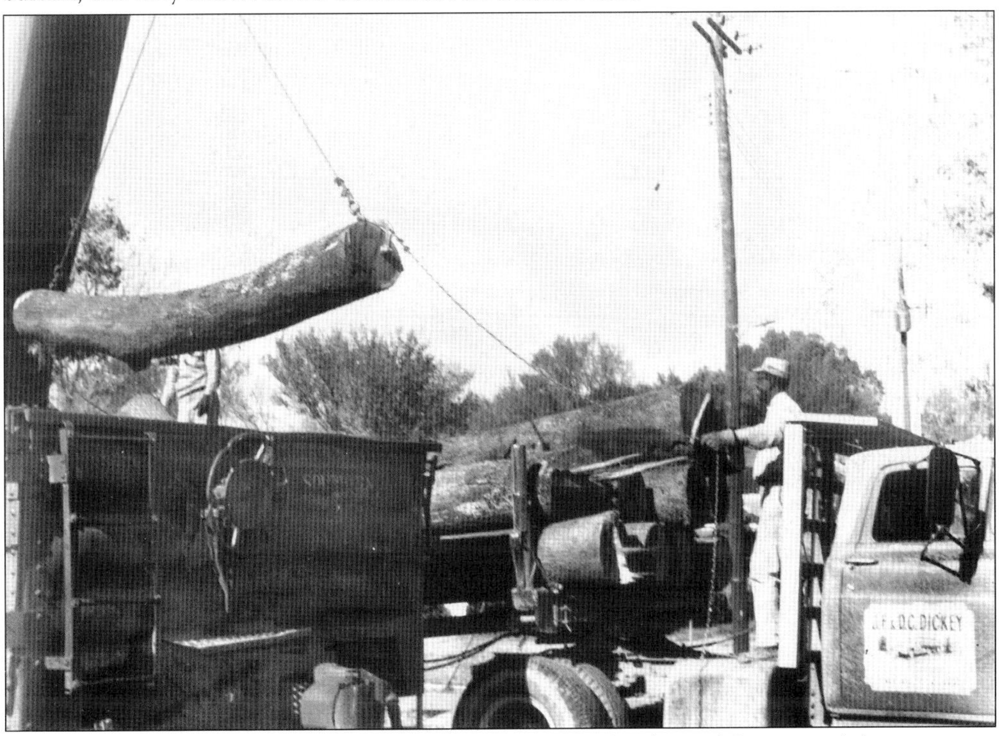

Sawmills in and around Collierville were commonplace as the demand for materials became more important to the growing community. In 1929, Collierville Lumber Company designed and built a form that molded 17 wooden blocks at one time. Mebane and Starnes Dimension Company cut hardwood blocks and sent them to Memphis to be kilned, and then they were shipped north where they were made into radio cabinets from timber cut in Collierville.

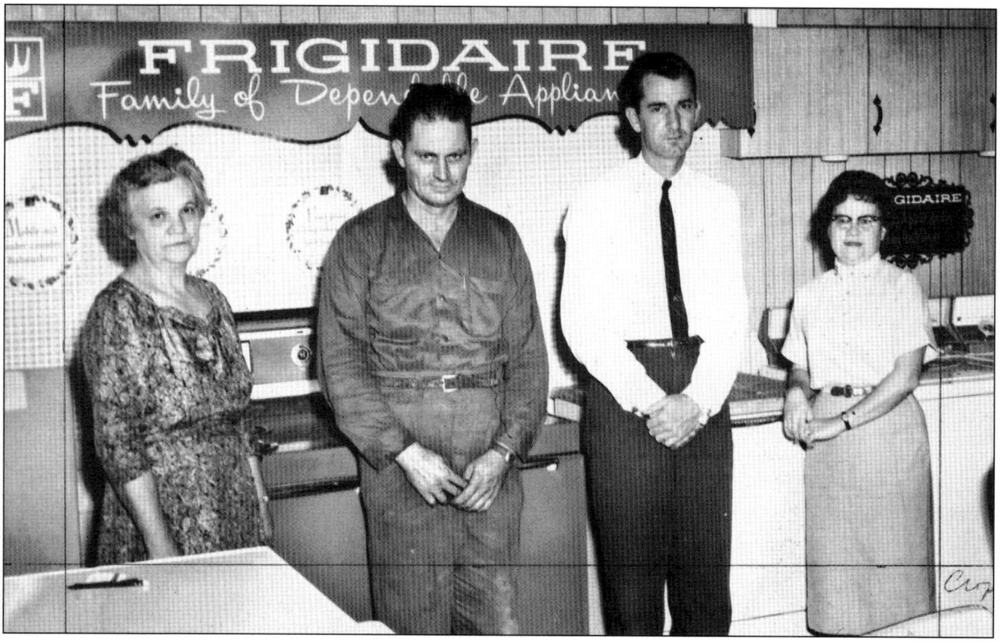

Wiley Sammons opened Sammons Furniture Company in the late 1940s on the north side of the Town Square. In addition to furniture, carpets, and linoleum, the company carried the latest appliances. Employees from the business are shown in front of the new Frigidaire washing machines. On the far right is Charlene Gray, niece of Wiley Sammons.

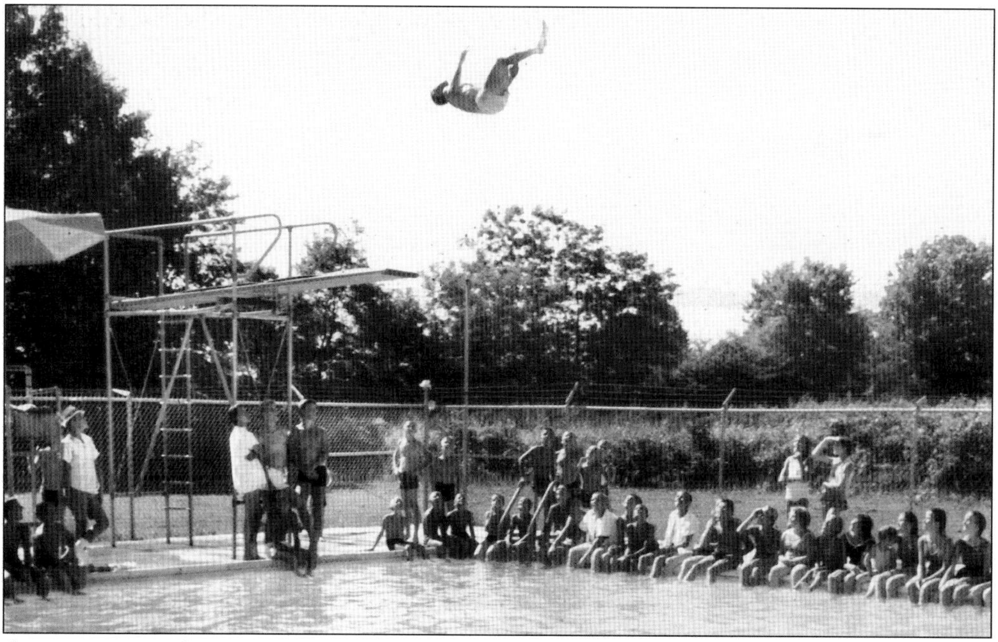

A swimming pool was constructed behind the local VFW Hall in 1957 and became a popular attraction for old and young alike. This photograph was run in the local *Collierville Herald* reporting on a swim meet and capturing a high dive. The swimming pool also provided employment for local residents and especially teenagers, including the current judge Craig Hall, who served as a lifeguard.

Kelsey Brothers, located on the north side of the Town Square, ran an advertisement in 1933 for a new shipment of fall dresses. The belted, below-the-knee, long-sleeve dresses also boasted of the fashionable wide shoulder pads. Summer, short-sleeve dresses sold for $1 each.

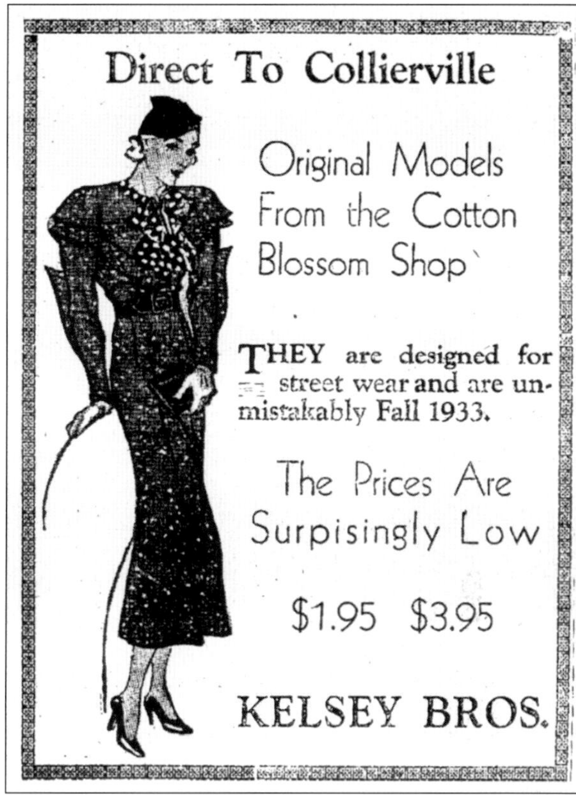

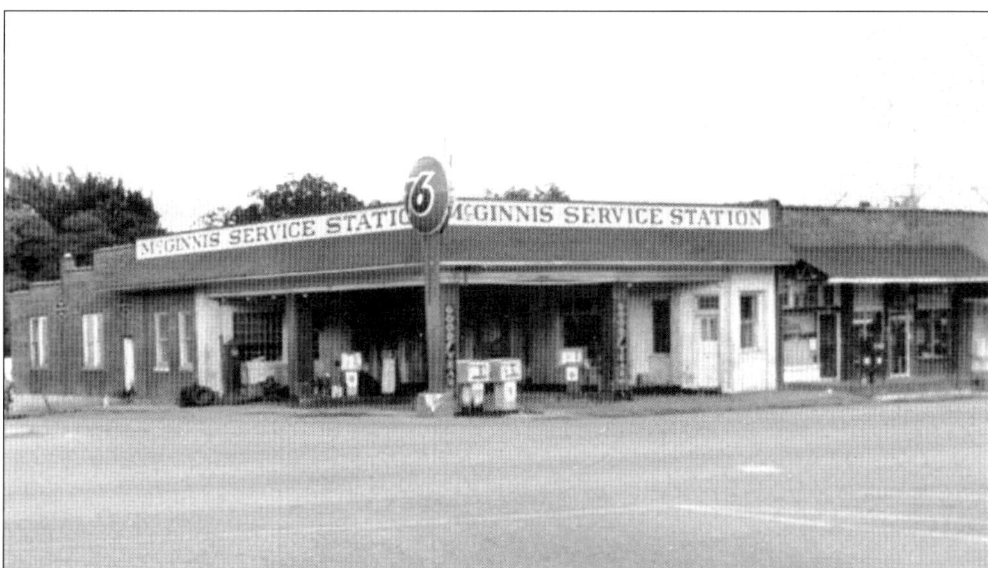

McGinnis Oil Company on the corner of Main Street and Washington Street has been in operation since being built by the family in 1927. In 1933, the merchants and businesses of Collierville agreed to close on Thursday afternoon at 12:00 noon, commencing June 15, 1933, until September 1, 1933. McGinnis Service Station still closes on Thursday afternoons.

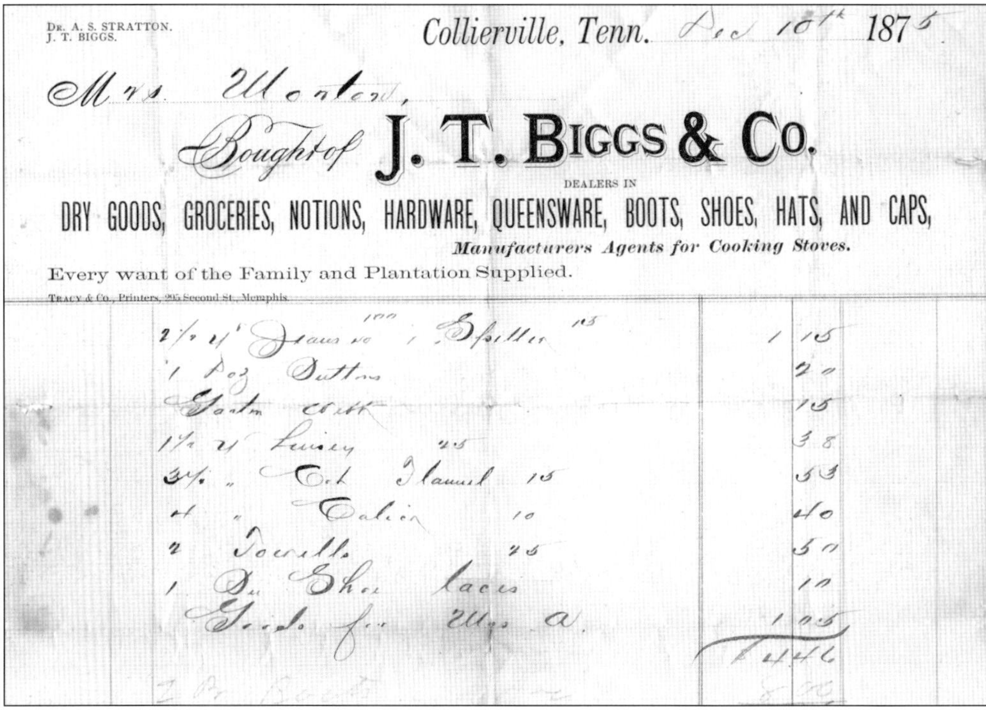

DR. A. S. STRATTON.
J. T. BIGGS.

Collierville, Tenn. Dec 1875

Mrs.

Bought of J. T. BIGGS & CO.

DEALERS IN

DRY GOODS, GROCERIES, NOTIONS, HARDWARE, QUEENSWARE, BOOTS, SHOES, HATS, AND CAPS,

Manufacturers Agents for Cooking Stoves.

Every want of the Family and Plantation Supplied.

TRACY & Co., Printers, 295 Second St., Memphis.

A receipt, dated December 18, 1875, is from the J. T. Biggs and Company located in Collierville. Biggs was a mercantile company that boasted "every want of the family and plantation supplied." Shoelaces on the receipt were 10¢.

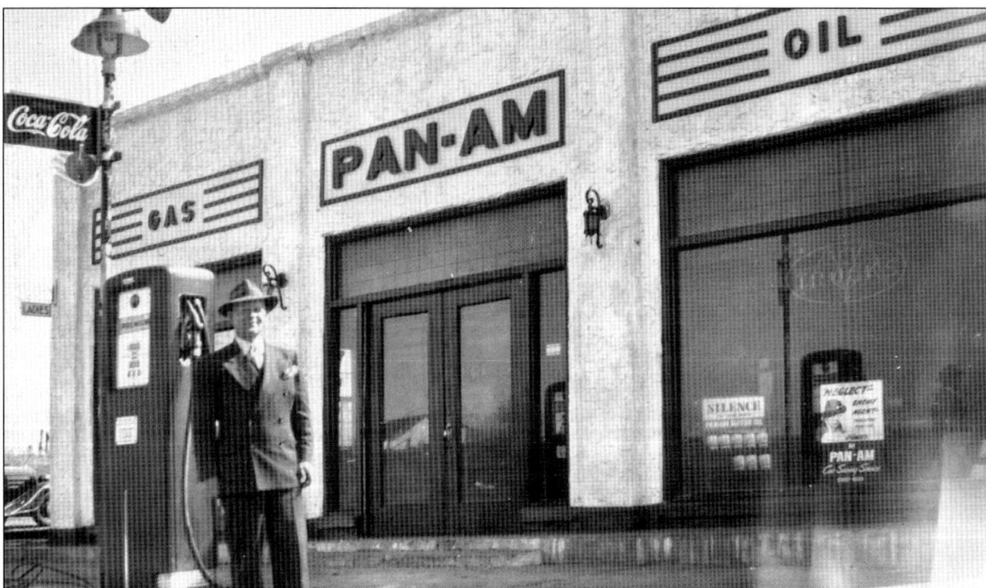

Elden C. Cooper, owner and operator of Cooper Motor Company, is standing in front of his station located on the corner of Cooper Street and Poplar Street (State Line Road). Mr. Cooper operated the station from 1928 to 1957. Today the building is used as an antique shop, and the exterior remains as it was in the 1950s.

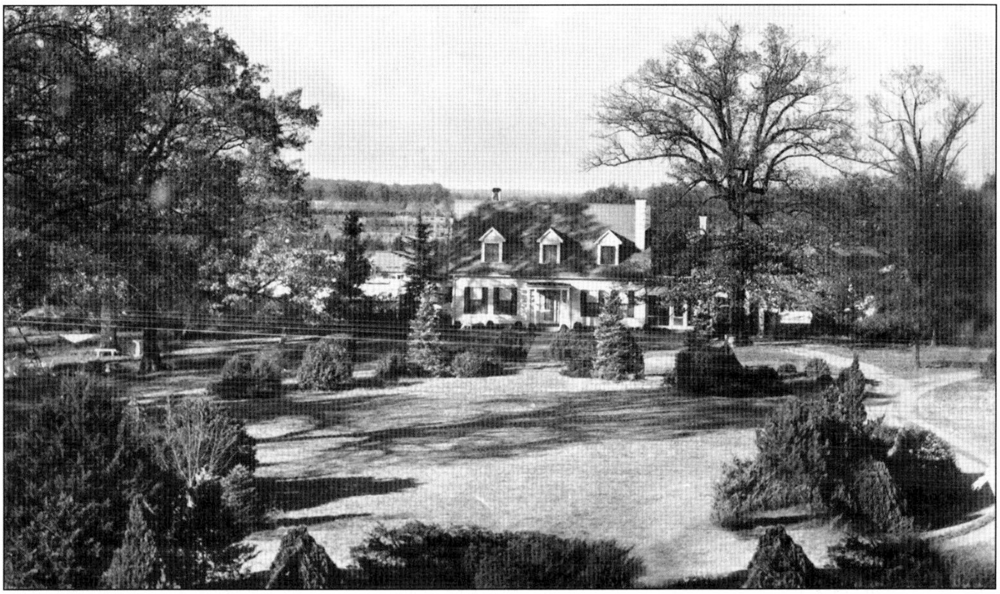

In 1935, the Cartwright Nursery was designated as one of the world's largest nurseries. The Cartwright home, located on the eastern edge of Collierville on Poplar Avenue, reflected much of the ornamental landscaping for which the nursery was noted. The nursery was started by A. D. Cartwright Sr. and continued by his son, David Cartwright. The nursery employed several hundred from the area. In 1999, the home was lost by fire.

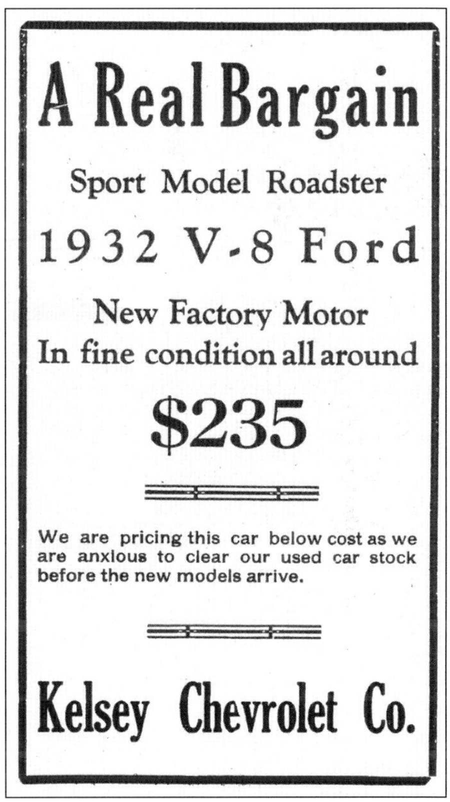

This advertisement ran in the *Collierville Herald* July 6, 1934. Kelsey Chevrolet was located on Main Street on the east side of the Town Square. Driving too fast has never been acceptable in town limits. In 1873, the town minutes show an ordinance stating it became a misdemeanor for any person to ride or drive any horse or horses within Collierville faster than at a moderate pace.

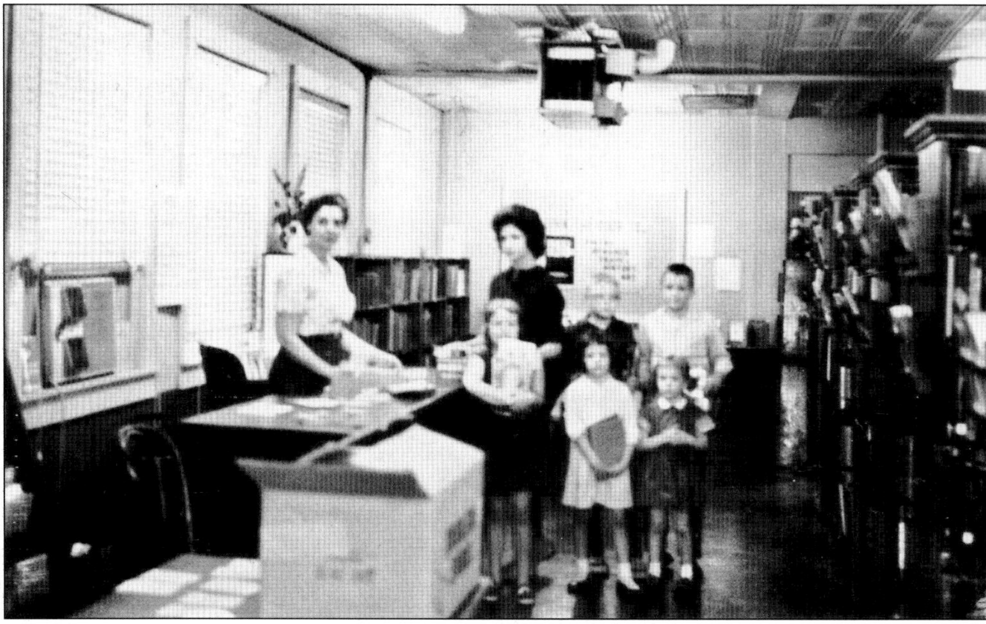

Mrs. James Cowan, librarian, is pictured in the town's library that was located on the corner of North Rowlett Street and the west side of Walnut Street. The library was a project of the Collierville Contemporary Club and the doors were opened to the public on March 5, 1956. Cowan served as librarian for 17 years.

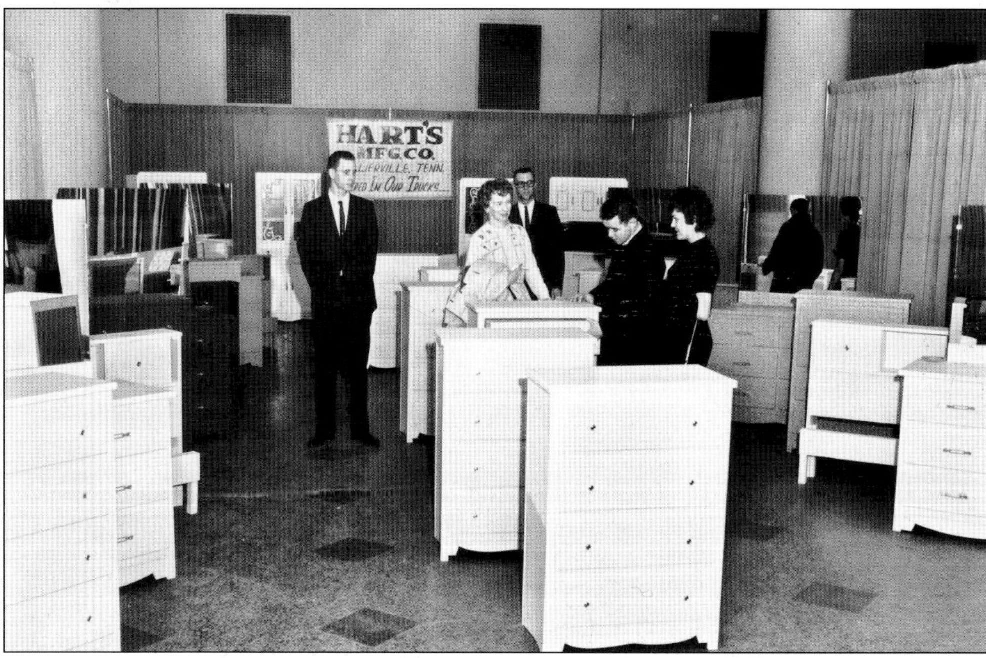

Hart's Manufacturing Company, located on Easley Street, began in 1945. Two brothers, Thomas and Fred Hart, started the company. By 1972, the company employed approximately 50 people. Hart's manufactured low-cost bedroom suites and odd chests. The company has diversified but remained in the family for three generations. The photograph shows the company displaying their furniture at market.

The 1947 and 1948 winters were extremely severe in Collierville. Memories of waking up in a cold house and running to dress by the fire are still familiar to the older generation. Some fortunate homeowners enjoyed gas heat with floor furnaces, but most of Collierville still used coal or wood. Many of the older homes in the area still have coal grates in their fireplaces. It is not unusual to step outside today on a cold morning and catch the scent of coal in the air.

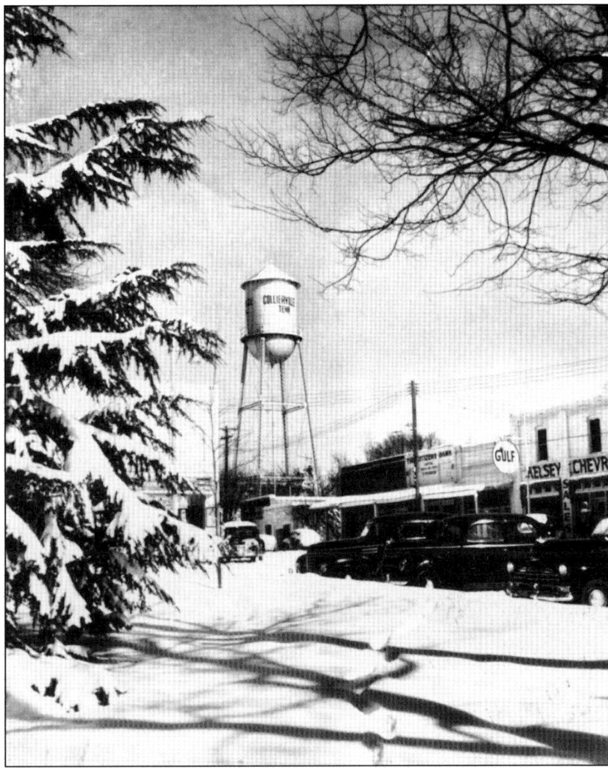

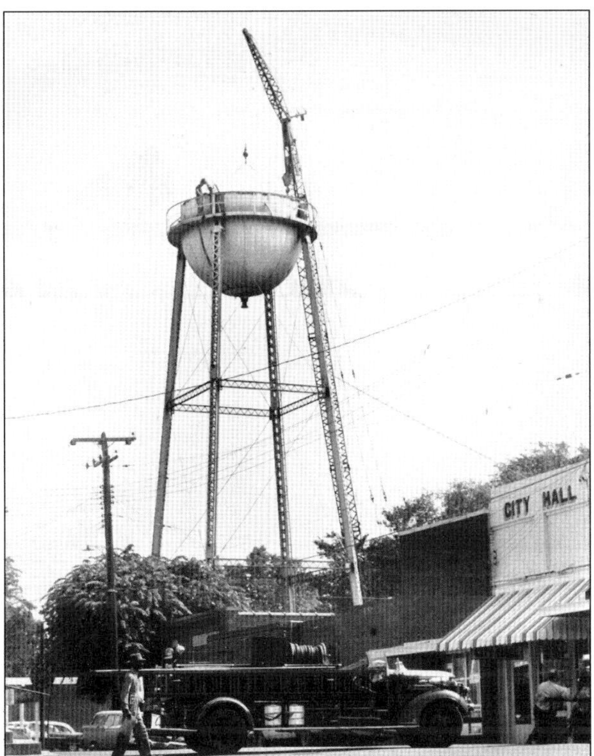

When the town's water tower was taken down and replaced with a new one, it was a major event in the community. As early as 1912, the town fathers had passed an ordinance making it unlawful to climb or ascend the tower or tank at the water and light company. The large crane quickly dismantled the icon, and a new one replaced it. Progress was coming to Collierville.

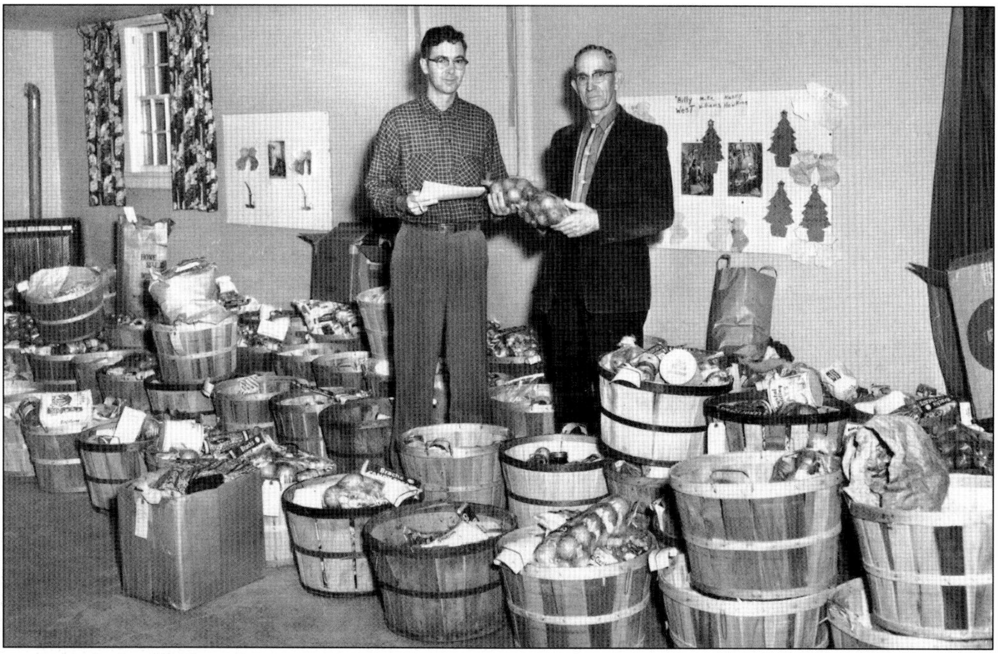

Carl Rutledge (left) and Claude Harris are pictured preparing Goodfellows Christmas Baskets for needy families. This practice still continues today. Collierville has been known for its generosity to those who are in need in any way. The Town of Collierville and local churches continue to operate the food pantry.

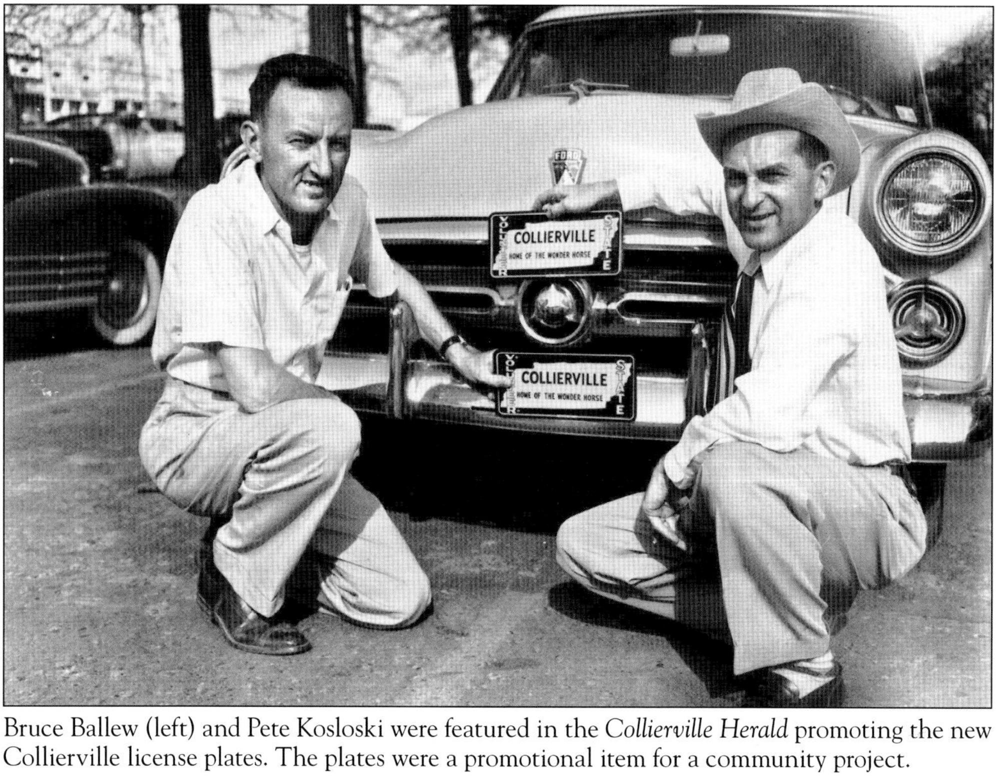

Bruce Ballew (left) and Pete Kosloski were featured in the *Collierville Herald* promoting the new Collierville license plates. The plates were a promotional item for a community project.

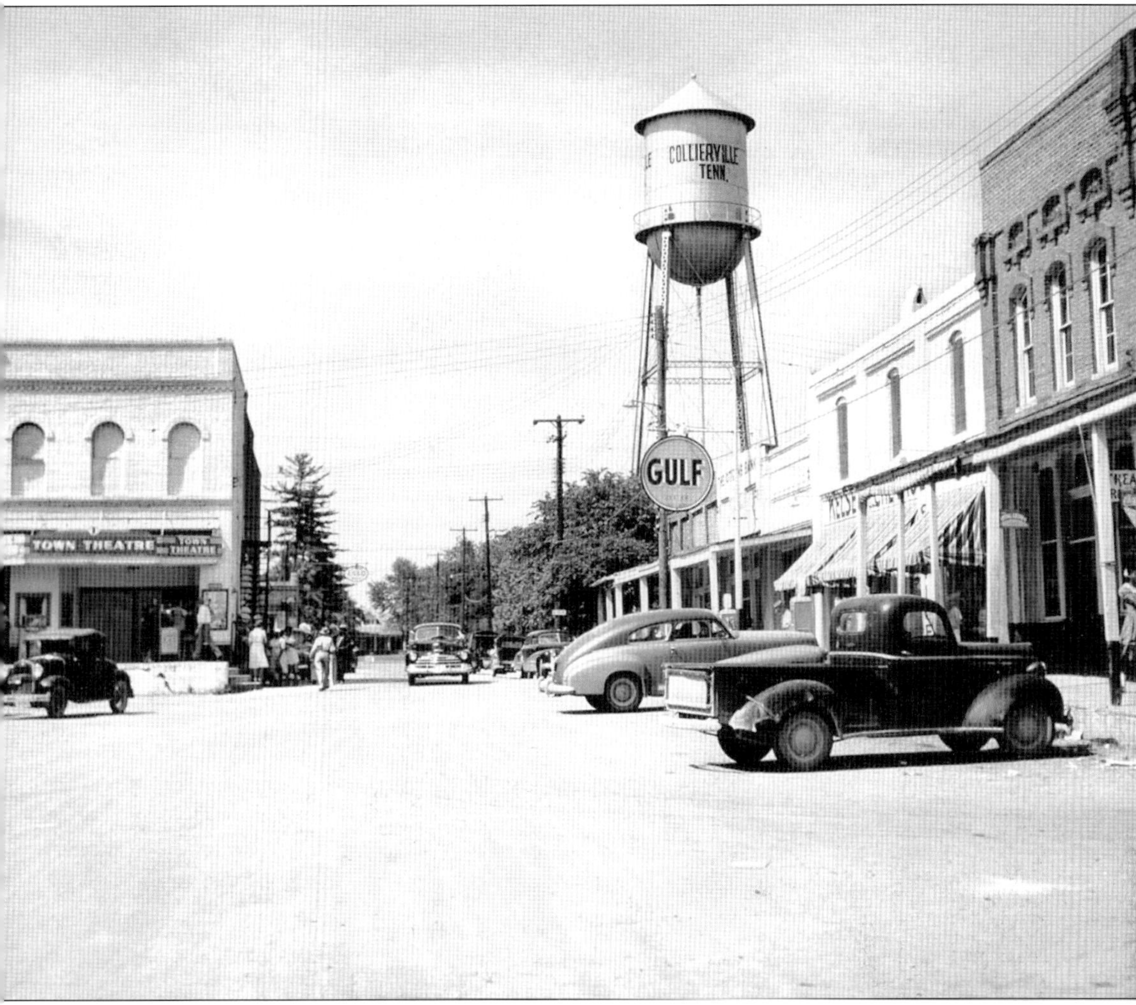

The skyline of downtown Collierville was defined by the large water tower that boasted the town's name. Although the town had grown, the 1943 town minutes reflect that the street tax was waived because so many young men of the town were in the service. Town improvements were on a limited basis.

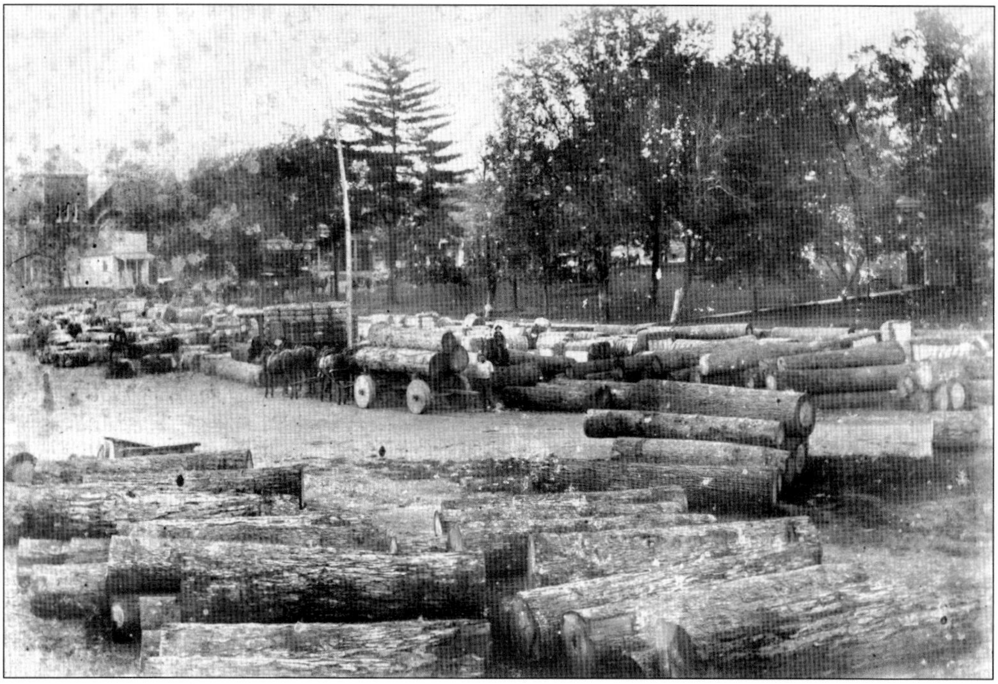

Logs are piled on the south side of the Town Square in the late 1800s. The logs would be taken to the Keough's Lumber Warehouse that was located nearby on Moore Street (South Main Street) and later shipped by rail.

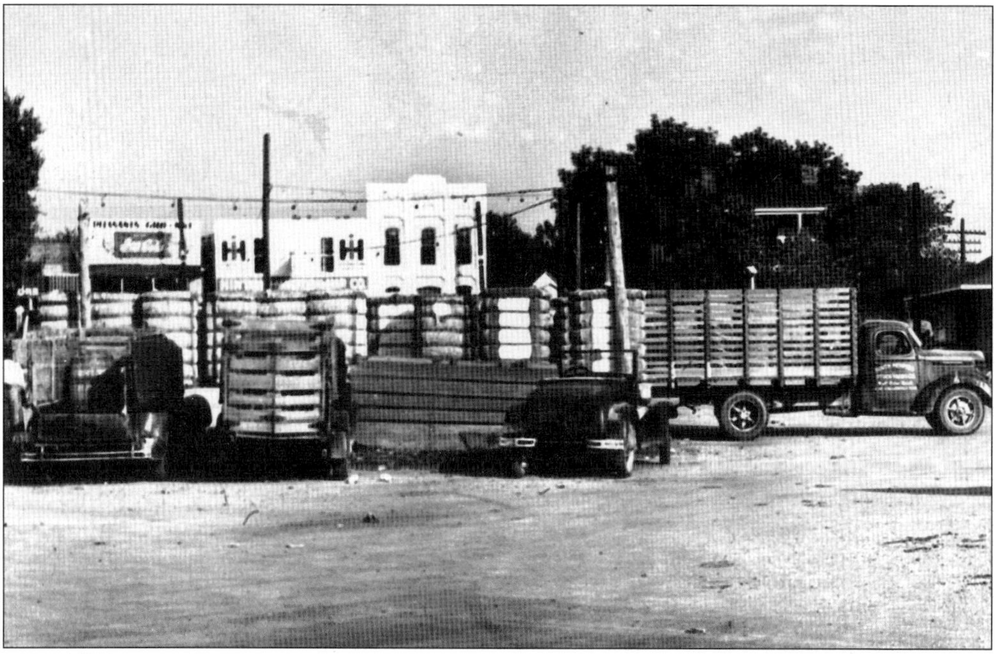

Busy fall days on the Town Square in the early 1950s show the old cotton platform and cotton bales ready for shipment. To the east of the platform stand buildings owned and operated by Boyd Pleasant, the Hinton family, and J. H. Swoopes. South of the Swoopes building, hidden by the trees, was the Hester Hotel.

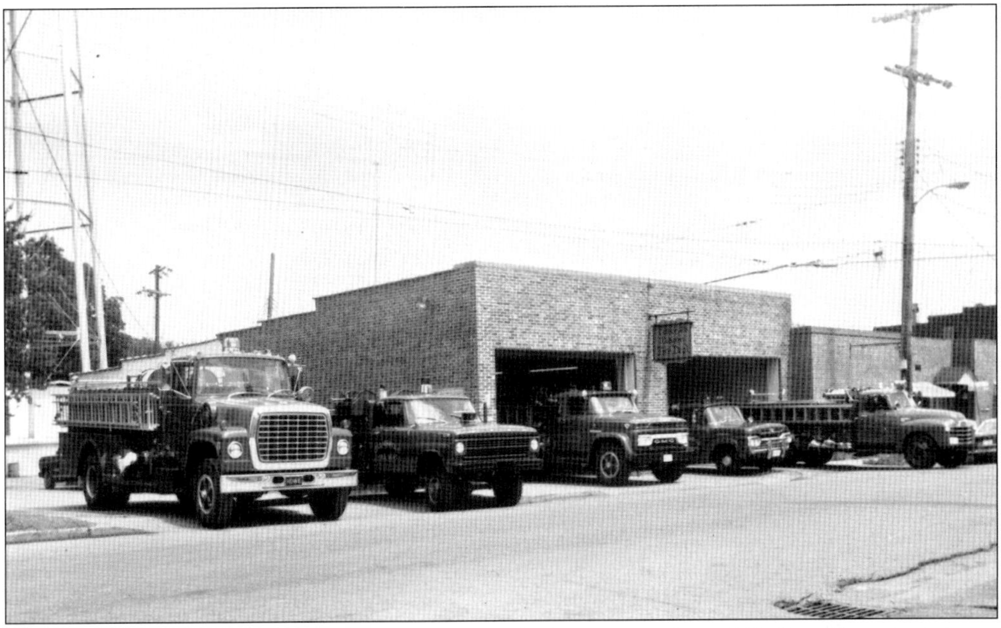

In 1902, Collierville had 15 volunteer firemen with the one handcart, 200 feet of two-inch hose, and a fire alarm system by bell and telephone. The hose cart was kept at the pump house located in the area of Fire Station No. 1 on Main Street in 1933. A new building was constructed in 1944 just north of the old station. The building has been recently renovated and houses a modern engine and dedicated employed firefighters.

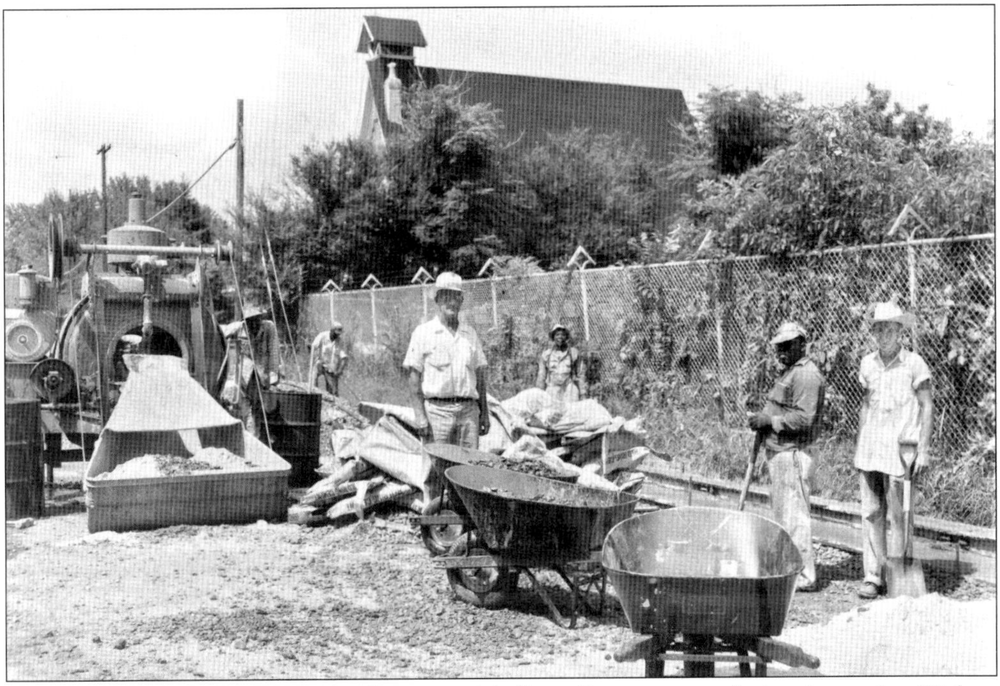

The Public Works Department for the town of Collierville is seen resurfacing the road on Walnut Street. The McGinnis coal yard is behind the fence area, and the St. Andrew's Episcopal Church is in the background. This photograph was in the *Collierville Herald* newspaper in the 1940s.

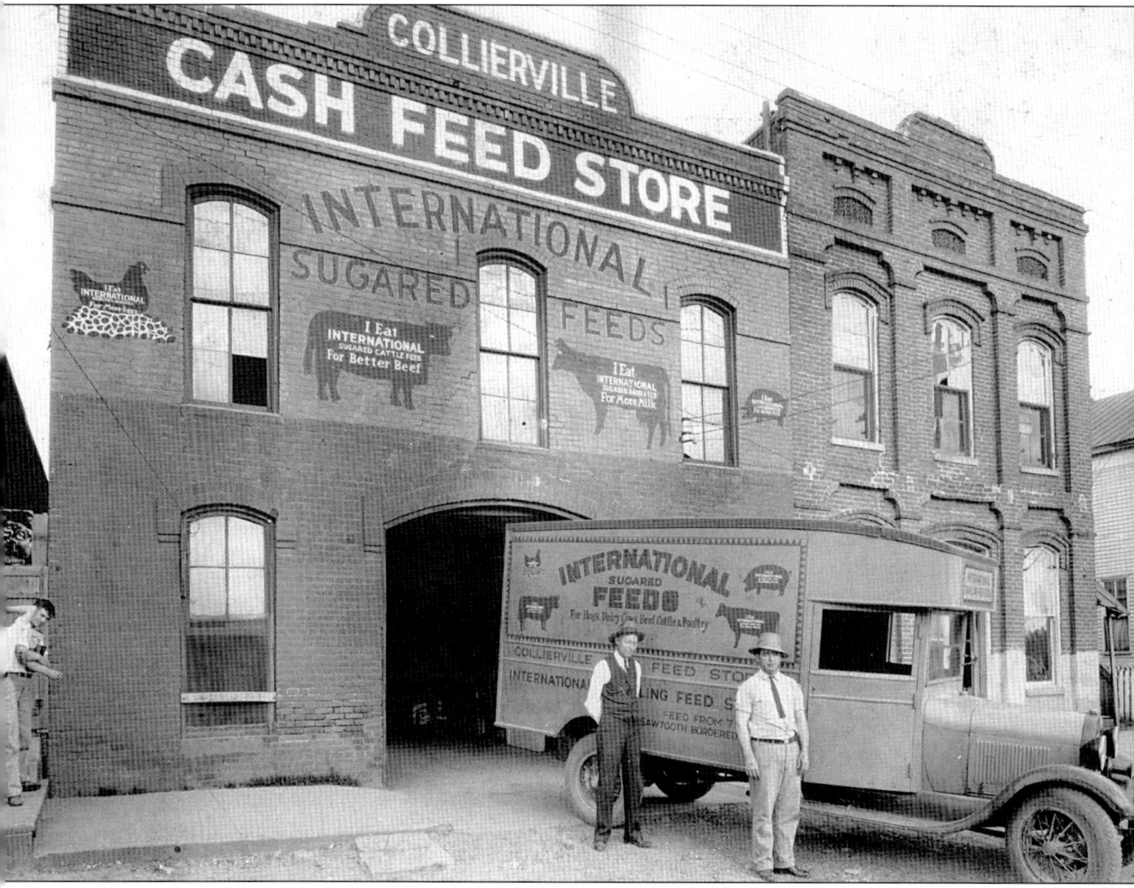

The Collierville Cash Feed Store, a dealer in International Sugared Feed, had its own delivery truck in 1929. Pictured are Edgar Herbert Russell (left), assistant manager, and J. C. Cook (right), manager. This same building is in earlier photographs as a livery stable and later Russell's Farm Supply Company. Today the building is being totally rebuilt using the same footprint and the exterior design of the original. The buildings in the historic district are required to follow the guidelines set forth by Collierville's Historic District Commission and the Town of Collierville Planning Department. Before a new structure can be built or an older building restored, plans must be submitted to the town.

Six

Architecture

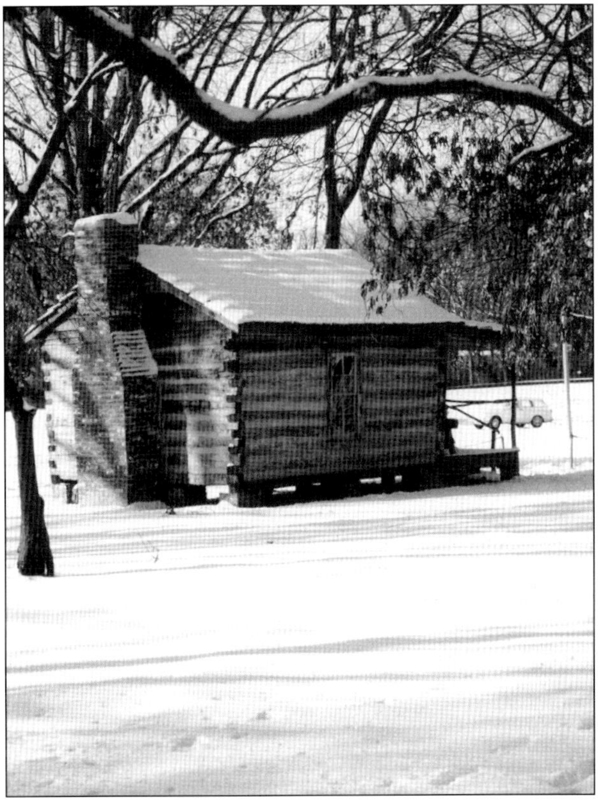

The small cabin in Confederate Park tells our early history. It was built in 1851 by the William W. Talley family south of the Memphis and Charleston Railroad on the Holly Springs Road, currently known as Byhalia Road and South Rowlett Street where Pepsi Americas is located. It had two rooms on either side of a dogtrot and served as a home and stagecoach stop. The date 1851 was inscribed on the chimney. The cabin was dismantled in the 1970s and rebuilt on the Town Square with a donation of $6,000 from the Miss-Ark-Tenn Corporation. Today the cabin is open for the public visiting the Town Square as they tour and learn about the community's rich history.

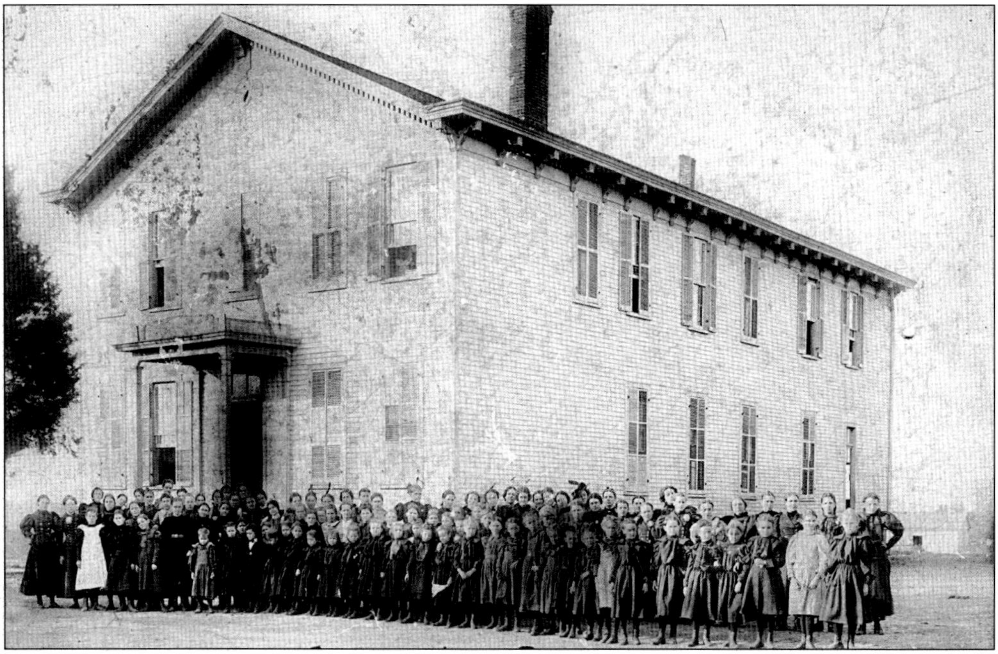

One of Collierville's earliest schools and large buildings was Bellevue Female College. This faded photograph, dated 1894, shows the school located at the corner of Walnut Street and Poplar Street (State Line Road). The lower rooms of the building were used as classrooms, and the principal's family and boarding students used the upper rooms. The large, two-story frame building was the first educational institution built at this site.

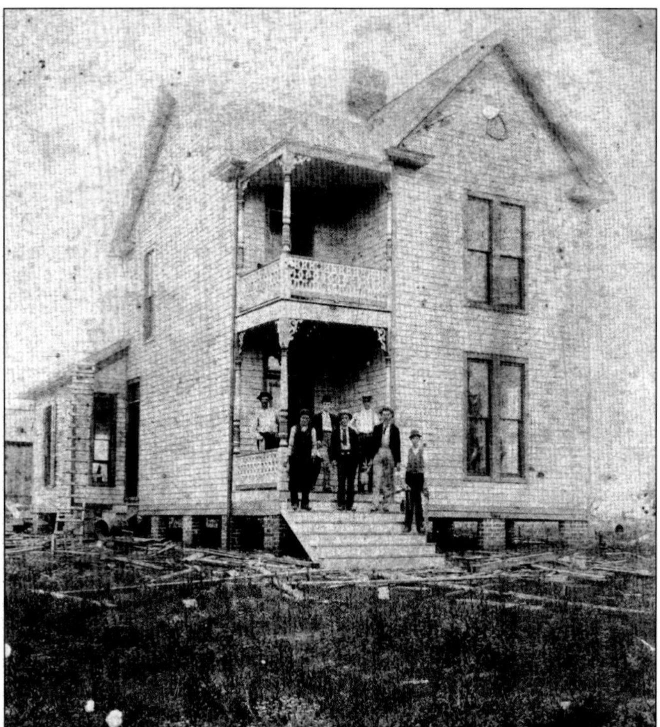

Wiley Washington McGinnis built many of the early homes in Collierville. His craftsmen are pictured on the front steps of a house under construction. There is no date on the photograph, but the details of the house indicate the late 1800s. The house is a frame building with double hung windows and transoms over the doors. The decorative trim on the upstairs and the downstairs porches indicate the Victorian design and era.

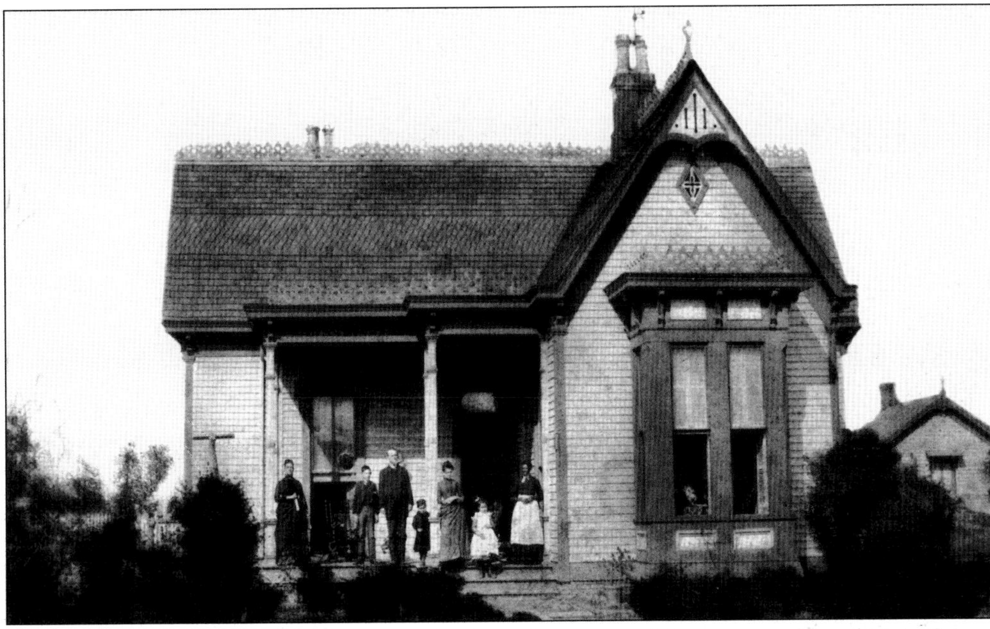

Dr. David Thompson Waddy's house was built in the center of five acres and faced Main Street. Dr. Waddy moved to Collierville in 1870. This photograph is thought to date to approximately 1880. The ornate gingerbread features on the front of the house were seen on houses around the late 19th century. This house remained into the 1970s.

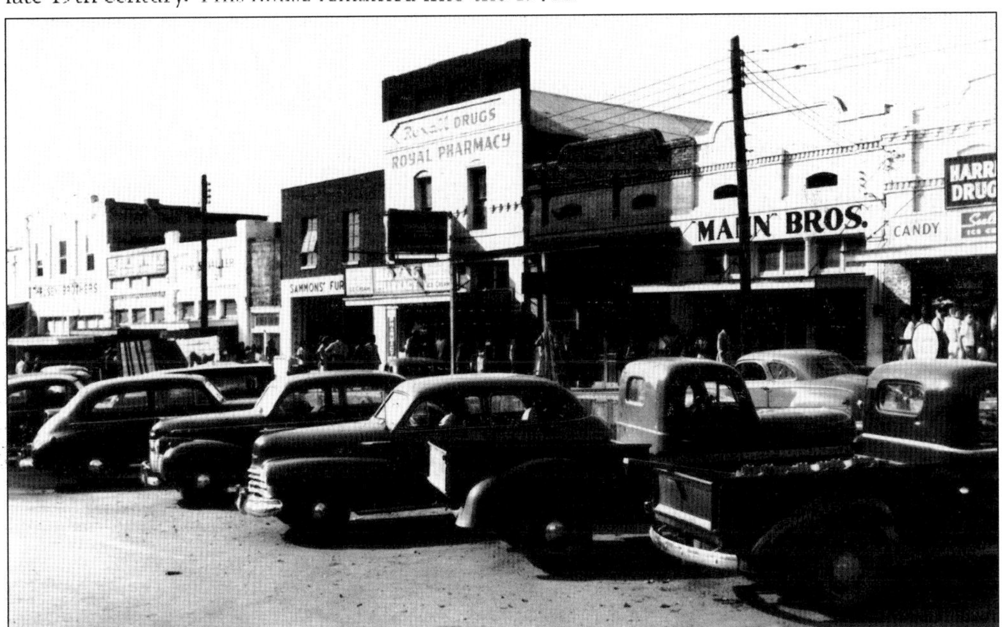

Collierville's first preservation plan in 1992 resulted in a streetscape program for the downtown area. The plan identified some of our most unique historic features of design. Featured above is one of the best-preserved facades in the commercial district today, which dates from the 1890s. This photograph shows the building partitioned for Mann Brothers in 1948. Today it has been totally restored by John and Patricia Ashworth for a retail shop.

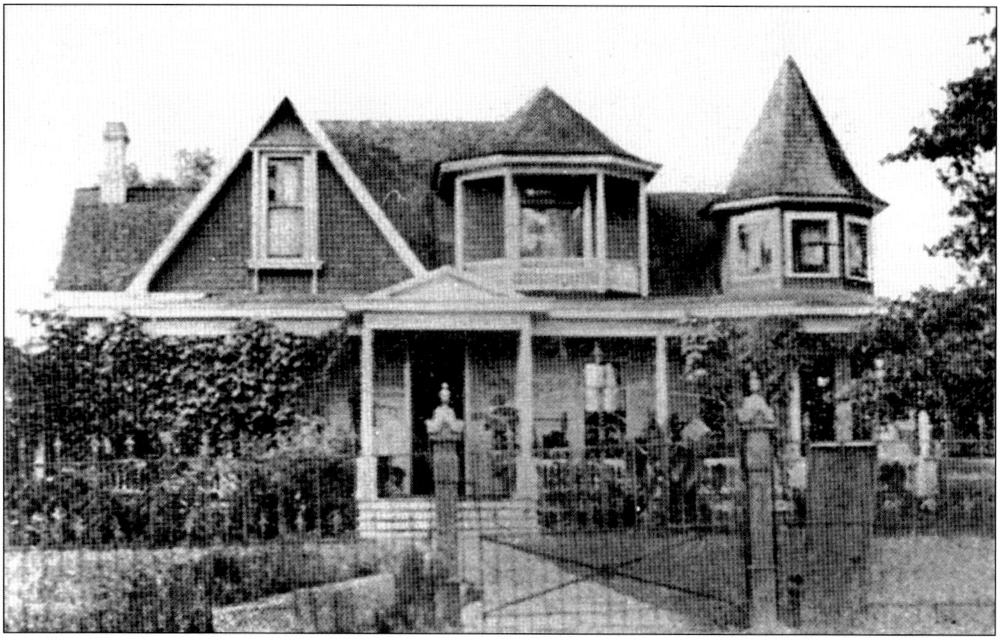

The home of James Buford and Alice Townsend Cartwright was on Poplar Pike. The home and 96 acres of land were bought from a Mr. Bray in 1883. The cottage-type house with porch and decorative banisters is decorated with wood scrolls at the top. The kitchen was separated from the house by an open brick walk. The home became part of Cartwright Nursery. This photograph was taken in 1910 after it was remodeled and the decorative turrets added.

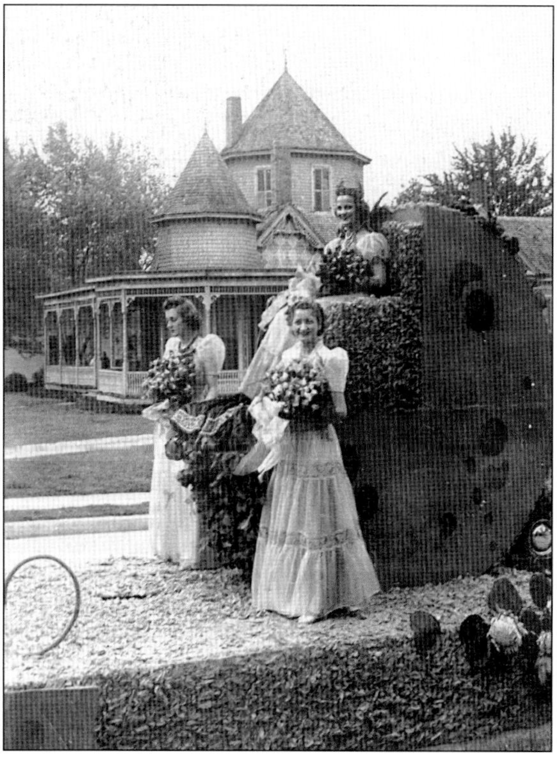

The home of John E. Stamps is pictured behind the float in the Cheese Carnival Parade in the 1930s. The house was built in the late 1800s and features conical turrets on the porch. The Stamps family lived in the home, which was located on the west side of Main Street, until the 1950s when it was torn down for a commercial building.

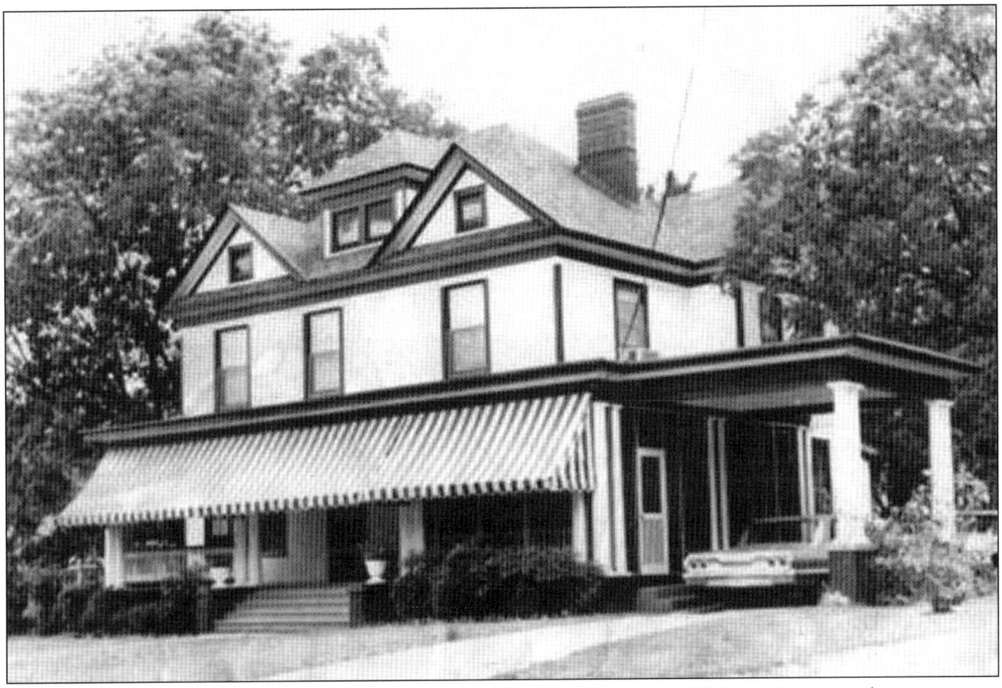

John and Nancy Andre presently occupy the Hinton House on Walnut Street. The two-story Colonial Revival house was built in 1909 and has Queen Anne and Eastlake features. A two-story bay window is featured on one side of the facade.

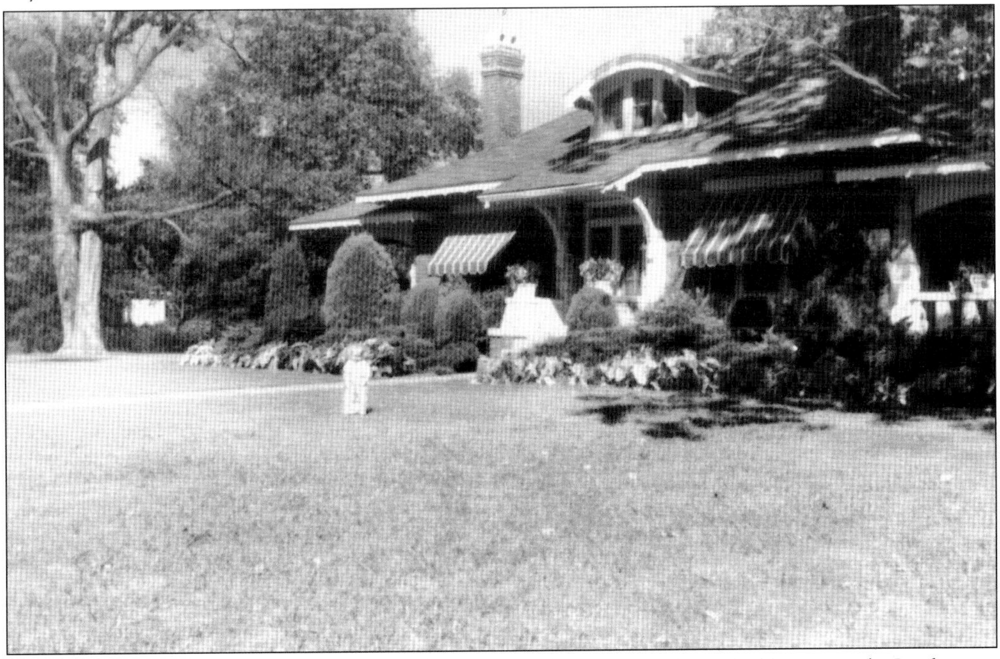

The brick bungalow built in 1910 by the Mann family is one and one-half story with Craftsman influence. The entrance is covered with a shed-roofed hood supported by curved major brackets and features a multi-light double-door topped by a multi-light transom. Corner porches flank the house. Mark and Alicia Free have recently renovated the attractive home.

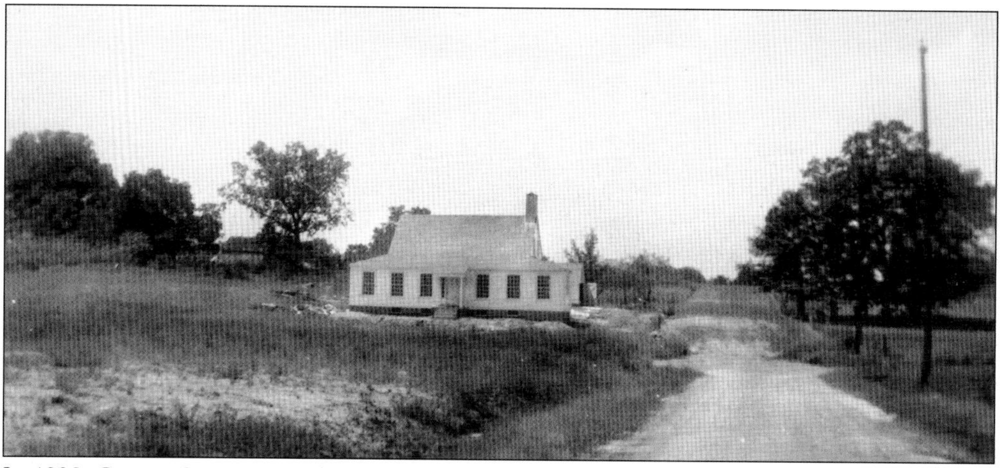

In 1928, Cooper Street opened and College Street was extended. John Dean built a new home at the end of West College Street in 1937. He had a road cut to North Rowlett Street so he could drive to town easier. Today additional homes have been built in the area, and large shade trees shade the quiet street. The Deans' daughter, Charlotte, lives in the house.

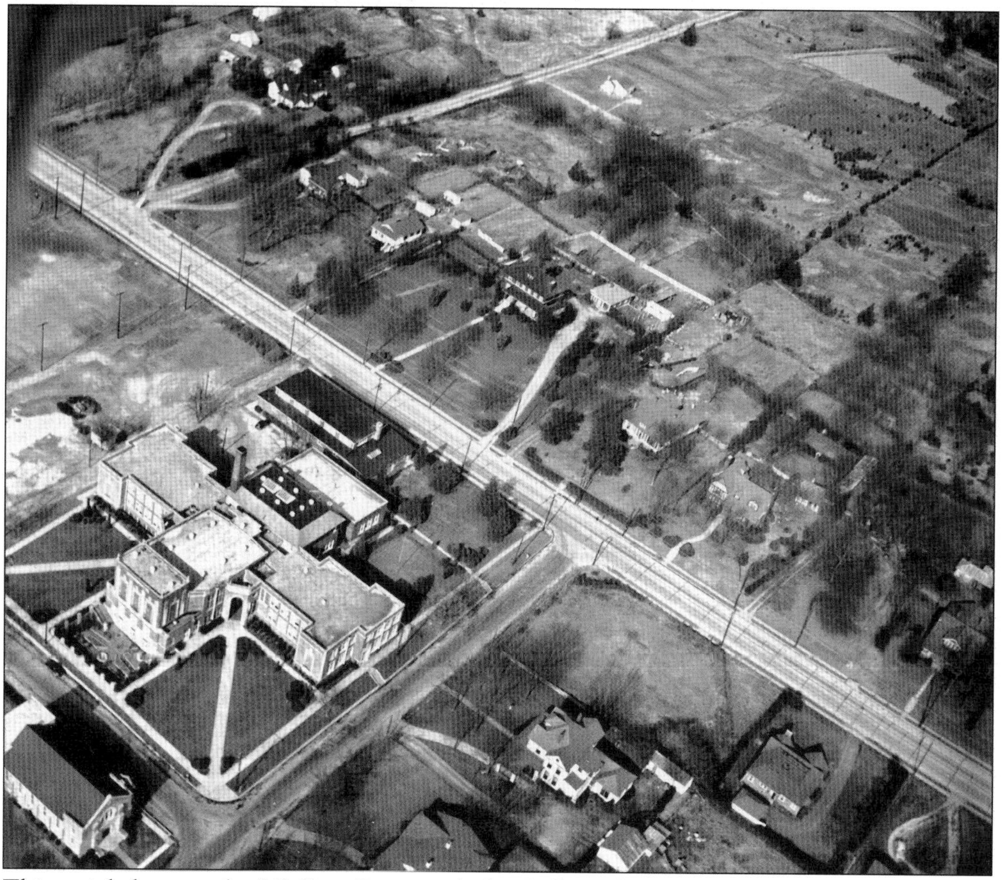

This aerial photograph of College Street with the Collierville High School in the middle shows the light development around the historic district. The wide road in the photograph, taken in 1948, is Poplar Avenue (State Line Road). The photographer is looking southwest.

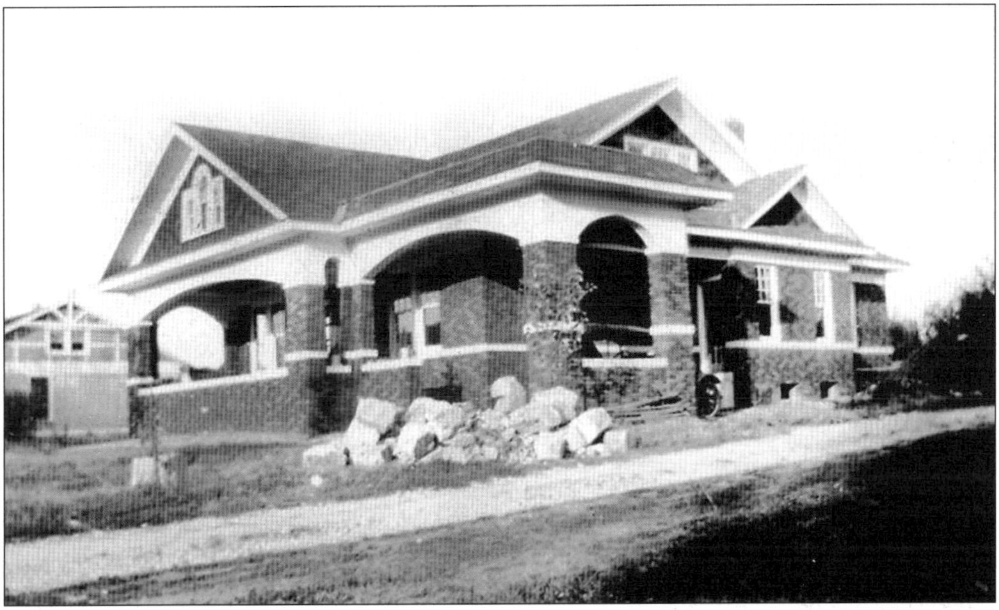

Wiley Washington McGinnis built the one-and-a-half-story bungalow with Craftsman influence in 1920–1925. The gable end contains a decorative Paladin-style window. There is a porch across the front with a porte-cochere to the side. Mr. and Mrs. Bill Felton and family have made attractive additions to the rear of the home. Construction was recently completed in this original photograph.

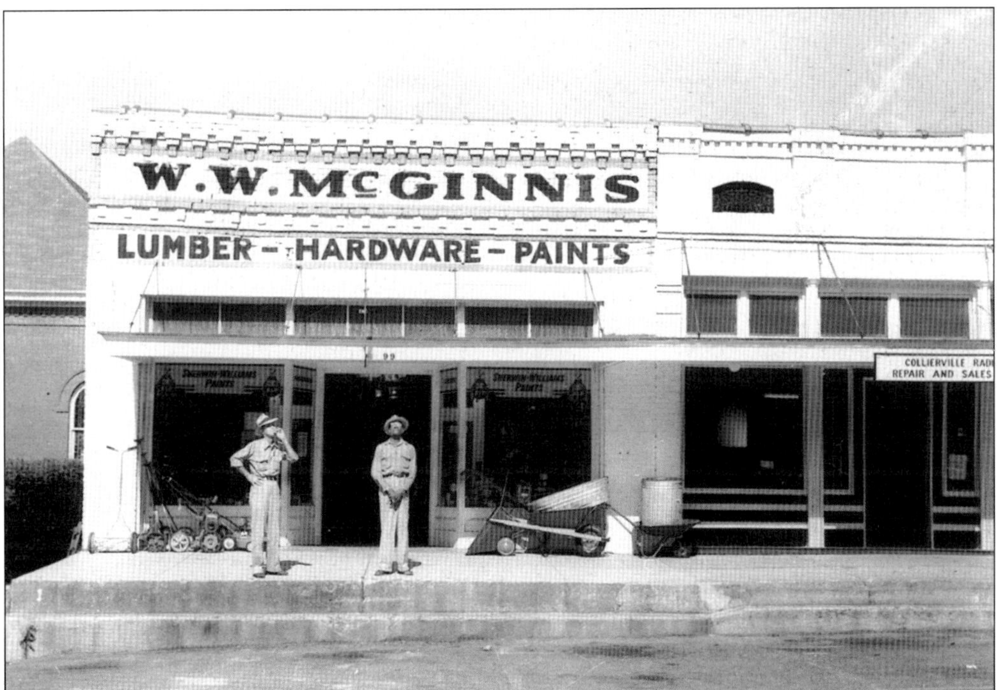

A 1948 photograph of the McGinnis Hardware building reflects the early architectural detail of the historic 1879 building. The transoms over the front windows and door, plus the architectural detail over the signage, are now hidden under later renovation.

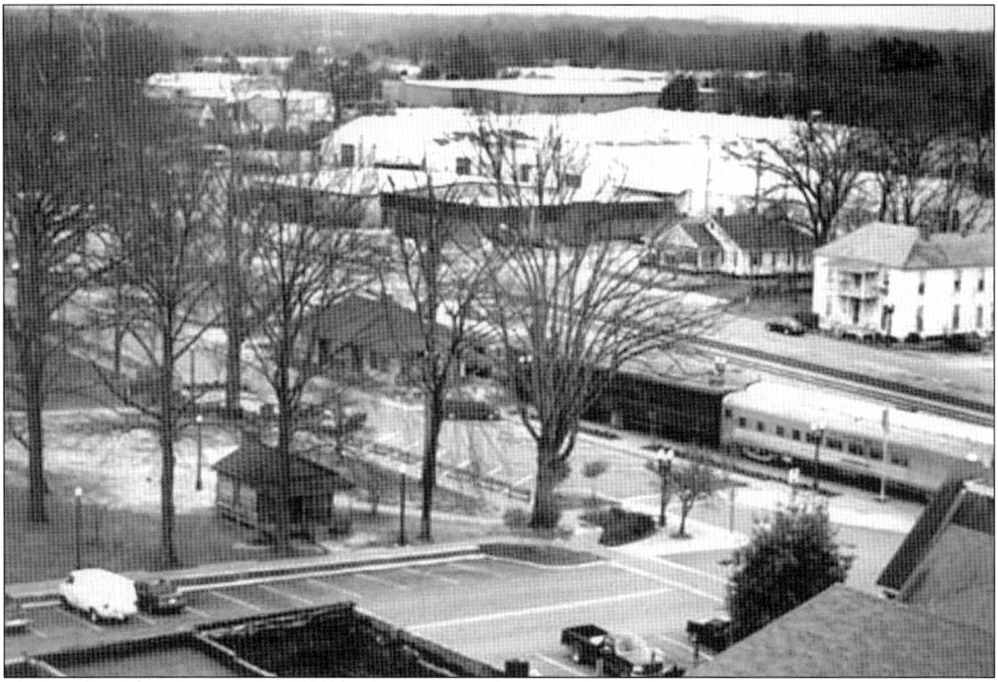

This photograph taken of the depot and Town Square captures the changes in the architecture of the business district. The two-story frame railroad hotel is seen in the distance. The building features a hipped roof with boxed cornice, covered with pressed-metal shingles. The two-story porch is covered with a shed roof supported by simple square replacement posts, with an open block spindle balustrade. The entrance, including the door to the second porch level, features a four-panel door topped by a three-light transom. The McGinnis Hotel was built in 1889.

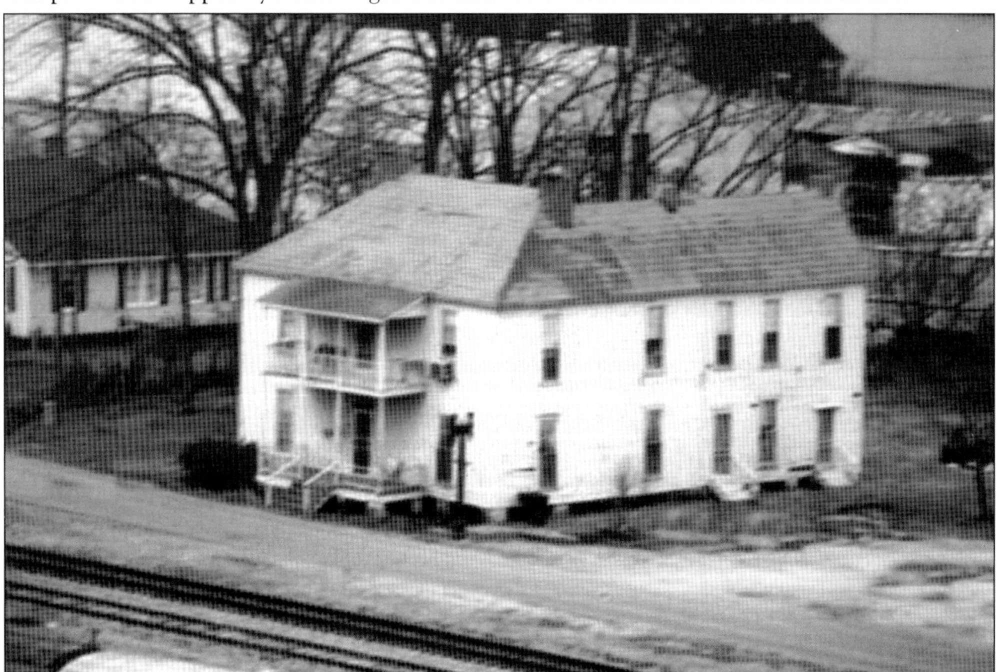

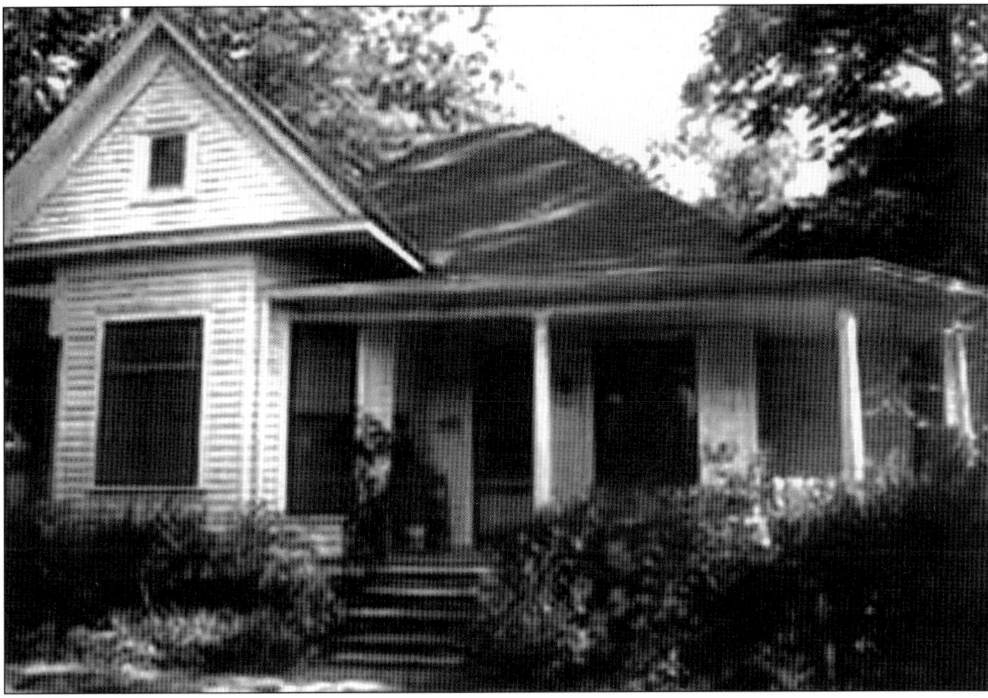

Thomas Dean built this home located on North Rowlett Street, west of Cooper Street, about 1907. The house contains two rooms that were moved from the neighboring Biggs home to create the dining room and kitchen. The Colonial cottage is located on property owned by the Dean family since 1874.

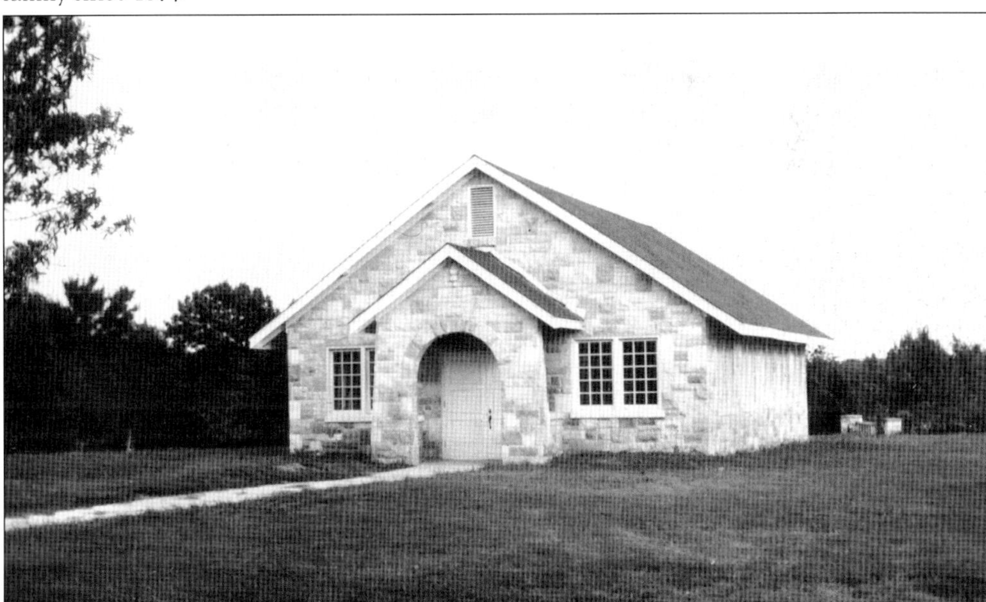

In May 1942, Mrs. Alice Townsend Cartwright was honored for her untiring efforts to improve the Magnolia Cemetery. The stone chapel and beautiful sunken garden were dedicated in her honor. The Collierville Contemporary Club restored the Summer House, built in 1882, in 1992 on its 100th anniversary.

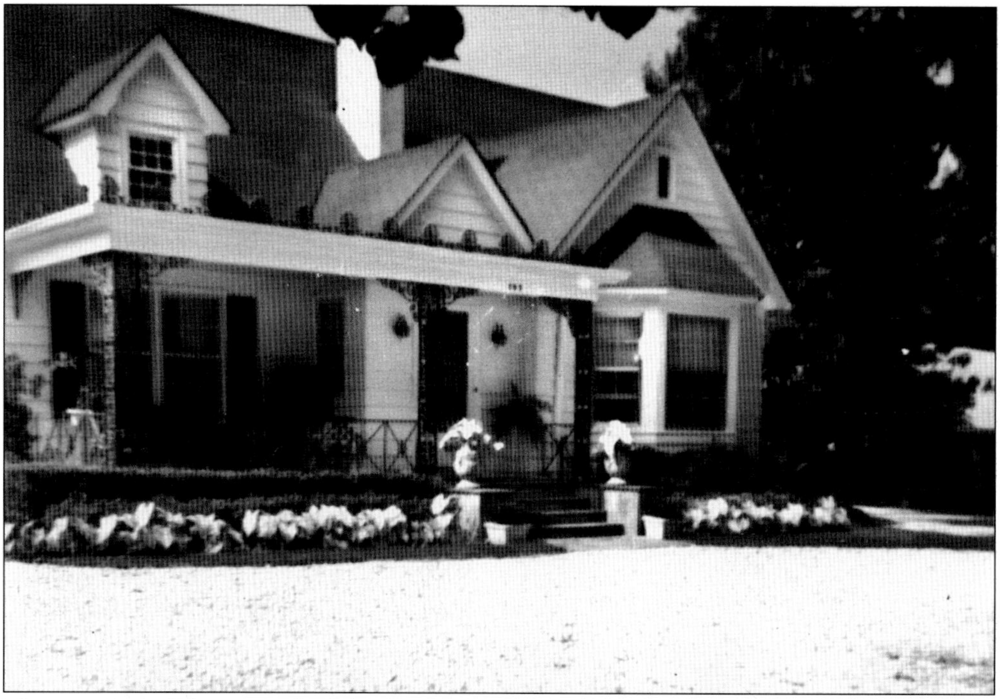

This cottage-style house was built by the Cartwright family in the 1930s and is located on College Street across from the middle school. Descendants occupy the home.

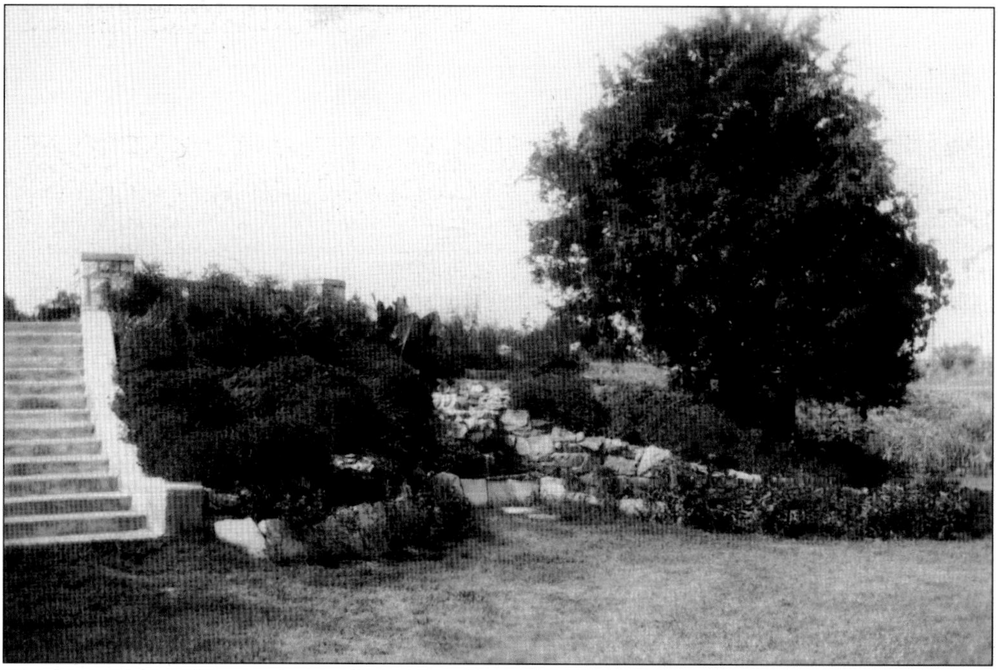

The beautiful sunken gardens, adjacent to the stone chapel in Magnolia Cemetery, featured stone steps that lead to a quiet retreat for meditation. The Cartwright Nurseries furnished many of the plants and flowers. The stone chapel is still in use today, but the sunken gardens no longer exist.

Mary Lou Cooper is standing with her father, Eldon Cooper, in the early 1940s. Mary Lou had her picture made here in front of their home every year. The house is located on the corner of College Street and Cooper Street. The columns on the front porch were once used for the principal's home that was adjacent to the high school.

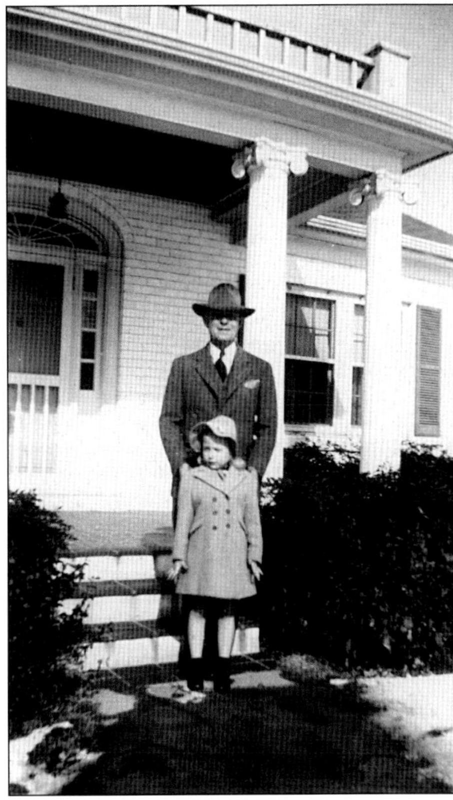

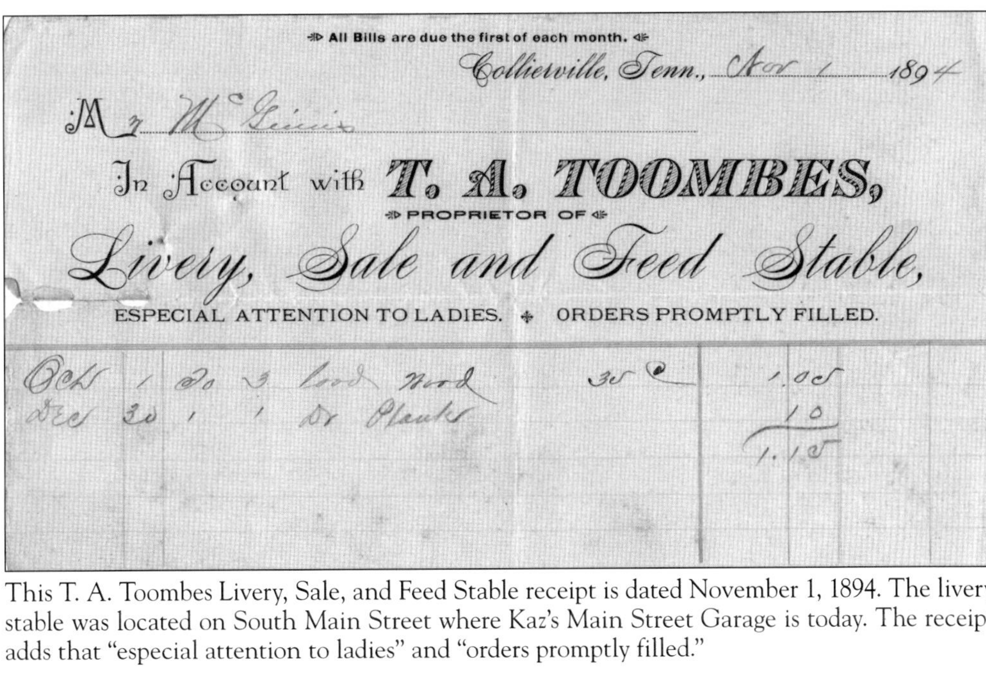

All Bills are due the first of each month.

Collierville, Tenn., Nov 1 1894

Mr McGinnis

In Account with T. A. TOOMBES,

PROPRIETOR OF

Livery, Sale and Feed Stable,

ESPECIAL ATTENTION TO LADIES. ORDERS PROMPTLY FILLED.

Oct	1	To 3 load wood	35	1.05
Dec	30	1 1 Dr Planks		10
				1.15

This T. A. Toombes Livery, Sale, and Feed Stable receipt is dated November 1, 1894. The livery stable was located on South Main Street where Kaz's Main Street Garage is today. The receipt adds that "especial attention to ladies" and "orders promptly filled."

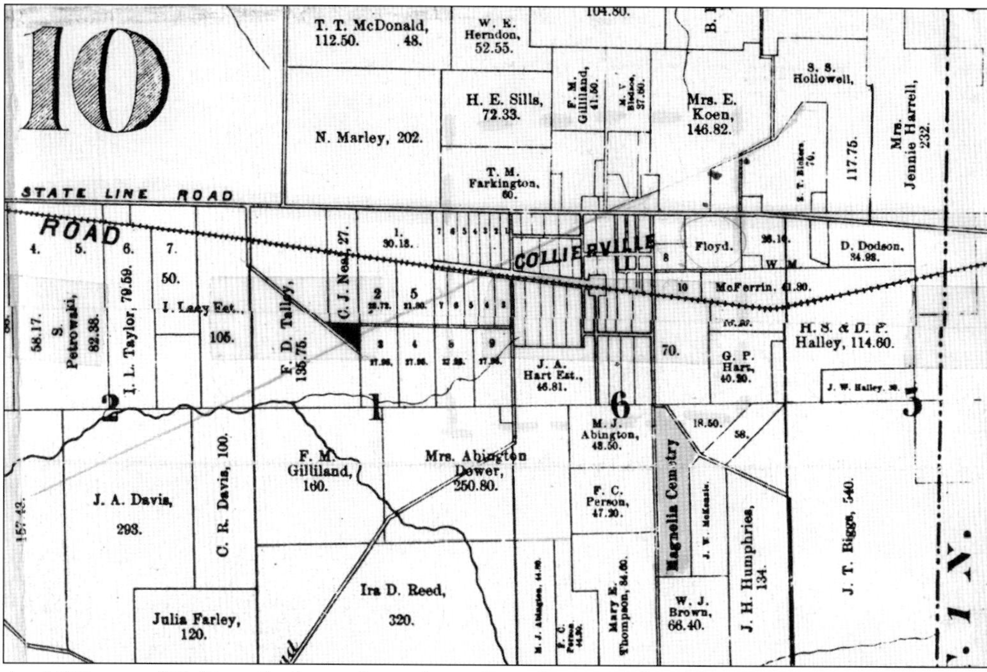

An 1890 map of Collierville shows the early roads in the area. The old American Indian trails were quickly disappearing, and some of them became well-traveled roads for the settlers. Collierville, also known as Oak Grove, was beginning to grow and be known as a healthy community surrounded by good cultivated land. The population was over 1,200.

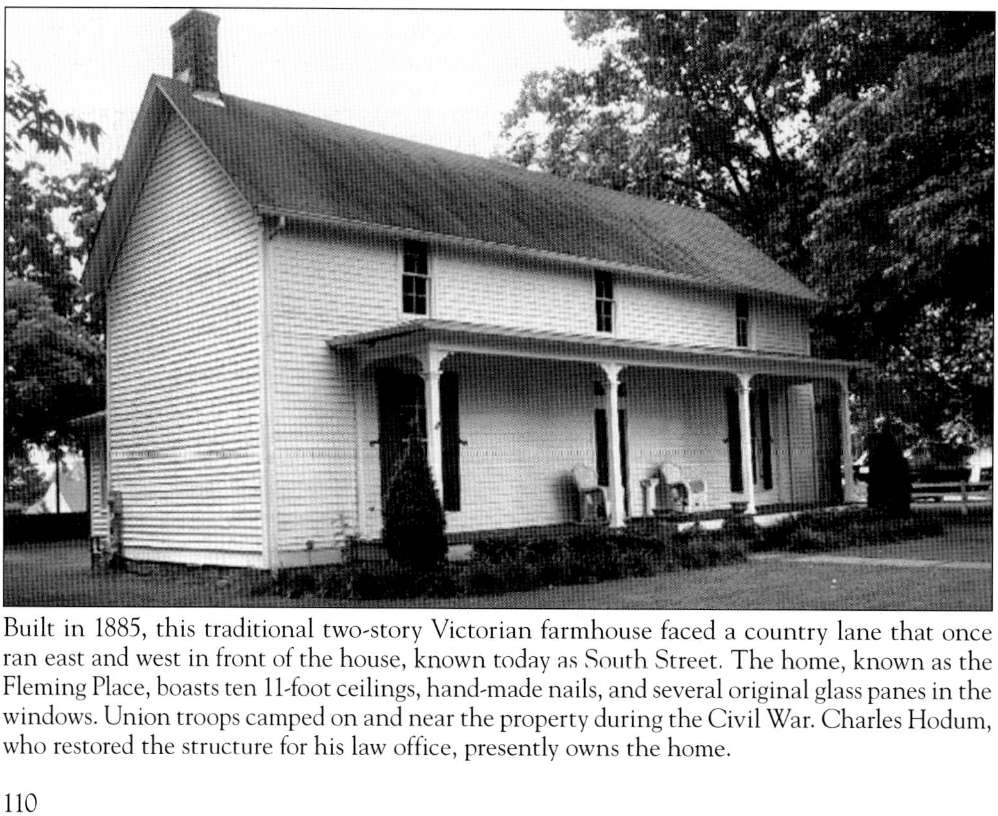

Built in 1885, this traditional two-story Victorian farmhouse faced a country lane that once ran east and west in front of the house, known today as South Street. The home, known as the Fleming Place, boasts ten 11-foot ceilings, hand-made nails, and several original glass panes in the windows. Union troops camped on and near the property during the Civil War. Charles Hodum, who restored the structure for his law office, presently owns the home.

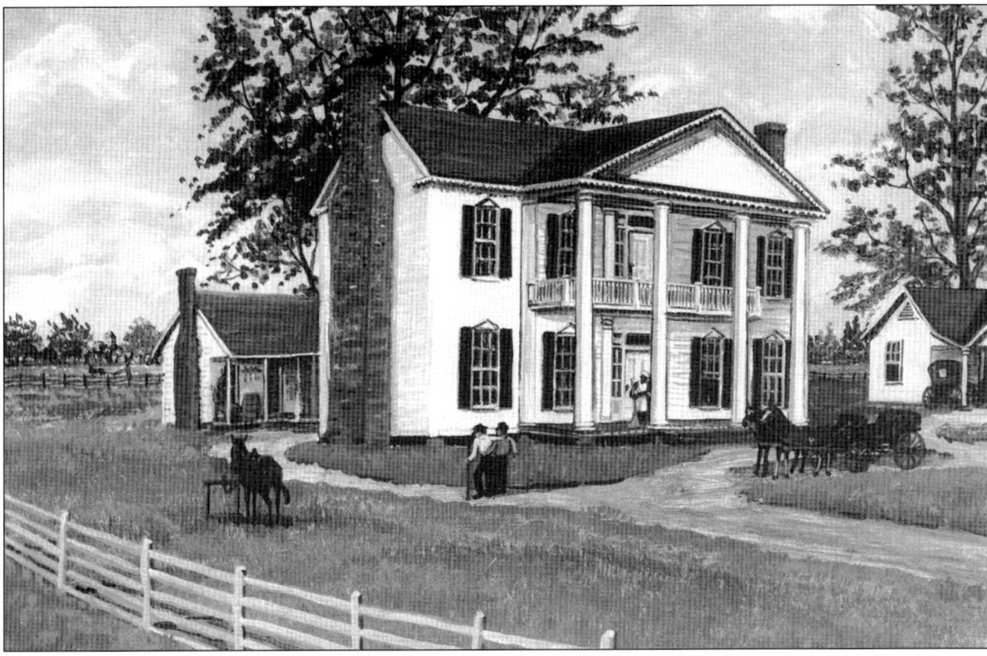

These early paintings are of Greenlevel Farm, which dates to the 1830s and is located on the north side of Wolf River. The top image features the house with the addition of the porch and columns, and the bottom picture shows the house at an earlier date without the porch. The house was sold to Bennett Bagby, who married Frances Leake in 1844 and later sold it to his brother-in-law, Dr. Virginius Leake. Leake and his wife, Martha, added the grand portico supported by four decagonal columns, all constructed from hand-hewn timbers cut from the property. The house served as a hospital during the Civil War. Today state senator Mark Norris, his wife, and family continue to preserve the charm and history of the home.

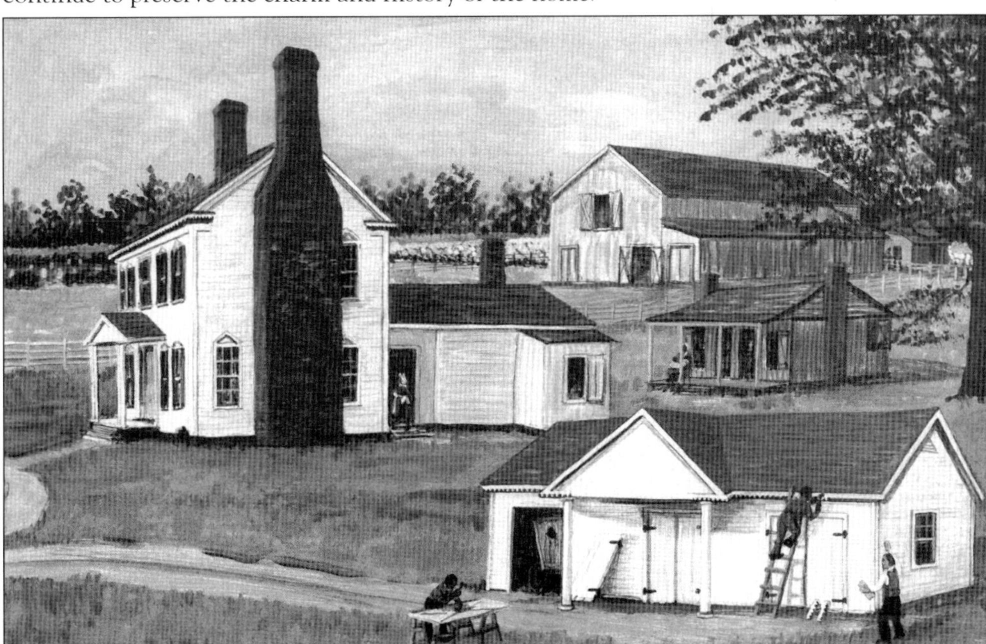

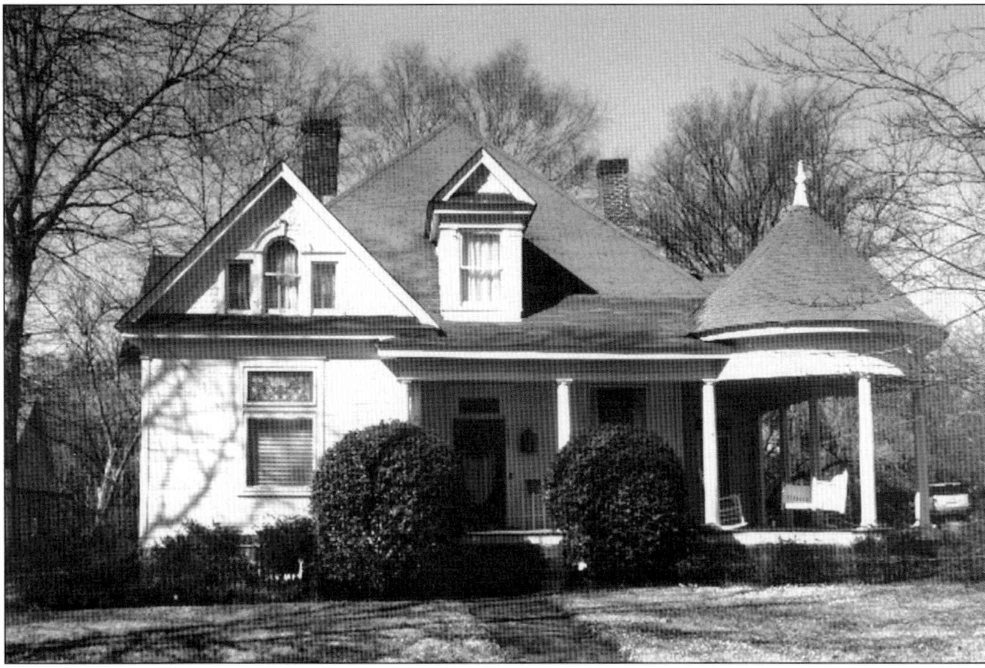

The historic McGinnis home on North Rowlett Street was built in 1905 and features a large extended porch topped with a conical turret. The frame house has stained-glass windows and 12-foot ceilings. Only members of the McGinnis family have lived in the home since it was built.

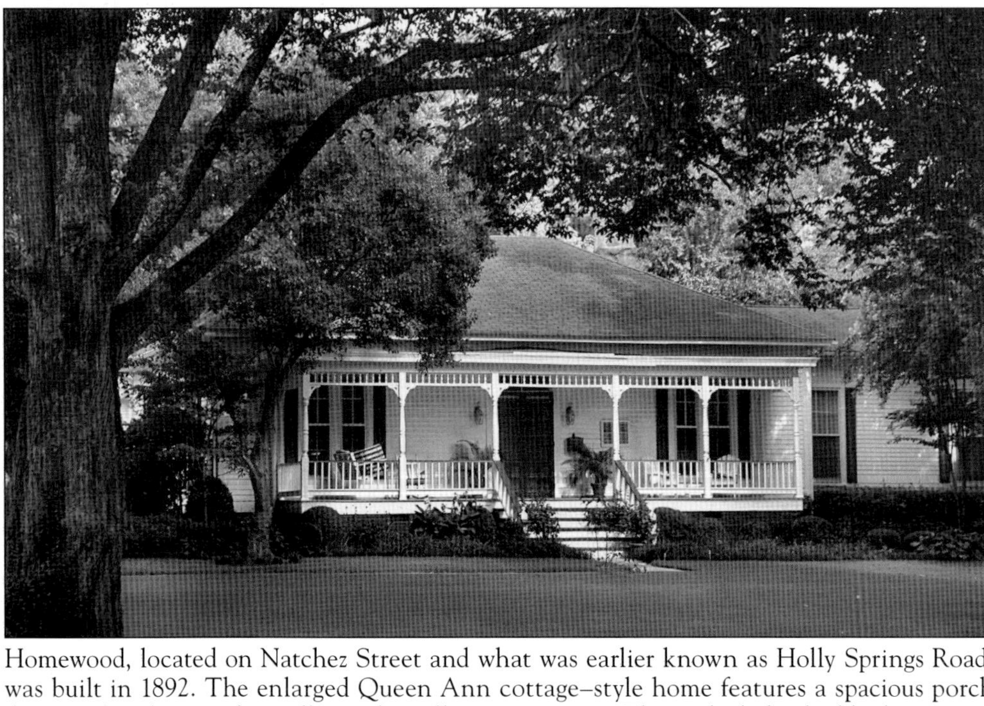

Homewood, located on Natchez Street and what was earlier known as Holly Springs Road, was built in 1892. The enlarged Queen Ann cottage–style home features a spacious porch decorated with turned spindles and scroll-sawn supports. The multi-light double doors open onto a 35-foot grand hall. Lyman and Sally Aldrich have expanded and restored the historic home for their family.

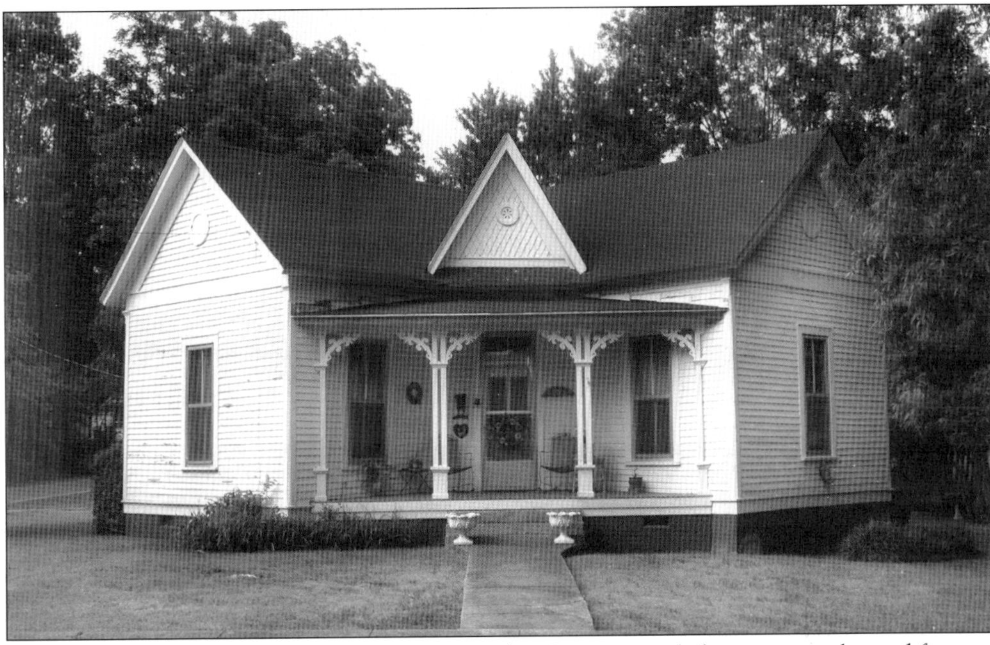

The Queen Anne cottage house located on Nathez Street is angled on a corner lot and features gingerbread trim that was common during the 1890s. The one-story frame building is a Y-plan with the entrance and triangular porch center between angular wings. Turner Harper Humphreys built the home, and it remains in the family.

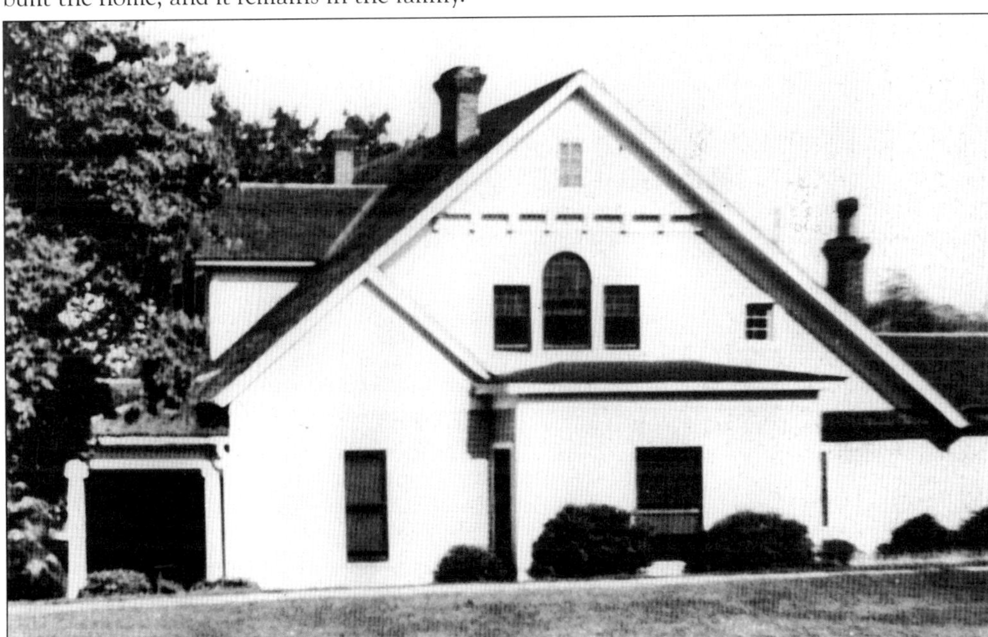

This is the only photograph that can be found of the principal's home located adjacent to the Collierville High School. Due to the condition of the house, it was torn down in the 1940s during Principal Charles H. Harrell's term. The demolition also gave space for additional parking. Since it was during the Depression, the school board was unable to build another house. The columns from the house were used in the Cooper home on College and Cooper Streets.

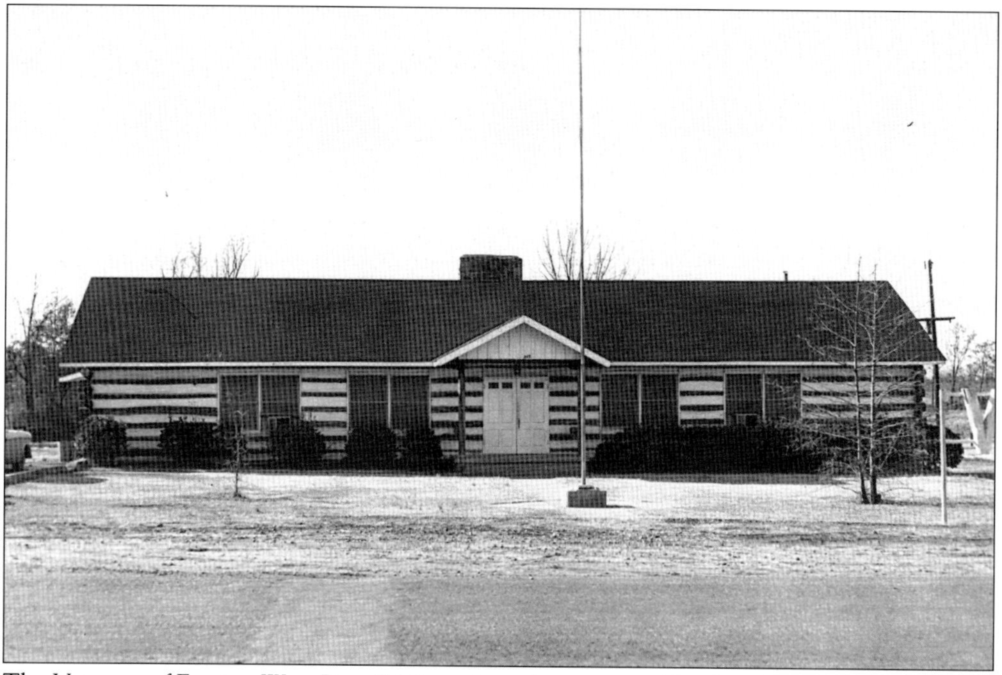

The Veterans of Foreign Wars Post 5066 purchased two acres of land on Center Street in 1948. The following year, they completed this structure. Constructed of logs, the Post Home presents a relaxing atmosphere with its exposed beams and huge stone fireplace. The mantle and the Cross of Malta over the fireplace were hand-carved and donated by Odie Bishop, who built the fireplace and chimney.

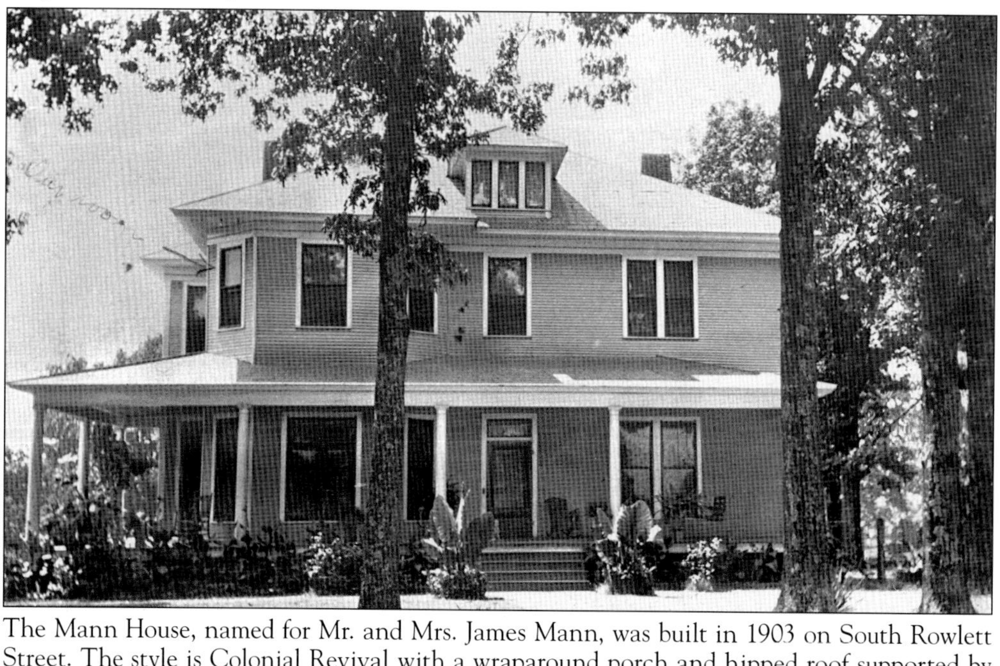

The Mann House, named for Mr. and Mrs. James Mann, was built in 1903 on South Rowlett Street. The style is Colonial Revival with a wraparound porch and hipped roof supported by columns with Doric capitals and Tuscan shafts. Othan and Donna Bailey are currently restoring the home.

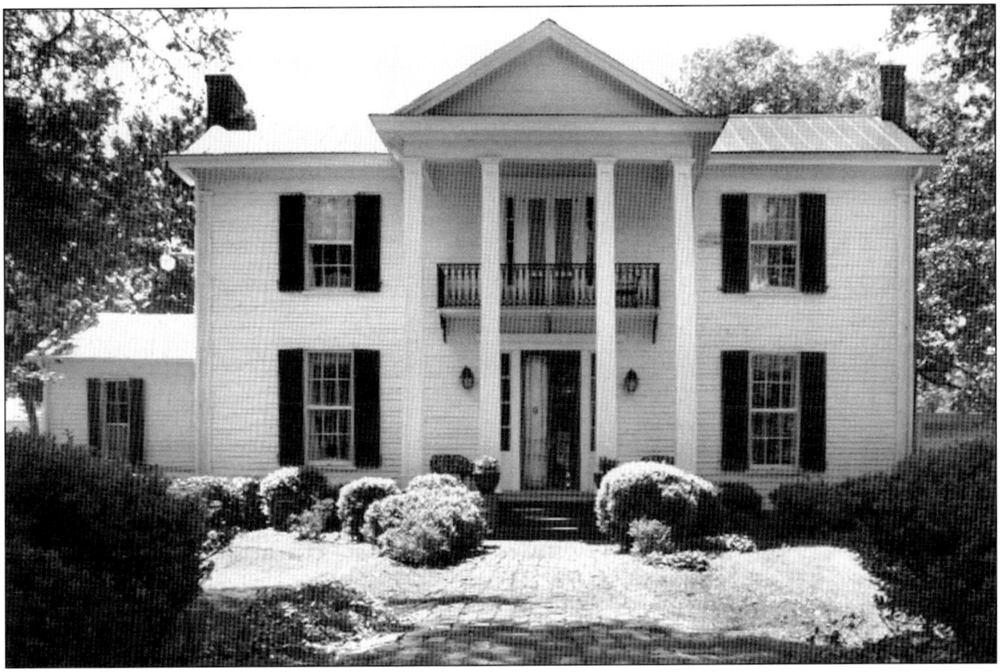

William Crain originally purchased this property from a Native American owner, She Mi O Kay, in 1836. After several owners, John and Mary Locke Porter purchased the property in 1945. The original features of the home have been preserved through the years, including the metal roof and original brick kitchen floor. A portico, supported by square columns and wrought-iron balcony, enhances the facade. The home remains in the family today.

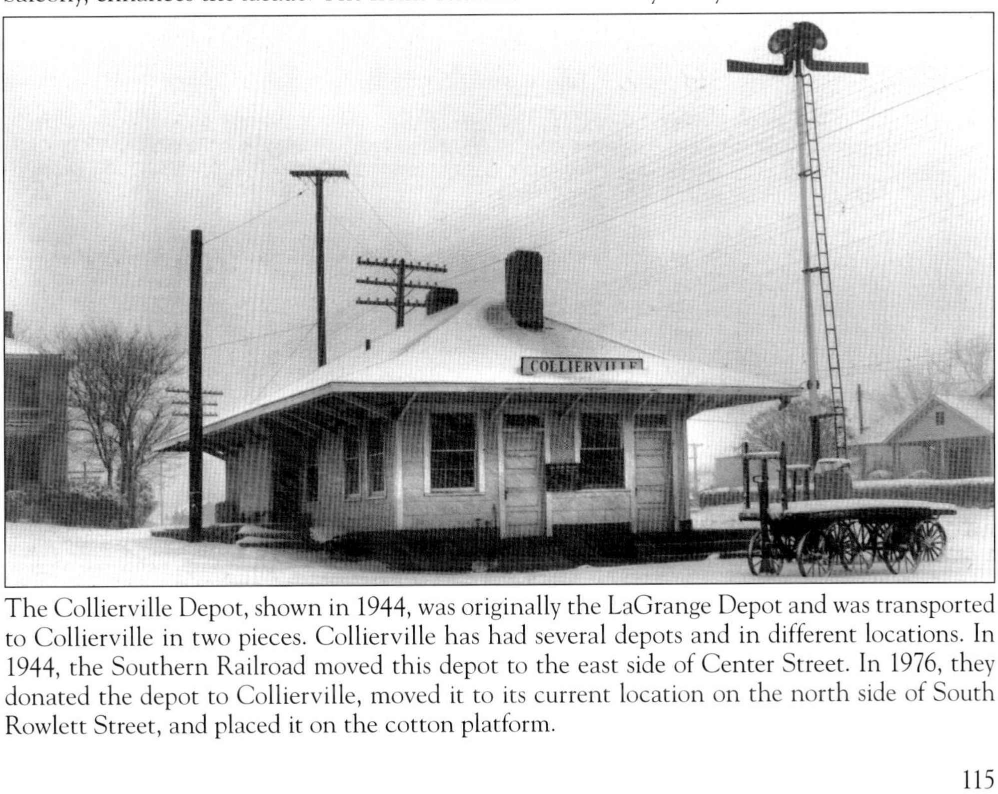

The Collierville Depot, shown in 1944, was originally the LaGrange Depot and was transported to Collierville in two pieces. Collierville has had several depots and in different locations. In 1944, the Southern Railroad moved this depot to the east side of Center Street. In 1976, they donated the depot to Collierville, moved it to its current location on the north side of South Rowlett Street, and placed it on the cotton platform.

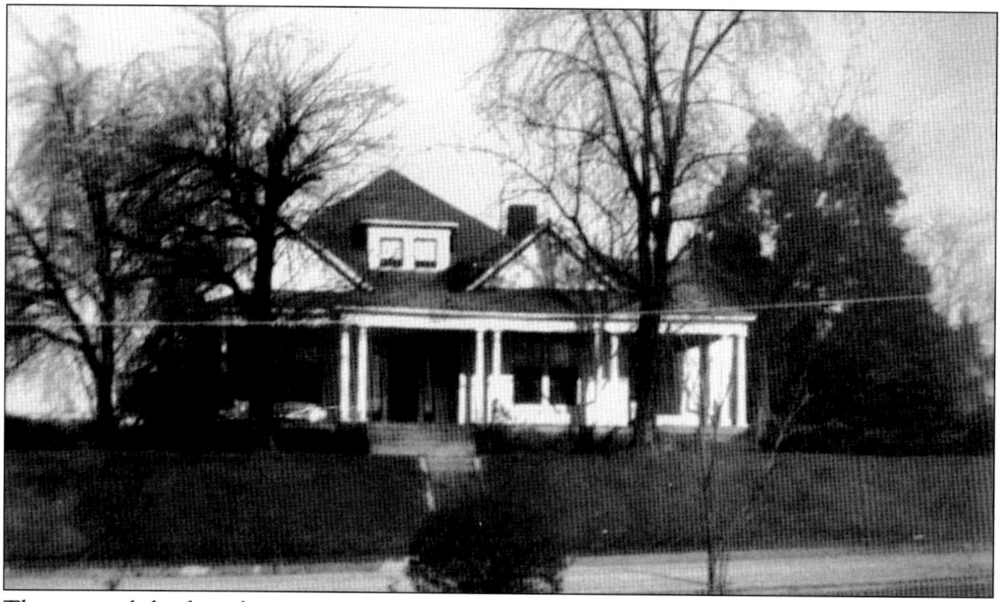

The original deed to this property is from 1879 when six acres of land located on State Line Road (Poplar Avenue) were first transferred. The white frame building has 12-foot ceilings and square nails from the original construction in the late 1800s. The home belonged to Squire J. F. Dudney, who was chairman of the Shelby County Quarterly Court from 1924 until his death in 1954. The house remains in the family and is located on the north side of Poplar Avenue and Burroughs Street.

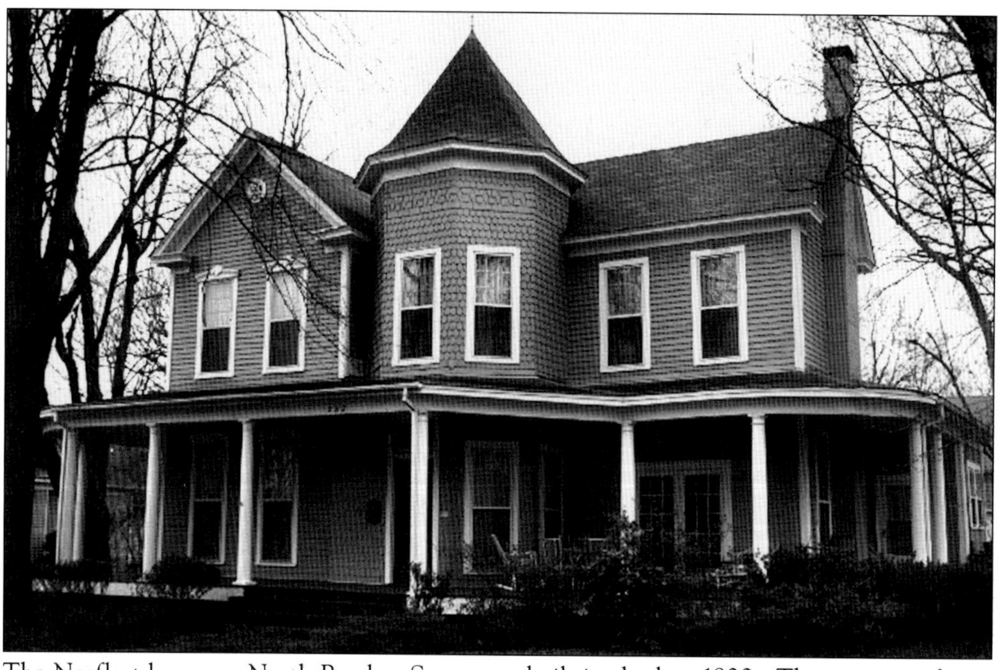

The Norfleet home on North Rowlett Street was built in the late 1800s. The two-story frame house features a covered wraparound porch and a second-story turret over the entrance. The Norfleet family added the Victorian features to the structure in 1910. Today Don and Nancy Bassett occupy the home.

Seven

Treasures Lost

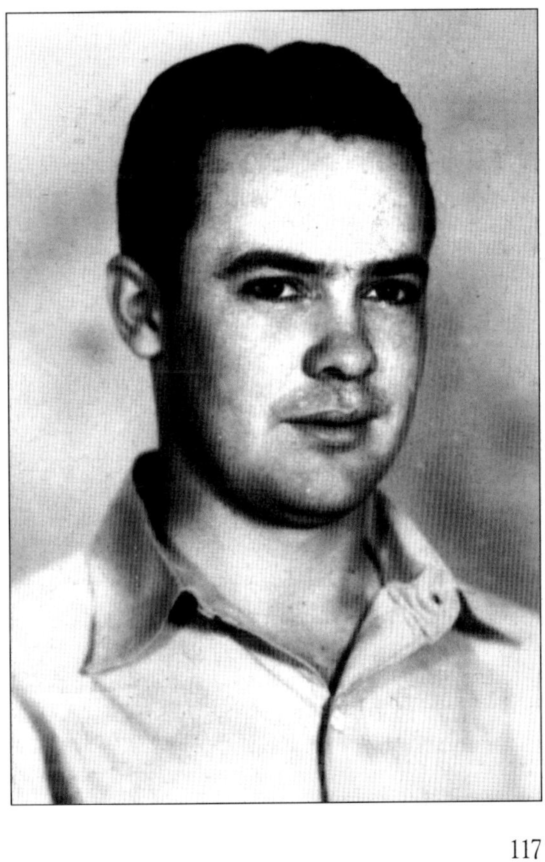

The most important treasures we have are the young people who live among us now only in memory. Robert Thomas Jamison was the first World War II casualty from Collierville. The local Veteran of Foreign Wars post on Center Street is named in his honor. A memorial marker is placed on the grounds of the Collierville Middle School for the students who lost their lives in service. Robert Jamison left a wife and two small children.

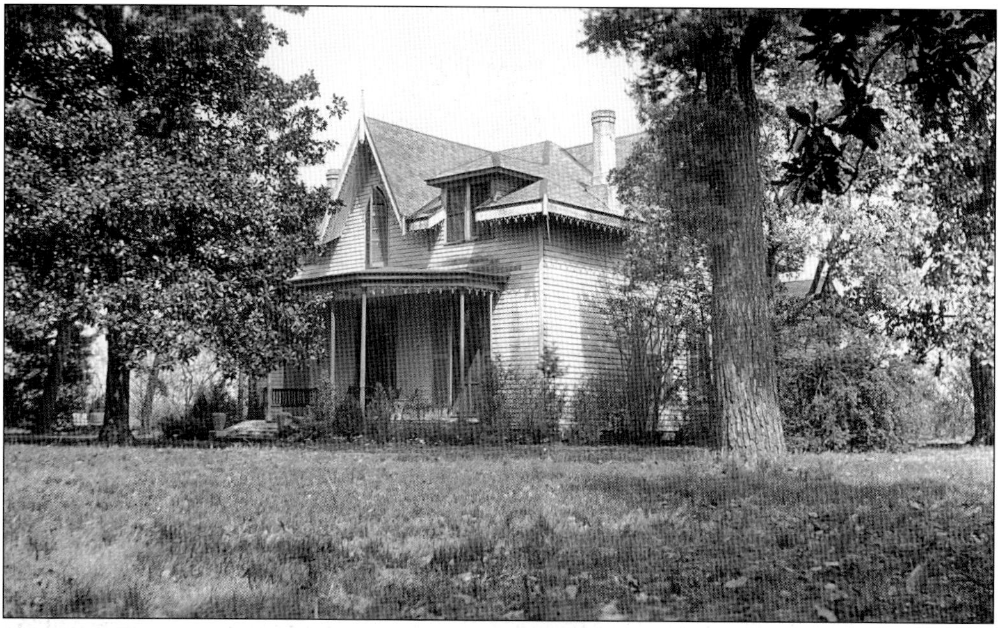

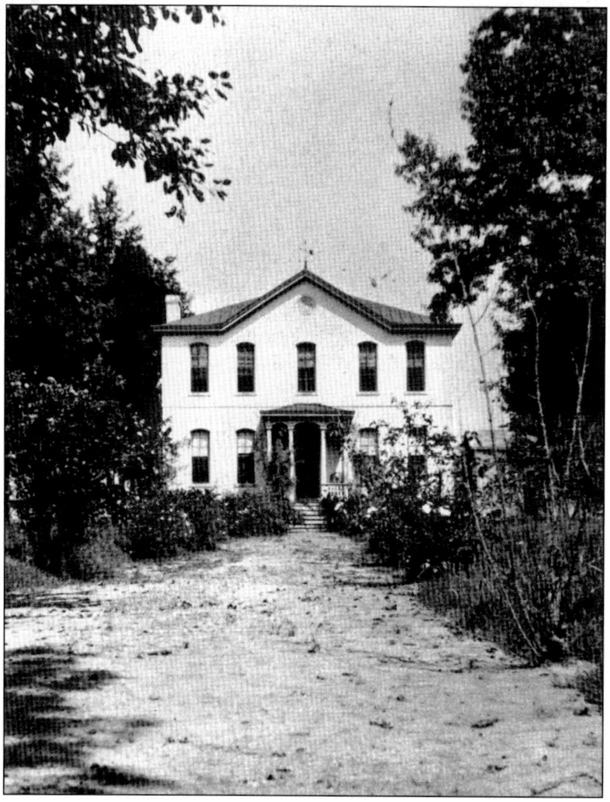

Deloach Place was built in 1840 by Thomas Peters. Josiah Deloach lived in the home, located on Poplar Pike, during the Civil War. This 1930 photograph shows the frame house that featured four brick chimneys and a large first-floor porch supported by iron columns. Baptist Hospital later purchased the home. Efforts were made to preserve the 160-year-old home that had survived the Civil War, but in a valiant last stand, it was not saved, moved, or preserved. The home was demolished in 2001. The historic Burch Home has also suffered at the hands of developers. The 1910 picture at left shows the home when it belonged to Walter Frank and was located in the area of the present-day Office Depot. The Lucius Burch family sold the home to David Halle, and as urban sprawl reached Collierville, the property was sold and the home was torn down.

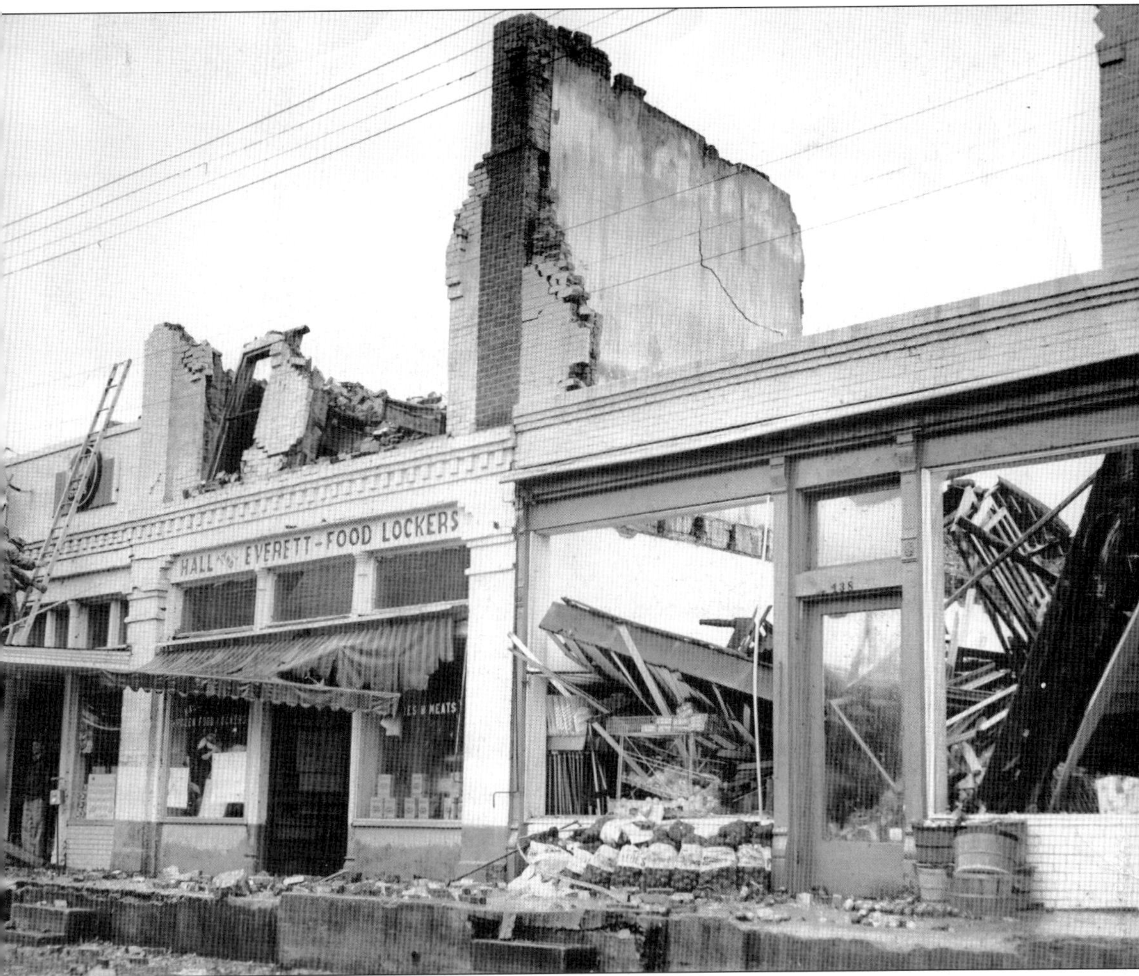

"Torrential rain still beat down when minutes after a high-velocity wind-spout raged across the town's heart. Collierville's citizens began clearing away dangerously remaining sections of four store buildings. In a matter of moments damage estimated between $300,000 and $500,000 was inflicted on the east Shelby County community. Only one minor injury was reported." This quote was from the "Memphis Commercial Appeal" article on October 29, 1955. The damage was to the northwest corner of the Town Square, the gazebo in the park, and a few private homes close to the area. Although the store buildings were repaired and continued to be in use, the original design and facade on some on the structures was altered. As the buildings are being restored today, efforts are being made to return to the original design. This photograph hangs in the front of the Silver Caboose restaurant as a reminder of the tragedy.

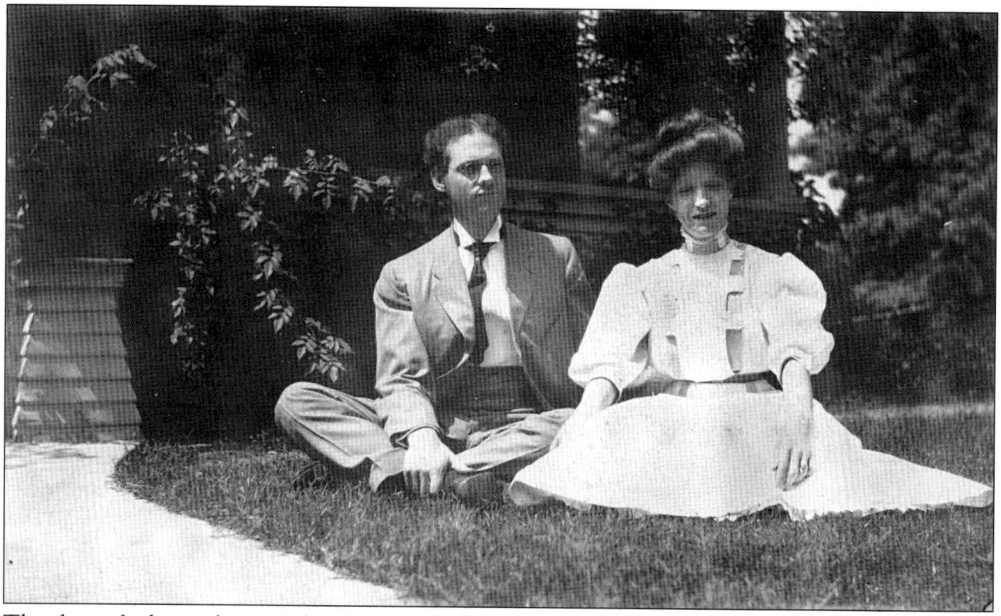

The days of a leisurely courtship have passed as this young couple reminds us. The photograph was taken *c.* 1915 and is from the scrapbook of Alice Cartwright Mann. The young people were her friends and are pictured in front of a home in Collierville that can't be identified. Many of the faded photographs in her scrapbook feature old Collierville and her young friends.

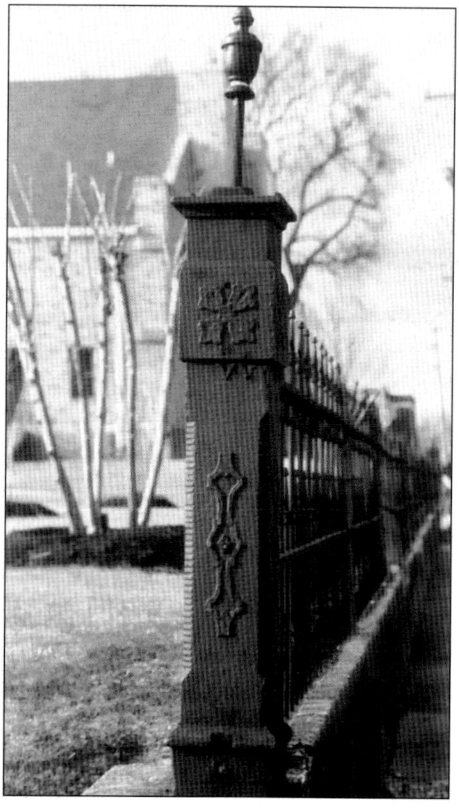

The decorative iron post and fence is all that remains of the historic Perkins home that was located on Walnut Street across from St. Andrew's Episcopal Church. The beautiful Victorian home was torn down to make room for additional parking at the Collierville Baptist Church.

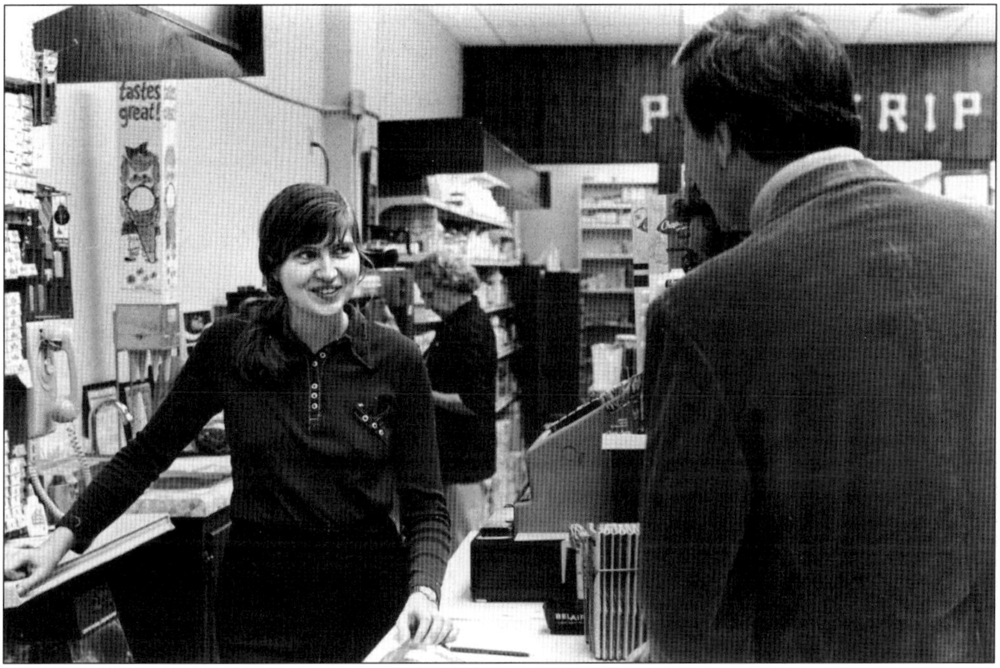

The old soda fountain still remains, but the drug store on the Town Square is gone. Harrell Pharmacy on Mulberry Street was the last to operate downtown, as larger pharmacies and grocery stores moved into the outlying areas. The Silver Caboose restaurant still uses the soda fountain and has restored the building and an adjacent building. It is one of the most popular businesses on the square.

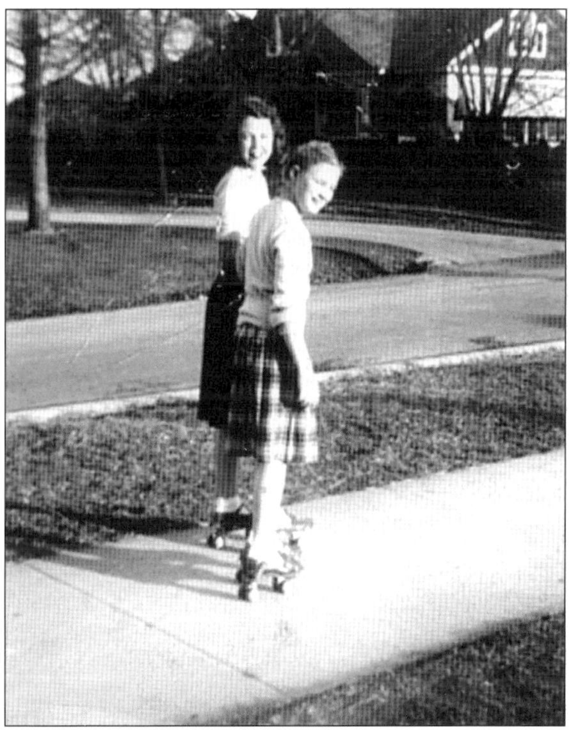

Young girls skating on the sidewalk is a scene from the past. Mary Jean Hall (right) and Carolyn Harrell are enjoying an afternoon on the sidewalks in Collierville c. 1950. Roller-skating was a common pastime for the young people.

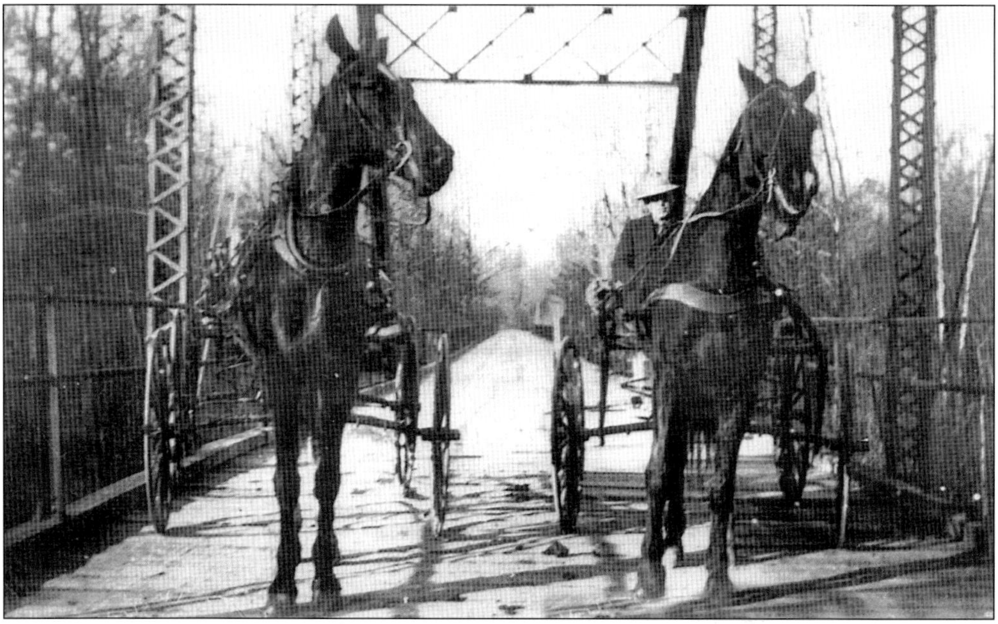

Elmo Edward Bryan (right) stops with his horse and buggy on the Wolf River bridge crossing on the Collierville-Arlington Road in Collierville. The date on the back of the photograph is 1929–1930. Today the bridge serves as a main artery to the Interstate 40 connection.

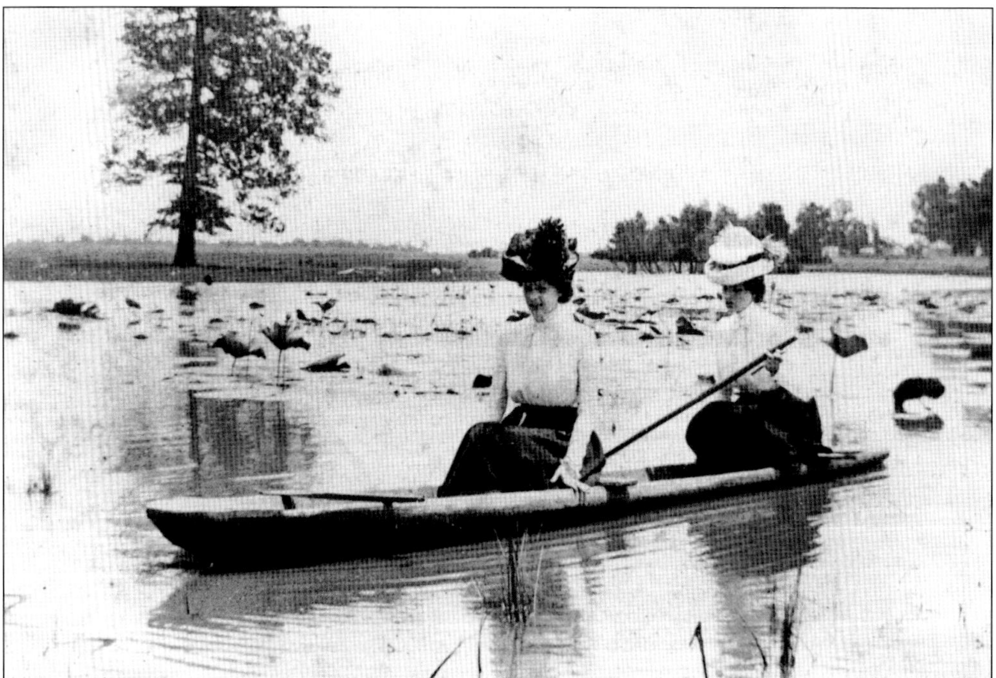

Frank's Pond in 1912 was where the young people of the Collierville area enjoyed fishing and canoeing in summer and ice-skating in the winter. The pond was west of the Lucius Burch home on Poplar Pike (Highway 72). The home can be seen in the far right side of the picture. The home was formerly the Frank home.

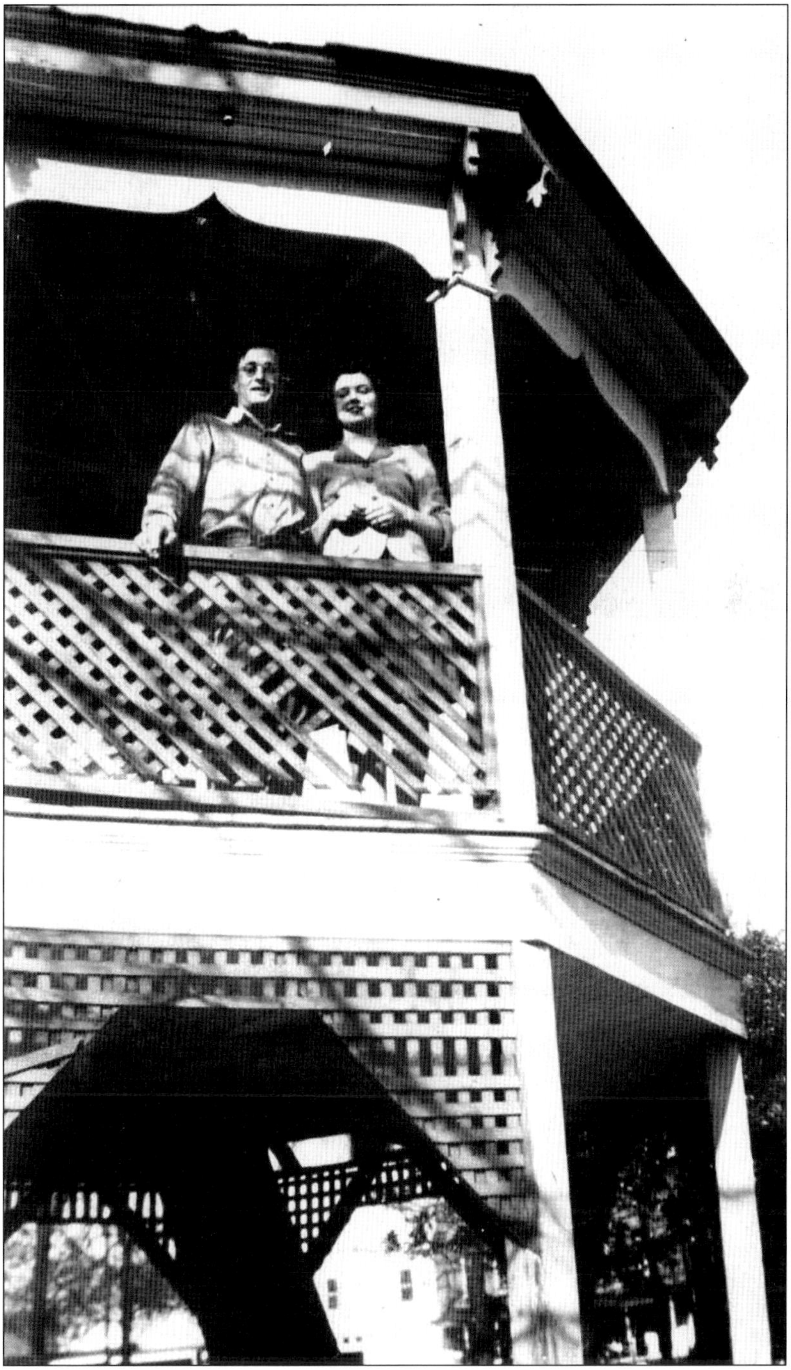

The two-story bandstand, erected in 1872, was destroyed by a tornado in 1955. Local artists including W. C. Handy performed from the bandstand's upper level. The square, a gathering place for many residents, has served as the venue for revivals, cheese and watermelon festivals, fairs, rummage sales, ice cream suppers, egg hunts, and picnics. The square's current bandstand, more commonly called the Gazebo, continues the traditions of hosting concerts, weddings, and other special events.

Timeline

1800	State Line Road (Poplar Avenue) is the southern boundary of the state
1818	Pres. James Monroe directed Andrew Jackson and John Shelby to buy land west of the Tennessee River from the Chickasaw Indians
1819	This land opened for settlement
1837	Court held in Collierville
1837–1838	Question on boundary line settled between Mississippi and Tennessee
1835	LaGrange and Memphis Railroad chartered
1838	Work begun on railroad
1840	Taverns, businesses, saloon, coach stop
1842	Railroad completed—ran from Memphis to Col. Eppie White's Plantation (six miles)
1844	Old Salem Presbyterian Church established three miles south of Collierville
1848	Collierville Lodge No. 152 organized
1848	Two stores, no churches, one schoolhouse (taught by Mary Elizabeth Chamberlain of Connecticut)
1850	Memphis and Charleston Railroad Company purchased the charter of the LaGrange and Memphis Railroad
1857	Memphis and Charleston Railroad opened in May—known in history as the "Wedding of the Waters;" Collierville had about 250 inhabitants
1861	War Between the States begins; the Wigfall Grays organized at Collierville April 15; took part in Battle of Shiloh, Chickamauga, and Missionary Ridge
1863	Battle of Collierville
1866	Dr. Virginius Leake and Harrison Irby bought 90 acres of land and sold lots, which moved the old site of Collierville on the State Line Road to the present site near the Memphis and Charleston Railroad
1870	Collierville incorporated
1870	Schoolhouse built on present Collierville Middle School site
1871	Salem Presbyterian congregation moved to Collierville and held joint Sunday school with the Methodists
1871	Christian church built
1872	Bellevue Female College built
1872	Town Square Park developed
1873	Baptist church organized and built
1875	First State Board of Education organized
1879	*Collierville Herald* published
1880	Miss Ann Holden's school for girls opened
1885	Main Street opened
1886	Miss Holden's Seminary and Bellevue Female College, both thriving institutions—enrollment over 300

1886	1200 inhabitants—good business
1890	St. Andrew's Episcopal Church built
1890	The Collierville Bank organized
1892	Shares sold in Collierville Water and Manufacturing Company
1893	First *Collierville Star* published
1895	Miss Holden's School sold to Shelby County for a boys' school
1896	Bellevue College burned
1897	Shelby County built new high school on same location as the college
1898	Racetrack built west of town
1900	Methodist church built on Town Square
1901	Cumberland Telephone established
1903	Collierville incorporated for the second time
1904	Electric lights, a few hours at night and early morning
1905	First car in Collierville owned by Dr. E. K. Leake
1907	Collierville Telephone Company organized
1908	Peoples Bank organized
1909	Baptist church burned
1911	First addition built to Collierville High School
1917	Citizens Bank organized
1924	A second addition to Collierville High School built
1928	Cooper Street opened and College Street extended to meet same
1933	Cheese plant opened by Swift and Company
1934	Present middle school (then high school) begun and completed in three years
1935	Rotary Club organized
1935	Cartwright Nursery is recognized as one of the world's largest nurseries
1936	Contemporary Club organized
1936	Sewerage system in operation
1936	Natural gas from Memphis and all-time lights
1936	Four-lane drive on Poplar Pike through town
1938	Stone wall built at Magnolia Cemetery
1939	Collierville Telephone Company sold to Minor Cormon
1941	Minor Cormon sold telephone company to Bell Telephone Company
1942	Piper Brothers John Deere first business built at Highway 57 and 72 junction
1945	Center Street opened to Highway 72
1945	Hart's Manufacturing Company established
1946	Wonder Products Company built
1947	First dial telephone installed
1948	Football field at Collierville High School lighted
1949	Primitive Baptist Church built
1950	Twentieth Century Club organized
1953	Dublin-Haskell Corporation opened
1955	Tornado struck town; park and buildings on Town Square are destroyed or damaged
1956	Church of Christ established
1956	Collierville Library begun, sponsored by Collierville Contemporary Club

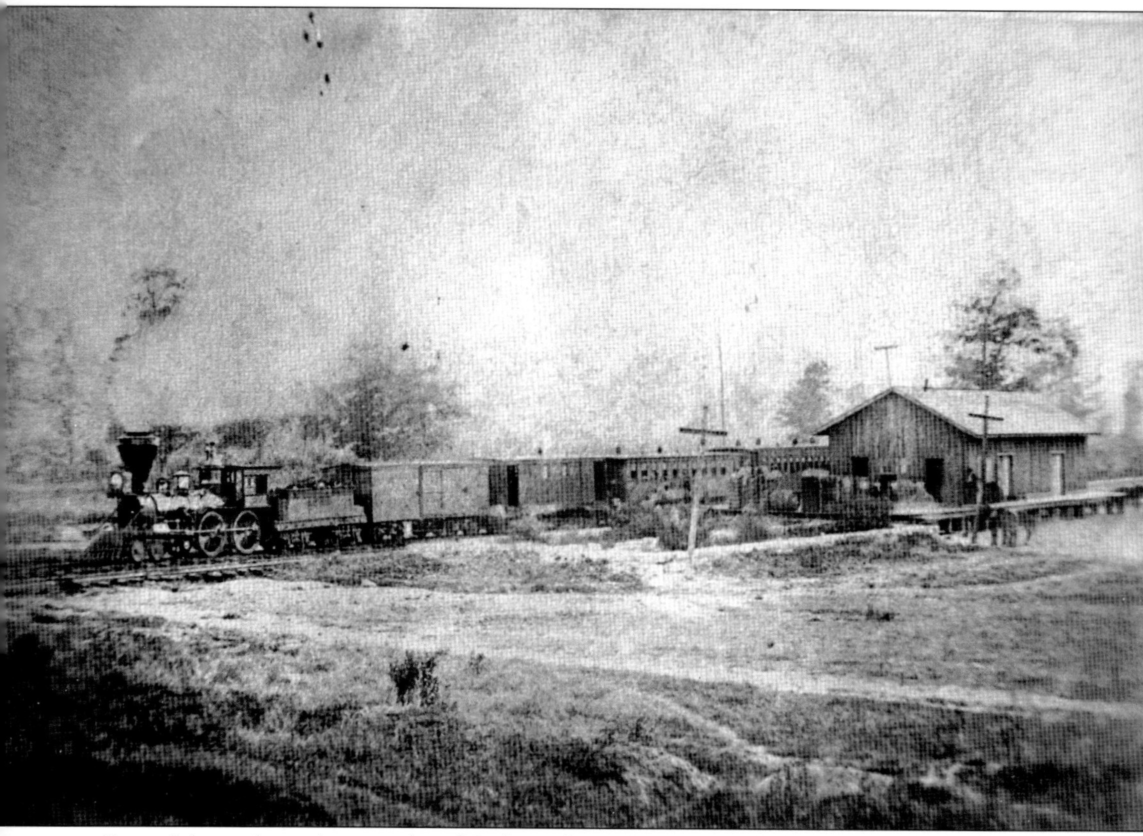

One of the earliest photographs of Collierville and the depot is dated *c.* 1890. This depot was built soon after the Civil War. It was the second of four depots that would be built or moved to Collierville.

BIBLIOGRAPHY

Baumgartner, Greg. "A Walking Tour of Historic Collierville, Tennessee." Collierville, TN: Main Street Collierville, 1992.

Collierville Alumni Association, *Collierville High School, 100 Years of History and Memorida 1905-2005.* Collierville, TN, Instant Publisher.com, 2005.

Collierville Chamber of Commerce, *Collierville Centennial Program.* July 31–August 8, 1970.

The Collierville Herald. Weekly newspaper. Collierville, January 1929–January 1936 and January 1941–December 2003.

The Contemporary Club, *Collierville: A Place Called Home.* Collierville, TN: Starr Toof Printing, 1999.

Hopkins, John Lynn. *Collierville Traditions: A Plan for Preservation of a Traditional Environment.* Memphis: John Griffin, Inc., 1992.

Russell, Clarene. *Collierville, Tennessee: Her People and Neighbors.* Collierville, TN: Chamber of Commerce, 1994.

Town of Collierville. *Historic Architectural Survey 2004,* Collierville, TN: Town of Collierville, 2004.